The Reforming Organization

In modern large organizations there is often a strong belief in reform – that it is possible to change organizational structures, processes and ideologies from above and by rational choice and design. Administrative reform is also a common feature of large organizations – some organizations go through a seemingly endless series of administrative reforms of different kinds and at different levels. The failure of old reforms that supposedly make new reforms necessary does not seem to reduce the belief in reform in general as a method of accomplishing change. Management consultants are professional reformers with an extensive market.

This volume sets out to explain three phenomena: that reforms occur (even if they show little sign of success), the *contents* of reforms (why reformers propose specific solutions), and the *effects* of reforms. In the reform perspective, the reformers, their intentions and abilities, as well as features of the reformed organization are considered important explanatory factors. In the book it is argued that more significant explanations can be found outside reformers and individual organizations.

Reforms are the result of attempts at modernization, shifts in administrative fashions, the existence of insoluble administrative problems in organizations, and the organizational tendency to forget previous reform experiences. The contents of reforms are determined by strong rationalistic conceptions of organizations as well as by strong administrative fashions. Reforms may stabilize and legitimize common conceptions of organizations, rather than leading to real changes and better results.

The book is based on a large number of studies of attempts of administrative reform in private and public organizations.

Nils Brunsson is Professor of Management at the Stockholm School of Economics. **Johan P. Olsen** is Professor in Political Science and Public Administration at the University of Bergen.

The Reforming Organization

Nils Brunsson and Johan P. Olsen

T179

London and New York

First published in 1993
by Routledge
11 New Fetter Lane, London EC4P 4EE

Simultaneously published in the USA and Canada
by Routledge
29 West 35th Street, New York, NY 10001

Typeset in Times by LaserScript Limited, Mitcham, Surrey
Printed and bound in Great Britain by
Mackays of Chatham PLC, Chatham, Kent

British Library Cataloguing in Publication Data

A catalogue record for this book is available from the British Library.

ISBN 0–415–08287–0
ISBN 0–415–08288–9 (pbk)

Library of Congress Cataloging in Publication Data
Brunsson, Nils, 1946–
    The reforming organization / Nils Brunsson and Johan P. Olsen.
        p.   cm.
    Includes bibliographical references and index.
    ISBN 0-415-08287-0. – ISBN 0-415-08288-9 (pbk.)
    1. Organizational change   2. Organizational behavior.
    I. Olsen, Johan P.   II. Title.
HD58.8.B784   1993
658.4′063–dc20   93-18708
                                                    CIP

Contents

Preface

Recently there has been a revived interest in how and why organizations adopt new formal structures and processes, whatever their impact on practical organizational activities or outcomes. Administrative reform is a common phenomenon in modern organizations. Tendencies toward standardization and homogeneity among organizations have been observed, as well as fairly strong and wide-spread fashions in forms of organization.

The concept of reform is based on the common conception of organizations as being tightly controlled by the free and rational choices of their leaders, owners or constituencies. This conception is often strong even when the need for reform stems from a perceived lack of precisely those elements of top control and rationality. We argue that the origins, contents and effects of reforms can be explained by factors other than leaders' rational choices. We also explain why the criticism of the perspective of control and rationality we present is not likely to change the reform idea in practical organizational life; why it will not prevent new reform attempts; and why, therefore, the understanding of reform will continue being of interest for those who wish to understand modern organizations.

The book is the result of the efforts of many people. Chapters 1 and 12 were written by the two of us together, Chapter 2 by Johan Olsen and Chapters 3 and 5 by Nils Brunsson. We have benefitted from the work of several colleagues. Chapter 4 was written by Anders Forssell, Chapter 6 by Karin Fernler, Chapter 7 by Nils Brunsson and Hans Winberg, Chapter 8 by Marit Wærnes, Chapter 9 by Björn Rombach, Chapter 10 by Barbara Czarniawska-Joerges and Chapter 11 by Olov Olson. Earlier versions of some chapters have been published elsewhere: Chapter 2 in *Governance* (1991) vol. 4 no. 2; Chapter 3 in the *Scandinavian Journal of Management* (1992) vol. 5 no. 3; and Chapter 10 in *Organization Studies*, (1989) vol. 10 no. 4. We are grateful for permission to use the material in this volume. We are also grateful for the assistance of several translators and editors who helped turn the text into English, as well as to the Study of Power and Democracy in Sweden which financed most of the work.

Nils Brunsson and Johan P. Olsen

1 Organizational forms: Can we choose them?

Formal organizations are important realities of our time. They appear in great numbers and penetrate almost every aspect of life. Organizations have also been getting larger, more professionalized, more differentiated and wealthier, all of which has made the question of controlling them a crucial issue. In a world dominated by formal organizations it is generally hoped that the behaviour and achievements of these organizations can be controlled not only by other organizations but also by individuals. It is often assumed that they can be controlled by their leaders: by top management, by politicians or by others to whom we have assigned the task of controlling them.

If organizations can be controlled from above, it would seem to follow that leaders can control and change the forms of organizations, i.e. their structures, working methods or ideologies, thereby improving their results. And indeed, large organizations today are often the subject of what we will refer to here as administrative reforms, that is to say expert attempts at changing organizational forms. Departments or whole organizations are frequently merged or split. Organizational charts are rewritten. Changes are often introduced in the systems for delegating authority, disseminating information or distributing responsibility. And leaders try to convince their subordinates of new ideas and ideologies. Reform projects have become a commonplace, in many organizations almost a matter of routine.

ADMINISTRATIVE REFORM AND CHANGE

The concept of reform brings a special perspective to bear on the processes of organizational change and the way organizations function, as well as on internal leadership and power. In a reform perspective administrative change is assumed to be the result of deliberate goal-directed choices between alternative organizational forms. The structures, processes and ideologies of organizations are shaped and altered, to help the organizations to operate more functionally and efficiently. (Re)organization is a tool used by the reformer or reformers. There is a continuous chain of cause and effect starting from the intentions of the reformers and proceeding through decisions, new structures, processes and ideologies to changes in behaviour and improved results. At the same time experience leads to learning. If results do not correspond to intentions, or if the conditions for action change, the process of reform begins anew.

The reforms we shall be discussing below are those instigated by politicians or other elected representatives, owners or corporate executives, or people supported by such groups. Reform can also be triggered from lower levels in an organization or from the broader mass of the people, but such changes can even verge on the revolutionary. Although they are naturally important they are no part of our subject here.

In a reform perspective organizations are regarded as instruments or means. Two qualities are seen to distinguish formal organizations from other types of social arrangement: they are set up to accomplish specific tasks and to advance quite precise objectives, and they have a formalized structure which determines the distribution of authority and the division of labour. An inequitable and undemocratic distribution of labour and working conditions, of authority, status, power and resources, is justified by reference to its role in promoting efficiency and achieving the objectives of the organization. The structure of the organization with its system of rewards and punishments encourages some types of behaviour and inhibits others. Looked at in this way, the organizational structure can be said to create a system that is rational in terms of its own previously determined goals, by channelling behaviour and resources in the direction of these goals. Organization and coordination allow for action and problem-solving far beyond what any individual members could achieve on their own.

This interpretation of change in terms of rational choice and of organizations in terms of instruments, stems from a hierarchical view of leadership and power. It is thus assumed that reformers have the right to organize, i.e. to make authoritative, binding decisions about organizational change, and that they have the power to crush any resistance, which means we can concentrate on the question of how correct decisions are made. Once decided, the implementation of reforms is fairly straightforward. A distinction is made between thought and action, between making a decision to reform and implementing that decision. The first is a task for the few, the leaders, and the second a task for the many, the non-leaders.

The reform perspective belongs to a rational, instrumental tradition in organizational research. Despite persistent criticism of the fundamental principles of this tradition over the years, it is still strong (Scott 1987). The rationality norm is also held in high esteem in political and economic life.

To many people formal organizations represent the very incarnation of their belief in control, rationality, leadership, power and order. This belief in the virtue of controlling social arrangements and societal development parallels man's aspirations to exert control over nature. Its models are the industrial process and the efficient machine, its catchwords are clear goals, design, implementation, efficiency and optimization, and its key actors are the social engineers.

How free is the choice?

This book is based on several studies of reform processes in a variety of formal organizations. From these it appears that in practice it may actually be difficult for reformers to make decisions on reform, to implement reforms once decided, to achieve the desired effects, or to profit from the experience of earlier reforms. This means that we shall be questioning the fundamental assumptions about rational calculation and social control (Dahl and Lindblom 1953) on which the rational-instrumental approach rests.

Instead of assuming that changes in formal organizations are the result of reforms and deliberate choices, we ask how much freedom of choice the reformers actually enjoy when they decide that a reform should or should not take place, when they determine its content and direct its implementation and its consequences. In raising this question we are associating ourselves with the classical debate on political control and the design of institutions. This was the issue launched in 1861 by John Stuart Mill, when he published his *Considerations on Representative Government*. In this book he also summed up years of discussion by distinguishing between two main standpoints, both of which are easily discernible in contemporary organization theory.

On the one hand Mill (1861/1962) identifies a school which sees institutional development as a practical matter, geared to the finding of effective instruments. A 'good' institution must have clearly defined objectives; the effects that different organizational forms will have on the chosen objectives must be assessed, and the alternative chosen that will best achieve them. Mill then identifies another school which sees the evolution of institutions as a natural and spontaneous process. Institutions are neither designed nor chosen. They emerge in a historical process, and represent a cultural development that is neither directed nor controlled by any particular group of reformers.

It is important to keep in mind the possibility that reforms account for a limited part only of the changes which occur in formal organizations. If it is true that the connection between change and attempted reform is a weak one, in the sense that many changes are not the result of reforms and many reforms never result in change, then there are two questions which must be considered.

One concerns the way in which an organization's structures and processes change, when the changes are not the result of reforms. What factors, other than the intentions of the reformers, affect the occurrence, the implementation and the consequences of change? An analysis of this question would also help to identify the conditions which influence the reformer's freedom of choice. The second point concerns the reform projects themselves: what do they mean and why are they so abundant in formal organizations if they are not associated with change? It is this last issue which will chiefly engage our attention in the present book.

Once we acknowledge the problematic nature of the relationship between change and reform, we can no longer assume that organizations are (always) instruments, and that the power relationship is (always) hierarchical between those attempting to reform – 'the reformers' – and those who are to be reformed – 'the reformees'. Many factors can affect the freedom that the reformers actually enjoy, but we will limit ourselves here to the institutional element in their situation. Thus, if formal organizations are perceived not as instruments but as institutions in environments which are also institutionalized, what implications does this have for the reformers' freedom of action?

INSTITUTIONALIZED ORGANIZATIONS

Organizations can be said to be institutionalized insofar as their behaviour is determined by culturally conditioned rules which manifest themselves in certain routines for action and which give meaning to those actions. They reflect relatively stable values, interests, opinions, expectations and resources (March and Olsen 1984, 1989). Every organization has a history, and in the course of time it evolves its own accepted ideas about what work is important and what results are 'good', and about how such results can be achieved. Some ways of thinking and behaving come to be seen as self-evident, thus excluding other interpretations and behaviours (Meyer and Scott 1983). Structures and processes also acquire an intrinsic value (Selznick 1957), and cease to be regarded simply as a way of achieving the variable objectives of the leaders.

Seeing organizations as having institutional environments means emphasizing that many of the rules in individual organizations are part of a wider rule-system in society. There are many norms for how organizations should behave that are not formulated or controlled within the local, individual organizations but are produced on a more general level and have a more general applicability (Meyer and Scott 1983; Thomas *et al.* 1987).

A well-developed institution generates a capacity for action. It facilitates effective co-ordination. But it also creates inertia or friction in face of attempted reforms. This phenomenon is well known in political theory. Wolin (1960), for example, compared classical Greek and Roman political philosophies, and tried to identify the types of leadership that are possible in an institutionalized world. Greek political philosophy saw the leader as hero. Individuals could leave their mark on institutions and even society as a whole. The conditions of leadership in ancient Rome were quite different: leaders had to adapt to existing institutions, with all the rules and expectations this implied. The individual – the 'great statesman' – thus had less impact and the institutions had more, as regards creating the capacity for action as well as setting the limits for its exploitation.

Institutional identity

The concepts of 'organizations' and 'institutions' stand for continuity and predictability. And it is just the creation of stability in organizations that is often regarded as a major problem (Zucker 1988). At the same time major changes in the organization population, and within individual organizations, are undeniably a prominent feature of contemporary social development. We see the achievement of change as the greater challenge.

Even if reform projects are commonplace or even routine in organizations, it is not unusual to find a combination of sweeping changes and abortive reforms. For all these reasons we have to distinguish between different types of change, and between resistance to change in general and resistance to one specific kind.

Changes which accord with the institutional identity of an organization – i.e. its basic values, interests and opinions – are carried out as a matter of routine. Any organization reacts constantly to political signals, criticisms, changes in market conditions, new technologies, new information, growth or recession, as well as to new leaders or staff with new kinds of qualifications. The changes are effected in local standardized processes, without arousing any particular attention in the higher reaches (March 1981b; Jönsson 1989).

Such changes may contribute to the establishment of stability and continuity, in that they reinforce the organization's institutional identity. Nonetheless, if many small changes all point in the same direction, they may ultimately lead to substantial changes in this identity. And an accumulation of minor unco-ordinated changes may also lead to so many inconsistencies that extensive reforms are called for (Mosher 1965; March and Olsen 1983).

However, sudden big changes which violate the identity of the organization are pretty rare, and when they do occur they are the result of crisis or the strong expectation of crisis (March and Olsen 1989). In other words, when the gap becomes too great between an organization's perform- ance and the expectations and ambitions that people attach to it, reforms appear on the agenda (Cyert and March 1963).

We can also expect that the way a demand for reform is interpreted and the reactions it arouses will be influenced by the correlation between the content of the reform and the institutional identity of the organization. If a reform is to succeed although it clashes with the organizational identity, its advocates will have to command a concentration of power far outweighing any resources and alliances that can be mobilized by those they intend to reform. This presupposes in turn a commitment on the part of the leaders of the organization and a willingness to devote considerable time and interest to the reform project. Usually, however, the leaders are already extremely busy and can afford very little time or attention for reform activities. Other pressing commitments may all too easily distract their attention from the implementation of the reform, which may come to a halt even if the reform itself does not meet with much resistance (March and Olsen 1983).

Because of the institutional nature of organizations, reforms are easier to initiate than to decide on, and easier to decide on than to implement. Imple- mentation is particularly difficult if a reform requires the active participation of the reformees, or if the co-operation of several organizations is necessary. It can sometimes be difficult to change organizational symbols, but it is much harder to change behaviour. And even if reformers succeed in changing behaviour, it may not necessarily be (only) in the way they intended. Reorgani- zation, for example, may have unexpected effects on the level of conflict and the patterns of contact within and between organizations (Christensen 1985, 1987, 1989; Egeberg 1989b). The reformers and the reformees can be expected to act on a basis of institutionally determined values, interests, opinions and resources. Strong institutional values and resources increase the reformers' capacity for action and pave the way for active policy as long as the reforms are consistent with an organization's institutional identity (Egeberg 1984, 1989a; Olsen 1988c), but has the opposite effect if there is no such consistency.

The reformees may resist reforms because they disagree with the re- formers in their definition of 'good' results or solutions. If it is assumed that there are correct solutions to organizational problems, and that the reformers know about them, then such resistance can appear irrational and reactionary, the result apparently of thinking in grooves or jumping to the defence of individual interests. This interpretation, which is a familiar one in the literature of organizations (Mintzberg 1979), probably reflects what happens in many attempts at reform.

However, an alternative interpretation is that the reformees do want their organization to work better, and that they often have more insight into organizational operations than the reformers. When they adopt a negative stand on a reform, they may be doing so because practical experience, which in turn may have generated institutionalized structures and processes, tells them that the proposed reforms are based on faulty premises, are self-contradictory or even destructive to the operations in question.

INSTITUTIONALIZED ENVIRONMENTS

Not only do people inside organizations have specific ideas of how their organization's operations should be organized. Also people external to the organization display the same interest. They are not simply or sometimes even primarily interested in the services or goods produced by organizations. Organizations are also judged by the use they make of the structures, processes and ideologies which significant groups in their environment consider to be rational, efficient, reasonable, fair, natural or up to date. Organizations live in partly institutionalized environments (Meyer and Scott 1983).

Companies not only have to grapple with legislation regarding structure, such as the Joint Stock Company Act, or laws about employee representation on company boards: they are also exposed to the quirks of fashion in organizational structure. To win the respect of shareholders, banks, clients, suppliers or government, it may be advisable on some occasions to boast a centralized organization and on others a decentralized, divisionalized or matrix organization. The way the organization spends money can also affect its external support. It might be wise to invest a decent sum in in-house training, environmental protection or cultural sponsoring, regardless of whether the outlay has any effect on production.

Similarly there are norms dictating the processes which organizations are expected or even obliged to use. For instance, ever since the 1970s large companies have been expected – by banks and other finance institutes, by the business schools and consultancy firms – to draw up budgets. They have also been exposed to strong pressure to base their investment decisions on increasingly numerous and sophisticated financial calculations (Lundberg 1957; Renck 1971; Tell 1974).

The organization's ideology, the opinions it expresses, may also influence its external support. It can lay claim to numerous positive qualities such as efficiency, service-mindedness and public spirit. Objectives are even more useful in this connection: if the organization falls short of the norms in some respects it may be a good idea to emphasize how hard it is striving to achieve certain goals that society or important sections of it hold in high esteem (Brunsson 1989).

All these norms are external to a particular organization in the sense that they are formed outside and apply to a larger set of organizations. But this does not necessarily mean that people within an organization consider the norms to be external. People in organizations, perhaps in particular at the management level, often share the norms: their ideas of what is decent, rational, etc. do not differ from those of important people outside the organization. This makes the norms particularly strong.

But whether reformers share external norms or not, such norms will restrict their choice of reform content. It is difficult to propose reform ideas that are generally considered as unfashionable, unfair, irrational or in-efficient. Society may be convinced that theatres should in principle be governed by administrative managers rather than public meetings, or that universities should be run by bodies drawn from many groups in the community and not just by professors. Theatres and universities often go along with such normative preconceptions, regardless of whether they make for better theatre, research or education. Sometimes the norms are even acknowledged when the people who work at the theatres and universities are convinced that they will impair the quality of their results.

Reformers may also find it difficult to propose reforms which would involve creating new norms and institutions. Grønlie (1989) has shown, for example, how an institutionalized organizational form long established in private industry, namely the joint stock company, became predominant in the organization of state-owned companies in Norway after World War II, although the reformers were always dissatisfied with this arrangement. A model was available, ready for use, while it was proving difficult to develop new forms of organization. Similarly, the organization of the Norwegian National Petroleum Administration reflected traditional principles of the organization of government departments and agencies rather than the par-ticular nature of petroleum operations. Once again the joint stock company form was adopted, albeit with some modifications (Olsen 1989).

Finally, the existence and change of external norms may be the very reason for reform. When fashion swings, organizations must change their forms if they are to be considered normal and up to date.

Decoupling

The demands imposed from outside on the organization's structures, processes and ideologies are often justified on the grounds that they will increase its efficiency and adaptability. But it cannot be taken for granted that what powerful groups in society consider to be good administrative forms will actually lead to good results in practice.

When environmental norms and perceptions do not coincide with what is required for effective action and production, we can expect organizations for which effective actions are important to develop two sets of structures, processes and ideologies – one for each set of demands. For the organization it is important that these parallel sets do not disturb one another, and they therefore tend to be decoupled, separated and isolated (Meyer and Rowan 1977).

In practice, the result is two organizational structures. The formal organization is the more visible one, and it is thus particularly important that it should be adapted to the institutionalized norms of society. It is relatively easy – basically with a couple of strokes of the pen on an organizational chart – to adapt the formal organization to changes in norms or new laws or fashions. At the same time the organization can use a completely different structure for co-ordinating its activities. This is often referred to as the informal organization.

Similarly, two sets of organizational processes also evolve, one concerned with the production of goods and services, and one which is displayed to the rest of the world but has little or no effect on production. These second processes can be described as rituals. For example, a company may abide by the rules of industrial democracy, obediently consulting its employees before making important decisions, but the consultations will not necessarily have any effect on the content of the subsequent decisions. Increasingly, numerous and complex routines are used in investment calculations, but they have little impact on the ultimate investment decisions (Jansson 1987). It is perfectly possible to draw up a budget, and not to follow it (Högheim *et al.* 1989b). It is possible to collect huge amounts of information, and not use it when decisions are made (Feldman and March 1981).

Organizations may also develop double standards, one ideology for internal and one for external use. The picture of the organization and its objectives that corporate management presents to the outside world, does not necessarily have to agree with the signals they send out to their employees.

These differences between formal and informal organization, these rituals and double standards can all be very important, if not essential, to a modern organization which wants to live up to society's demands for respectability and rationality, while also effectively producing co-ordinated action (Brunsson 1989).

The existence of decoupling means that organizations influence the strength of external support, or the amount of resources, freedom or criticism that will come their way, by altering their structures and processes and ideologies, regardless of whether such changes increase their production or improve their efficiency. Similarly, it is possible to affect people's picture or perception of an organization by talk, changing a name or projecting an image through symbols without (necessarily) changing any structures or processes or altering productivity or efficiency.

In this light reform projects can be seen as one step in moulding public opinion, and the very fact that reform is being attempted tells the outside world that the organization is open to change and renewal. A visible willingness to change may then make it easier for the organization to acquire resources and support, and to shield itself from criticism and external intervention. Such an interpretation helps to explain why so many reforms are attempted, even though they have little effect on structures and processes, let alone on results.

Modernity and fashion

The institutional environments of an organization may have been profoundly affected by long-term historical and cultural processes, significant trends which, although not answering the intentions of any specific group of reformers, nonetheless determine developments. 'Modernization' is an example of such a trend, and we can expect that any reform accepted as 'modern' will have a greater chance of success than many others. Being 'modern' is associated in our culture with improvement, progress and development, which makes it extremely difficult to argue against reforms aimed at modernizing an organization. But these profound and long-term trends do not only block the opponents of reform: they also determine in part what the reformers can include in their reforms, thus restricting their freedom of choice.

Institutionalized environments are also affected by other shorter-term fluctuations, the swings of fashion. Democracy and efficiency are certainly values central to economic and political life, but the balance between them can vary greatly, often within a short time. During the 1970s, for example, many reforms were aimed at making organizations more democratic. In all kinds of organizations in many countries, campaigns were launched to extend participation and representation, to make information more available and to extend rights of control to more members. Then during the 1980s the normative framework changed radically: reforms associated with democracy and co-determination became increasingly rare. The focus switched to efficiency, instead, and the model for attempts at reorganizing the public sector was an idealized picture of private enterprise. The aim of most reform attempts was to improve efficiency by adapting to market forces and encouraging competition.

Such fluctuations in fashion also affect the content of reform proposals, as well as limiting the number of acceptable arguments and choices available to both advocates and opponents. During the 1980s it was easier than it had been ten years before to justify and win support for reform proposals implying an improvement in efficiency, and more difficult than it had been in the past to argue for increasing democracy.

The creation of meaning

The idea of the institutionalized environment, characterized by significant long-term trends and short-term fluctuations in fashion, provides an alternative or complement to the rational-instrumental perspective when it comes to interpreting the effects of attempted reforms or trying to explain why changes occur without their being the result of reform. When the environment is institutionalized, the primary effect of attempted reforms may be the creation of meaning and the moulding of public opinion. Attempted reforms can then be regarded as part of a cultural struggle for norms, world views, symbols and legitimacy. Reform processes are characterized more by the creation and reshaping of aims and preferences than by the transformation of predetermined aims into new structures and processes.

In such situations attempts at reform are only loosely connected with any direct improvements in structures, processes or results. Both reformers and observers may see the reform as successful, even though it results in few material changes. The participants are not even particularly interested in implementing the reform. Nor are they especially interested in following up any effects it may subsequently have on behaviour or results.

The perception of institutionalized environments and attempted reforms as elements in the creation of meaning and norms in a society also gives us an alternative approach to the question of why changes occur in formal organizations. It is less a matter of sudden big changes stemming from explicit choices and reforms, and more one of gradual transitions resulting from changes in world views and norms.

A gradual redefinition of an organization, of its objectives and the criteria on which outsiders should assess it, may also help reformers to create a crisis, a major discrepancy between ambitions and performance, which in turn motivates a call for sweeping reforms. The tendency in the late 1980s to describe all kinds of organizations, including government agencies and universities, in terms previously reserved for industry, and to cite economic efficiency as the paramount criterion, can be seen as just such an attempt to launch a process of redefinition.

The redefinition of the tasks, the objectives and the performance of an organization can be brought about by rational discourse, involving argument and the development of ideas (Wagner and Wittrock 1989). But world views and norms can also be changed in a process involving slogans and propaganda, myths and symbols. In formal organizations the production of ideology and attempts to change organizational cultures by influencing norms and ideas, are being used deliberately and increasingly as a management technique (Czarniawska-Joerges 1988a, 1988b).

CHALLENGING A HEGEMONY

In the subsequent chapters we will use the insight that both organizations and their environments can be institutionalized when analysing administrative reforms. This is in sharp contrast with how reforms are normally presented. Most advocates of reform base their arguments on a rational-instrumental way of thinking. The norm is to define objectives in order to determine the organizational forms which would be most effective and functional in terms of those objectives. The interpretation of change as reform and formal organizations as instruments, and the assumption of a hierarchical relationship between reformers and reformees, together possess a sort of normative hegemony. It is difficult for other interpretations of the processes of change and attempted reform to make any real impact or even to be taken seriously.

One important reason for this is that, when we challenge the rational-instrumental mode, we are also challenging some of the most influential norms and conceptions prevailing in our modern society. This applies particularly to the belief that historical development and society's organizational arrangements are, and should continue to be, the result of control, rationality, leadership and authority. Consequently we have no expectations that the studies presented in this book will unsettle the hegemony of the rational-instrumental philosophy. But it is important to bear in mind that the rational-instrumental model has long been the subject of criticism, and that some of its assumptions are particularly unrealistic in our contemporary open society with its multiplicity of power centres and its high rate of change.

An important task for organizational research is to try to understand to what extent organizational forms can be chosen, and how far reformers can achieve their goals with the help of deliberate, directed changes in administrative structures and processes. Our analysis starts from the recognition that formal organizations and their environments are often institutionalized, which means that ways of thinking and acting are governed by culturally determined rules. Consequently organizational research needs to explore the question of how institutional factors affect change processes and attempts at reform, and how far they account for the weakness that sometimes exists in the links between reform and change. However, we shall be saying very little here about how changes occur when they are not the result of reforms. We will concentrate on possible interpretations of reform projects, regardless of whether or not they lead to the intended change.

The insight that institutionalized organizations and environments will restrict the reformers' choices has some paradoxical consequences. On the one hand, it might help to scotch the illusion of the reformers' freedom of choice and the myth that the future can be fairly easily influenced by designing rational, efficient organizations today. On the other hand, this view may help reformers and others to see more clearly just how much freedom of choice they actually have. And this should make it easier for all parties to make sensible choices. People would also be better equipped to defend their interests and achieve their goals if they based their actions on realistic institutional conditions, instead of ignoring the institutional framework within which they nonetheless have to act.

At the same time an institutional perspective draws attention to the fact that attempted reforms are largely about things other than making decisions and changing structures, processes and behaviour with a view to raising the efficiency of production. Institutions are the bearers of meanings, norms and ideas. Reforms and institutional change processes are thus part of a historical-cultural definition process which gives meaning and order to our perceptions of society and social development. Reform processes can affect what participants and observers regard as possible, true and right. They can contribute to the creation and alteration of objectives and preferences. The study of reform can thus help us to understand who has the power to mould public opinion in individual organizations and in society as a whole.

We cannot understand reform without studying some examples of it. In this book we base our discussion on empirical studies of reforms. These studies include many different types of organization and a variety of reforms. We have looked at companies, banks, various kinds of public agencies, governments, government commissions, special-interest organizations, county councils and municipalities which have acted as reformers or themselves been the subject of attempted reforms. We have studied attempts to alter the institutional affiliation of organizations, their company missions and strategies, their organizational structures and their accounting and budgeting systems. We have studied reforms that turned out well, and others that turned out less well.

As reforms generally take a long time and involve many people, studies of reforms require a good deal of empirical work. Knowledge of the history of an organization is often required if we are to understand even its most recent reforms. The facade that an organization presents to the world may have little to do with its internal structures, processes or ideologies. This is particularly true in connection with reforms. It is important that researchers do not simply register facades; they should also look behind them.

Reforms are concerned with ideas and practices and the relationship between them. In order to understand reforms, it is necessary to study both sides of this relationship, and to distinguish between them. Some of the following chapters are based on the study of ideas and practices, while others concentrate on what we have found to be the most important aspect of reform: ideas about organizations.

In the next chapter we use the example of public sector modernization programmes in exploring further what the view of organizations as institutionalized may mean for our understanding of administrative reforms.

2 Reforming institutionalized organizations

For decades governments worldwide have provided students of public administration with ample opportunity to study the processes of reform. Though there have been cycles of enthusiasm and disappointment, governments seem to remain convinced that public administration can be improved by means of explicit choice and design. In recent years, many governments have embarked on a new round of reforms. Working on an assumption that major surgery is needed, they have put comprehensive administrative reform on the national political agenda, formulating policies both to reshape the public sector and to redraw the boundary between the public and the private sectors. Across a range of political, economic and cultural settings, there is a great deal of overlap in the problems that have been identified and the solutions that have been proposed.

Public administration is generally criticized for being too complex, centralized, interventionist, powerful, bureaucratic, rigid and incompetent. It is thought to be inadequately responsive to elected leaders and citizens, and too sensitive to pressure from organized interests and groups, while devoting too little attention to cost-effectiveness, results, efficiency and productivity. There is a general disenchantment with the performance, structures and processes of public administration, which has arisen after numerous attempts over a long period to modernize and rationalize the structures of public administration. We must therefore question whether the ideas, concepts and theories underlying those reforms have been adequate (Brunsson 1985, 1989; Olsen 1986, 1988a, 1989b; Knott and Miller 1987; Kooiman and Eliassen 1987; Sjøblom and Ståhlberg 1987; Campbell and Peters 1988; Crozier 1988; Dente and Kjellberg 1988; Peters 1988a; Brunsson et al. 1989; Egeberg 1989a; March and Olsen 1989).

For most of its history, public administration has been a practical art rather than a theoretical discipline. In administrative reform, applied, institution-specific knowledge and political pressure have been more influential than theoretical models (Sjøblom and Ståhlberg 1987). Advisers have seldom accounted explicitly for their assumptions and methods (Scharpf 1977). Yet progress in explaining change and inertia in political institutions is likely to depend on the development of better theoretical ideas and concepts in order to understand the nature of reforms as explicitly designed and controlled modifications in organizational structure in order to achieve pre-stated goals.

Recent reform programmes may encourage a return to some old and central questions in political theory concerning the role of administration. They might also help to restore government structure and administrative variables as legitimate focuses of research (Campbell and Peters 1988). Recent reform programmes provide students of comparative public administration with the opportunity to update their theoretical framework for analysing organizations and their formation. Do the structures of governmental and political institutions matter? If so, what are the effects of different organizational forms? Why have the current forms developed? How can we explain their origins, development and endurance?

This chapter explores how modernization programmes are affected by the characteristics of existing institutions. First, we argue that contemporary modernization programmes are based on an instrumental view of organizational decision-making and change. The following section elaborates one part of the alternative perspective presented in the previous chapter, namely the idea that organizations are institutionalized. Then we examine some of the implications of this idea for the study of modernization programmes. Finally, we show that while the instrumental view of organizations dominates the way reformers talk and write about modernization, an institutional approach is a better explanatory tool in analysing the activities of reformers and the outcomes of reform efforts.

MODERNIZATION, RATIONAL ADAPTATION AND COMPETITIVE SELECTION

What does it mean to be, or to become, modern? Modernization as a concept suggests a society heading towards a better state, a development towards progress and maturity (Bendor 1977; Eckstein 1982; Offe 1987). 'Modern' society, as compared with 'traditional' or 'primitive', implies a rational approach, effectiveness, efficiency and improvement. Ideas of reform defined as modern are difficult to challenge. Individuals who resist reform are easily labelled old-fashioned, outmoded, obsolete, obstructive, irrational or reactionary. For change to be embarked upon, a country's public sector should be seen to be 'lagging behind' the public administration in other countries or the private sector.

Modernization is a disputed term, but there seems to be agreement on two basic issues related to decision-making and organizations. The first is that modernization implies individual choice based on utilitarian calculation, which is extended at the expense of rule-prescribed behaviour derived from custom, habit and prescriptive roles. The underlying principle of behaviour in modern society is the choice of optimum means (including organizational forms, processes, leaders and time allocation) in pursuit of self-determined goals

The second area of broad agreement regarding organizations is that the sphere of formal organizations, as deliberately designed instruments for the attainment of specified goals, grows at the expense of traditional bonds and forms of social organization like the family, the local community and the religious community. Formal organizations are seen as the most rational and efficient form of social organization. They are fundamental to modern civilization, an expression of the high value modern society places on means-end rationality, effectiveness and productivity (Etzioni 1964). Because the rational and the traditional are seen as opposites, breaking with the past becomes a central aspect of modern culture. In order to be effective and productive it is necessary to be able to adapt to changing circumstances, whether past or anticipated. Change is normal and a sign of modernity.

Whereas public administration traditionally pursued absolute organizational principles, the structure-performance hypothesis of organizational theory suggests that structures are contingent on circumstance. Depending on the aims and the environment of an organization, some structures are more effective and efficient than others. Success depends on constructing appropriate links between an organization's structure and its shifting context. Thus, the problem of organizational design is to improve adaptability to changing conditions (Lawrence and Lorsch 1967; Galbraith 1973, 1977). Organizational effectiveness becomes one of the main determinants of structure, and the organizational forms which exist in a society are the ones that are most effective and efficient within that society (Basu *et al.* 1987). Increasingly efficient interaction with the broad environment is attained through one of two processes: rational adaptation or competitive selection.

Efficient reform and rational adaptation

In this section, our focus is on single organizations. We start from the premise that organizational forms can deliberately be chosen. Changes in structure are explained as willed design.

Organizations are consciously planned to seek specific goals. They continually evaluate their activities and respond to new opportunities and challenges by means of deliberate restructuring (Etzioni 1964). Organizations may either adapt to resource dependencies (Pfeffer and Salancik 1978), or to norms and beliefs in their environment (Meyer and Rowan 1977); or they may restructure themselves in order to reduce transaction costs (Williamson 1975, 1985). Reformers are assumed not only to know what they want, but to be able to diagnose what is wrong with the organization and its performance; to be able to dictate how structures should be changed in order to meet objectives, as well as to have the authority and power to implement reforms.

Efficient environments and competitive selection

Here we consider changes within a population of organizations. The survival of an organizational form or an individual organization depends on how well they match their environment. Yet within this tradition individual organizations are seen as prisoners of their past with no capacity to transform themselves. Alternatively, changes have little adaptive value, in that they do not improve an organization's performance or its chances of survival. Structural change and variation are dictated by the environment, and better matches are achieved through the development of new, individual organizations and organizational forms which, over time, replace older and less well-adapted ones (Stinchcombe 1965; Hannan and Freeman 1977, 1984). Assuming a context of efficient, competitive selection, neoclassical economists see particular structures as optimal outcomes of the current balance of competing forces. In explaining variations in structure, the static equilibrium theory of maximizing behaviour under perfect competition need not consider the past, the process through which a structure is generated, or the characteristics of reformers trying to adapt an organization to its environment (Basu *et al.* 1987).

How helpful are the ideas of rational adaptation and competitive selection when it comes to understanding change and reforms in public administration? There is no reason to suppose either that reformers are always successful in adapting organizations to contingencies or that competition and selection mechanisms are always effective in weeding out organizations that are not optimal. The next section argues that when adaptation and selection processes are inefficient, it is more productive to view political organizations as institutions than as instruments.

BOUNDED MORALITY, INTELLIGENCE AND POWER, AND THE RELEVANCE OF INSTITUTIONS

It is easy to imagine conditions under which reformers or environments are inefficient. Reformers may be unable to formulate precise, consistent and stable goals. Their analytical capabilities may be overwhelmed by the complexity of a situation or by the pace of change. They may lack the power to implement their choices. At the opposite extreme, contextual constraints on administrative reforms may be overestimated. It might require time to achieve equilibrium, or there may possibly be a number of different equilibria. An institutional analysis of political organizations must consider the boundedness of morality, intelligence and power.

Bounded morality

The concept of bounded morality challenges the idea that organizational improvement can be evaluated on the basis of a shared purpose or fixed individual preferences. Organizations routinely make decisions without the kind of preferences that would satisfy models of rational choice and rational adaptation (March 1981a). Individuals may maintain goals for an organization, but goal ambiguity and goal conflict are normal. Individuals can co-ordinate their actions and co-operate without agreeing on goals (Cyert and March 1963; Keeley 1988). Organizational structure and decision-making also affect goals; and changing (endogenous) preferences make it difficult to apply the Coase theorem (1937, 1960), which suggests that organizational structures are to be evaluated by their contributions to lowering transaction costs. One implication of endogenous preferences is that it becomes more difficult to evaluate the performance and improvement of organizations (March 1978; von Weizsäcker 1984).

Bounded intelligence

While the idea of bounded rationality is well known, the problems of experiential learning have only recently been explored in studies of formal organizations (March and Olsen 1975; Levitt and March 1988). Both ideas seem relevant to the study of public administration, in which the paucity of evidence stands in sharp contrast to the firmly held ideological convictions aroused by alternative organizational proposals. There is still no firm theoretical basis for organizational design, and proposals for change therefore tend to be contradictory (Simon 1957; Kaufman 1977; Seidman 1980). When research indicates that structure affects participation, patterns of interaction, response levels, the nature of conflicts, the balance of power within organizations or their capacity for innovation, the authors usually emphasize the tentative and provisional nature of their findings. Others are more disillusioned, and point to the scarcity of testable hypotheses and generalizable explanations as well as to the problems of describing, measuring and classifying today's mixed organizational structures. The essence is captured by Peters (1988a), who argues that the structure of administrative systems is the most frequently manipulated and perhaps the least understood aspect of public administration. Reformers themselves are rarely interested in a thorough evaluation of what reforms have achieved (Brown 1979; Feldman and March 1981; Steinman and Miewald 1984; Røvik 1987; Levitt and March 1988).

Bounded power

Structural change is often resisted because those affected do not perceive it as beneficial and progressive. Instead, reform proposals are regarded as being disruptive, painful and threatening, and a drain on resources, especially in its effects on the organization's internal structures regulating status, power and policy.

Organizational reform is an exercise in the acquisition or use of political power (Peters 1988b), and it is unlikely that conflicts can always be resolved by reference to 'the presence of one or more power centres which control the concerted efforts of the organization and direct them toward its goals' (Etzioni 1964: 3). It is also unlikely that conflicts can always be resolved by the overriding influence of competition and selection. Environments may be more or less competitive, complex or simple, benign or harsh. They may change slowly or rapidly. Organizations vary as to their power to select, influence or survive within their environments. Where there are large numbers of incompatible interests, and thus multiple variables with conflicting design implications, a public organization must choose which part of the environment to adapt to (Child 1977; Child and Kieser 1981; Nystrom and Starbuck 1981). Government, in particular, is in the business of forming its environment rather than adapting to it (Hood 1979). Thus, creating commitment and winning support are key aspects of reform processes. We need to study the institutional arrangements and the interests, resources, cleavages and alliances organized around modernization issues, as well as the value-, interest- and power bases of organizations to be reformed.

Organizations as institutions

In a world of bounded morality, intelligence, and power, political organizations may be conceptualized as institutions rather than as instruments. When political organizations are analysed as institutions, they are seen to be collections of rules. These rules define legitimate participants and agendas, prescribe the rules of the game, and create sanctions against deviations, as well as establishing guidelines for how the institution may be changed. Institutions create a temporary and imperfect order. They influence and simplify the way we think and act, what we observe, how we interpret what we observe, our standards of evaluation and how we cope with conflicts.

The specific perspective on institutional analysis suggested here differs in important ways from an instrumental perspective in (a) its interpretation of how decisions are made, (b) what is at stake in organizational reform efforts, (c) how change takes place, and (d) when structures are likely to change.

Within that perspective (March and Olsen 1989):

- Political actors are driven by a logic of appropriateness built into standard operating procedures, conventions and rules of thumb rather than (or in addition to) a logic of calculated self-interest.
- Organizations are built around the construction of meaning as well as (or instead of) making choices. Reforms may have as much to do with affecting the interpretations of participants and onlookers as with affecting effectiveness and efficiency.
- Organizational structures cannot easily be metamorphosed to any arbitrary form. Adaptations to environments are not instantaneous or efficient, and equilibrium between environmental contingencies and organizational structures are rare. An organization may survive in spite of the fact that it would not be chosen if decision-makers could select without the constraints of the organization's origin and history (Basu *et al.* 1987). It may persist even though no individual benefits from it (Akerlof 1976).

The assumption of organizational inertia is a priori not more useful than the assumption of perfect flexibility through rational adaptations or competitive selection. There is a need for history-dependent process models which could explain both flexibility and change. There is still an inadequate understanding of when structures change and what stimulates change. The institutional analysis we present here suggests that major structural change takes place at long intervals. It arises as a consequence either of crises, related to declining performance or increasing expectations, or of conflict between the rights and duties granted by different institutional rule systems. The next section addresses some possible implications of this view: implications for when change will take place, which parts of an organization will change more easily than others, who are most likely to be successful reformers, and what are the likely results of reform efforts.

IMPLICATIONS FOR STUDIES OF MODERNIZATION PROGRAMMES

The structures of public administration are simultaneously both stable and fluid. Political organizations are not entirely rigid; nor are they immortal. Nevertheless, comprehensive reforms often fail. Change takes place without explicit decisions to change: there is no prearranged plan and there are no architects (Sait 1938). Change is sometimes explained by means of a life-cycle analogy associated with the birth, maturation, decline and death of organic systems (Kimberly and Miles 1980; Cameron *et al.* 1988). Changes occur before decisions are taken. Decision-making does not produce change, or it leads to unanticipated, unintended or unforeseen changes (March and Olsen 1976, 1983; March 1981b; Romanow 1981).

In order to understand the intricacies of organizational inertia, change and reform, we need to analyse the interaction of the intentions of reformers, organizational structures and transformations in society. Organizational change is shaped by neither reformers' intentions nor environmental transformations, though both have a role to play. This view is reflected in the debate of to what extent organizational change depends on the normative match between reform programmes and established organizations, the match between reform programmes and the normative drift in society, the degree to which reform intentions are well-defined or ambiguous, and the organization of reform processes.

The normative matching between reforms and institutionalized organizations

Organizational responses to external reform efforts are affected by the degree of consistency between the value basis and beliefs underlying a proposed reform and the value basis and beliefs of an organization (March and Olsen 1975). Organizations have their own dynamics. Incremental transformations through routinized processes which relate the organization to its environment (March 1981b) will succeed as long as they are consistent with the established institutional identity of the organization. Organizations mobilize their resources and their allies to resist external efforts to change those parts of their structures which relate closely to their institutional identities. Similarly, individuals who identify with established organizations – because, for example, they have been in power for extended periods and are seen as the architects of current structures – are unlikely to propose and seek to introduce comprehensive reform programmes inconsistent with established institutional identities. For them, creating new agencies will be more attractive than changing an established institutional identity. Since creating new organizations is easiest in times of slack resources, reforming existing organizations becomes a likely response to performance crises, primarily in periods with little slack.

The more an organization is integrated into a larger political order so that changes in one organization require changes in several others, the less it is likely that deliberate change will occur (Krasner 1988). Constitutional reforms, i.e. those affecting the political order regulating the exercise of public authority and power, are difficult to achieve.

The normative matching between reforms and society

Reformers are more likely to succeed if they try to change organizations in ways consistent with long-term trends in society, both international and national, than if they try to go against the tide. Modernization, democratization, bureaucratization and professionalization represent aggregate processes which constrain the options available to reformers. Moreover, the normative drift of society is not necessarily consistent. In the most extreme case, reformers may try to adapt public administration to conflicting trends or demands that are not reconcilable.

What can be achieved in reforming organizations is a long-standing question in political theory. One view is that people should be taken as they are, with their self-chosen values and individual choices. As argued by Madison (Hamilton *et al.* 1787-8/1964), if men were angels no government would be necessary. But humanity is not angelic, and it is neither possible nor even desirable to eradicate all evil from the face of earth. Therefore we need to design political institutions which control and regulate the negative effects of human selfishness and immoral choices by individuals by letting selfish ambition counteract selfish ambition through competition.

A contending idea in political philosophy since Aristotle is that public organizations and laws are not adequate in themselves to ensure virtue. Civic education is necessary to establish moral standards of justice and fairness and to balance principles of public virtue against self-interest (Morrisey 1986; Goldwin 1986). Thus, an alternative to changing public organizations is to change individuals and the demands they make upon public administrations. The weaker civic education is in a society, the more likely it is that public administration will be asked to do things which cannot be done whatever organizational form is adopted. Reform cannot be successful.

The ambiguity of intentions

The outcome of modernization programmes depends on the intentions of the reformers as well as on organizational responses and environmental factors. Reformers are more likely to succeed if their plans are focused and well-defined rather than broad and general.

When there is a poor match between reform aims, institutional identities of organizations and environments, reformers will confront conflicting demands. As a result, they will find it hard to take the initiative and present their plans clearly. More generally, the aims of a reform may themselves be uncertain because the merits of that reform appear to be ambiguous. Politics and public administration reflect a precarious balance between the need for change versus the need for stability. The recent government obsession with change has to be held up against the traditional concern in political analysis for order, predictability and reliability, and the destructive effects of institutional decline or breakdown (Wolin 1960; Leazes 1987).

There is a dramatic scenario in which reform attempts create conflict and lead to the breakdown of established values, identities and relationships. It is more common for the search for new structures to conflict with an organization's capacity to perform predictably and accountably. There is a balance to be found between exploiting known structures and exploring the potential benefits of new ones (March 1989). The results of organizations that undergo frequent or protracted reorganizations may be limited, and those organizations have little chance of survival (Hannan and Freeman 1984). Governments in particular may be unwilling to devote much time and energy to introducing comprehensive reforms as opposed to debating the need for change. This is the case when the expected adaptive value is modest because means-end relationships are uncertain, the environment is ambiguous, performance is difficult to measure or evaluate, opposition is likely, or it takes a long time to transform a structure.

The tensions and contradictions inherent in modernization programmes may also affect the willingness of governments to embark on such efforts. For example, representativeness, neutral competence and executive leadership are competing values in the organization of public agencies. Improvement in one sphere often makes it difficult to improve on the others. One period's horror story of bureaucracy is the next period's ideal. While the reformers of public administration in one period focus on creating incentives for initiative, innovation, and willingness to take responsibility, the bureaucrats of a later one are expected to act in accordance with political dictates rather than in an entrepreneurial style (Kaufman 1956; Jacobsen 1964, 1966).

Why then do reformers keep trying if the improvements in terms of effectiveness and efficiency are so unpredictable and difficult to achieve? Citizens will support a set of norms, beliefs and practices embodied in public administration, and reform programmes may be a part of the creation of meaning or even as propaganda (March and Olsen 1976, 1983, 1989;

Brunsson 1985, 1989). It is often difficult to legitimize reforms by demonstrating that particular decisions will produce appropriate results. Thus, legitimacy depends as much on the willingness to reform, on rhetoric and on the nature of the reform process as it does on eventual outcomes. Structural, process or personnel measures are treated as surrogates for outcome measures, and it becomes of vital important for organizations to maintain normatively approved forms (Meyer and Rowan 1977).

Modernization programmes may be seen as part of a long-term redefinition of politics and society. On the one hand, legitimacy effects may be valuable, independent of structural changes, making reformers more interested in rhetoric than in implementation. On the other hand, ignoring the constraints of bounded morality, intelligence and power can create unrealistic expectations and overselling the need for reform. Reformers may exaggerate the defects of existing forms and overrate the benefits of new proposals. Possibly, reforms cannot successfully be marketed unless they promise more than they can deliver (Schick 1977).

Using rhetoric to change peoples' attitudes and beliefs in order to create a normative climate may however also facilitate future structural change. While Marx (1845/1976) viewed the interpretation of history and the changing of history as opposites, it is possible that the two processes are closely related. Debates about reform programmes may alter the values of the state, the purpose and meaning of governmental actions, the rationale and legitimacy of organizational boundaries, the way in which conflict is regulated and the conditions under which different interests can be pursued (Poggi 1984; Dyson 1980).

The organization of reform

To succeed, comprehensive reform requires the backing of a strong organization capable of maintaining support for the reform and of overcoming resistance. Any goals of comprehensive reforms that are not apparent in the organization of the reform process itself are unlikely to succeed.

Change can occur when the inherent authority and power of the public administration does not conform to actual influence and control, i.e. cannot cope with critical contingencies (Pfeffer 1978). But public administration does not respond instantly to minor deviations in power: it tends to maintain the status quo until the external demands for change are substantial. Comprehensive reforms in public administration are likely to succeed only if there are significant inefficiencies in the historical development of those organizations; that is, if the authority and power exercised by policy-makers deviate markedly from the levels they would have held in a state of equilibrium (a 'clearance of the power market' (March and Olsen 1989)).

Political leaders have succeeded in introducing reforms where reorganizations have been given top priority and ordinary procedures have been bypassed (Roness 1979; Christensen 1987; Egeberg 1984, 1987, 1989a). However, such success have generally been restricted to the reform of specific governmental agencies. Comprehensive reforms tend to attract more opposition and trigger processes with complex and unforeseen consequences. If the organizational structure cannot protect reform efforts from short-term fluctuations in attention, comprehensive reforms are more likely to become 'garbage can' processes and to be derailed or defeated (March and Olsen 1983).

The process of change itself may to a certain extent be institutionalized and rule-bound. In addition, organizations are likely to resist what they see as inappropriate reform procedures. If comprehensive reform presupposes a perceived performance crisis, political pressure and confrontation may, under some conditions, be more productive than merely defining reform as a technical issue. Where there is a history of gradual, consensual reform (such as in the Nordic countries), governments may be less successful in introducing reform under these conditions.

In the next section these speculations are assessed in the light of evidence from some recent reform attempts. To date, there is no comparative study of modernization programmes in a representative sample of countries. The case studies available from single countries or specific organizations have not yet been reviewed and analysed, nor will they be here. Instead, our theoretical speculations are illustrated by specific observations, primarily from studies of modernization efforts in Britain and in the Nordic countries. Given our focus upon normative matches, it is interesting to compare British reforms after the Thatcher victory in 1979 with the reform efforts of the Social Democratic governments of Norway and Sweden.

SOME OBSERVATIONS

While some have announced the coming of a post-modern era, modernization programmes are strongly influenced by a vision of modernity, including a conception of organizations as instruments and change as deliberate policy. Such programmes assume that the problems of public administration can be solved by reorganization. Comprehensive administrative policies imply that governments, in order to achieve their political ends, can apply a coherent set of ideas and practices to the organizational structures and processes of public administration. This entails two assumptions: first, that organizational form is a significant determinant of administrative performance; and, second, that choices made by political leaders are important determinants of organizational forms.

The latter concept emphasizes that human will, reason, effort and power are all involved in the transformation of society. The former represents a view of public administration as part of modern technology, as illustrated by the use of such mechanical metaphors as 'instrument', 'tool', 'apparatus' and 'machinery' of governance (Olsen 1988a). In general, the normative world of modernization programmes is characterized by rationality and control. The enthusiasm for rational management techniques remains high although they have produced few striking successes and several failures in the public sector (Landau and Stout 1979; Wittrock and Lindström 1984; Goodsell 1985).

In contrast, the behavioural world of modernizers is more complex and less easy to predict or control. There is a marked lack of alternative organizational models and uncertainty about their effects. For instance, there is a scarcity of literature on the distinctions between public and private organizations, or between centralized or decentralized structures. Reformers often argue that administrative policies should be seen as experimental and conscious attempts to learn from experience. Nevertheless, changes are seldom followed by systematic efforts to assess successes and failures:

> Little information has been made available by any reporting country on the evaluation of results of their modernization efforts . . . . Most countries have yet to incorporate full-scale evaluation in their reform efforts.

> (OECD 1989: 9)

Modernization programmes (at least in OECD countries) are collections of reform ideas rather than coherent doctrines with a unified strategy of change. Yet the international tendency in the 1980s was neo-liberal, and was critical of many of the developments in the post-World War II (Social Democratic) welfare state. This was replaced with 'more managerial thinking and market mentality' (OECD 1987: 117). The private sector became the role model, and public administration was seen as a service to citizens as clients and consumers. Programmes reflected both the penetration of the microeconomic, cost-benefit approach to public administration (Colvin 1985; Downs and Larkey 1986) and the renewed interest in the economics of organizations (Moe 1984).

There was widespread agreement among governments regarding the need to reshape the public sector in order to increase efficiency and improve public services. The goals of public administration were to be specified precisely; and better methods for monitoring results and measuring efficiency and productivity were to be sought. Citizens' desires were to be met through prices and markets rather than by means of formal representation, advocacy and rules. The introduction of market-style forms in the public sector would create more competition and increase the citizen's freedom of choice. The administrative culture was to be transformed. There was little support for the Weberian idea that bureaucracy was the most modern, rational and efficient form of administration (Weber *et al.* 1924/1978). What was to be achieved was more important than how (in terms of procedures and rules), and incentives and performance were to be more closely linked. A modern public administration was supposed to delegate and decentralize in order to improve its flexibility. The possible benefits of stability and the trade-offs between stability and adaptability were barely considered. The programmes also reflected a strong belief in the value of information technology and electronic data-processing equipment.

Modernization programmes varied in their proposals for redrawing the boundaries between the public and the private sectors. Some governments wanted to reduce public sector expenditure and employment; others were 'pragmatic' or reluctant to commit themselves on this point, but none advocated major growth in the public sector.

From the viewpoint of normative matching, these observations are not surprising. While a concern with economy and efficiency is common to most governments, the issue of privatization was linked to a major cleavage in the organizing politics of many countries. It was predictable that the Thatcher government, with its neo-liberal goals and negative attitudes towards the public sector, should be in the forefront of modernization efforts. It is not surprising that this government emphasized both privatization and value-for-money.

As expected, the Social Democratic governments in Norway and Sweden showed little enthusiasm for reforming public administration along neo-liberal lines. Social Democratic programmes focused upon reforming the public sector in order to make it perform better, rather than upon privatization. The Swedish programme more than any other accentuated the need to widen democratic participation. Yet even in Sweden the private sector became the role model for civil servants (Czarniawska 1985) and for the symbols and logos employed by the state (Petersson and Fredén 1987).

Modernization programmes tended to lack explicit structural analyses, for instance of what organizational options were available to reformers in modern society. When options were discussed, they were usually seen as dependent upon economic developments. The idea of a normative mismatch between reforms and general trends in society may, however, help explain why it is often difficult for reformers to deregulate (Christensen 1989) or to implement the management-by-objectives features of some modernization programmes.

Modernization, involving as it does a reduction in the effectiveness of informal control via shared standards of appropriateness, creates a need for more detailed, formal rules and more powerful enforcement mechanisms. As society becomes more fragmented and specialized, with less common socialization, less frequent contacts between social groups and more utilitarian calculation and strategic behaviour, there will be a wider demand for formal rules and contracts in order to resolve conflicts (North 1984). It follows that attempts to reduce the number of formal rules may be unlikely to succeed in modern society. Many of those likely to lose out in bargaining over private contracts may prefer public regulation. Similarly, techniques like management-by-objectives may be difficult to implement in modern society because the participants do not share common goals. In a plural society, one group of actors cannot easily force its goals upon another.

Recent reform efforts are responses to a situation where many public programmes have built-in, quasi-mechanical increases in expenditure, where citizens-as-taxpayers are seemingly unwilling to pay more, and yet citizens-as-clients and consumers demand new services as well as higher service efficiency and quality (OECD 1989). The idea that a proper response is to reform public administration and thereby provide better services for less money has to be attractive to elected politicians. However, it is not obvious that this idea is viable, i.e. that better services for less money can be achieved simultaneously in any public organization.

It is quite probable that, through the long period of growth in public administration, some organizations accumulated excess resources and became inefficient. However, it is unclear how much waste there is in public administration today (Kelman 1985). Improving efficiency may also be relatively unimportant in the context of solving a nation's economic problems. The running costs of government departments are small in comparison with expenditure on public programmes (Fry 1988). As it is uncertain what can be achieved through reorganization, modern society may need to consider the possibility of coping with the current demands through civic education and of initiating public debate about the realism and legitimacy of those demands.

The conflicts between the international neo-liberal trend and their own ideologies and traditions have created difficulties for the Social Democratic governments in the Nordic countries in clearly defining their intentions as well as their criteria for improvement and success in public administration. Reform programmes promised better service, a better and more efficient economy, improved workplaces for employees, and greater democracy through increasing the influence of elected leaders and the public generally. Programmes were founded on a rhetorical claim of serving common, apolitical goals of economy and efficiency. They retreated from politically divisive issues like privatization and whether reforms would serve particular groups. For instance, the Danish government promised that life would improve for Danish citizens. The Swedish government said it would take the citizens' part against bureaucratic inefficiency. What was lacking in such statements was any explicit consideration of whether the goals appeared consistent and achievable in light of the dilemmas and conflicts inherent in comprehensive administrative reforms. The programmes primarily address how public administration could improve its practices in choosing means. There was little assessment of the values being pursued or of the particular concept of welfare underlying the modernization programmes (Mellbourn 1986; Olsen 1988a, 1988b; Bentzon 1988; Hansen 1989).

By contrast, the intentions of the Thatcher government were clearer, although at first even this government had difficulty stating precisely what it wanted to do. There was no blueprint for action, no master plan. Goals evolved over time. Neither were there any ready-made, reliable indicators of performance. It was difficult to develop measures that were not ambiguous, misleading or open to manipulation, to define aims and to measure the value of services and programmes, as well as to measure the efficiency with which resources were used. In short, it was difficult to say whether citizens were getting good value for their money (Beeton 1987; Harrison and Gretton 1987).

During this period, reform ideas were not universally accepted. Governmental processes in the Nordic countries and Britain differ both in how they cope with conflict and how they organize reforms. In the Nordic countries, modernization efforts provide illustrations of the limitations of parliamentarian and ministerial hierarchy. Governments were reluctant to spend large sums on administrative reform. Reform agencies were politically weak and of low status. Resources crucial to the success of administrative policy were often controlled by other state organizations. The ambitious aim of a comprehensive administrative policy was not built into the reform process (Mellbourn 1986; Olsen 1988a). In contrast, in Britain secretariats attached to the Prime Minister's office directed and co-ordinated reforms from the highest level of political authority.

Similarly, there were differences in reform styles. In the Nordic countries, where there was a commitment to consensus, conflict was avoided. This was particularly so where opponents claimed that reform proposals broke with the post-World War II development of the welfare state and raised constitutional questions (March and Olsen 1989).

The Thatcher government, on the other hand, employed a confrontational and ideological style, making its era a traumatic one for the career civil service and the trade unions (Hastings and Levie 1983; Metcalf and

Richards 1987; Fry 1988). There were profound changes, and it was claimed that the Thatcher reforms constituted a turning point in the evolution of British government from which there would be no going back (LeGrand and Robinson 1984; Gray and Jenkins 1985; Wass 1985; Harrison and Gretton 1987; Metcalf and Richards 1987). It was less clear whether the promised improvements in efficiency were achieved, and in particular there were doubts about the benefits of changing public monopolies into private monopolies (Kay and Thompson 1986).

Since 1945 the Nordic countries have shown a considerable capacity for reform, although it is difficult to determine what has really been achieved in terms of structural change (Mellbourn 1986; Winther 1987; Bentzon 1988; Olsen 1988a, 1988b; Hansen 1989). The concepts and data employed in the modernization process have been more appropriate to rhetoric and image-building than to rational analysis and choice. If we see reform processes as part of a struggle for control over peoples' minds, the efforts to date can be regarded as attempts to create a new consensus about the role and organization of public administration. On the other hand, the debate about modernization may have prepared the ground for major changes in public attitudes towards and understanding about the public sector, so perhaps facilitating future structural change.

Postscript

Although the observations offered in this chapter do not provide a strong test of the theoretical speculations we have presented, we believe they show some promise. In a world of bounded morality, intelligence and power, public organizations may be understood as institutions, rather than as instruments deliberately designed and redesigned. Processes of rational adaptation and competitive selection would not therefore dictate the form of public administration, but they would be relevant in institutional transformation. History could have direction even if it is not determined or directed by the intention and explicit choices of reformers. To argue that public administration can change but that it is not easily transformed to any arbitrary form is not to assert that political leadership through explicit choice and design is impossible.

In the remainder of this book, we discuss three main issues in relation to administrative reforms: their origins, contents and implementation. These issues must be analysed in order to answer the question we posed in the first chapter as to the freedom of action and power of reformers. Control over reforms consists of the power to initiate them, to determine their content, and to implement them so that they have the desired effects. When discussing these themes it is important to consider the institutional qualities of organizations analysed in this chapter. But in the next four chapters we will also describe how organizational environments are institutionalized and how this phenomenon affects the conditions of reform.

Determining the origins of reform involves asking why reforms are ever initiated in organizations and what makes reforms such frequent phenomena in modern organizations. This is the subject of the next chapter. In Chapters 4, 5 and 6 we discuss how the content of reforms emerges. Chapters 7 to 11 deal with the implementation of reforms. In the final chapter we use the analyses offered in the previous chapters to draw some conclusions as to power over reforms. We argue that reformers are much less powerful than is supposed in the reform idea.

3   Reform as routine

Administrative reforms are often presented as dramatic, unique changes in organizations. In this chapter we argue that reform can be regarded as an aspect of organizational stability rather than of organizational change. Reforms are common in large, modern organizations; reform is often a standard, recurring activity. Reforms are routines rather than interruptions in organizational life. Many studies claim that reforms are difficult to implement (Pressman and Wildavsky 1973; Hanf and Scharpf 1978). We argue that it is fairly easy to initiate reforms. Indeed, the very ease with which reforms can be launched may be one of the reasons why so few are completed. Reformers often claim that reform is necessary to adapt the organization to important changes in its environment. We argue that both fairly mundane, common and stable aspects of internal organizational life and various stable and common features of organizational environments can also produce reforms. One of these factors is reform itself: reforms tend to generate reforms.

Our argument is based on certain features of both reforms and organizations themselves, none of which are necessarily universal but which are common enough to be useful explanatory tools in many cases. There are four common basic attributes of administrative reforms which, together with certain organizational characteristics discussed below, aid the introduction and pursuit of reforms in organizations. The first is simplicity and clarity: the ideas proposed in the reform are less complicated and more clear-cut than most organization members consider the current organizational practices to be. Reform ideas consist of principles rather than detailed descriptions, theories rather than perceptions, i.e. reforms present ordered ideas which cannot encompass all the complexity of the real world, but which therefore seem more clear than reality. Second, reforms are normative: they represent attempts to bring order into a chaotic reality rather than to report upon it. Third, reforms tend to be one-sided: each reform invokes a single set of consistent values and perceptions of the world, in contrast to organizational practices which often have to deal with inconsistent values and perceptions. A fourth characteristic of reform is future-orientation: a reform is a process of idea elaboration, persuasion and implementation rather than an immediate action, so it cannot be expected to produce instant results. Instead it promises future benefits, sometimes when implementation has been completed and sometimes much later.

Since reforms contain ideas concerning both problems and solutions, they are dependent upon an adequate supply of both. That supply may support more reforms if each problem can be addressed and each solution can be used several times, which is made possible by what we call organizational forgetfulness. The supply of problems, solutions and forgetfulness in organizations is discussed below.

THE SUPPLY OF PROBLEMS AND SOLUTIONS

Reforms benefit from problems. The perception of problems in the current functioning of an organization can initiate the search for reforms and offer a strong incentive for attempts to implement them, as well as providing arguments to convince those whose support is needed.

There tends to be an ample supply of perceived problems in modern organizations (Starbuck 1983). A changing or malevolent environment can generate many problems, but there are also many internal sources. Administrative reforms can be proposed to remedy almost any such problem, including low profitability, increasing competition or poor management. Administrative reform, it can be argued, will make the organization more efficient, more profitable and more market-orientated, or it will make management perform better. But administrative reform is regarded in particular as the obvious response when an organization's problems are perceived as being administrative or directly concerned with its internal functioning. There is an ample supply of administrative problems in modern organizations.

A major source of administrative problems is the tension between the way an organization is presented and the way in which it actually works (Brunsson 1989). When presenting their organizations to the outside world, organizational leaders tend to stress unity, coherence, consistency, action and control. The organizations are portrayed as working towards a single goal or a set of consistent goals, as systems for producing action in accordance with these goals, which are maintained by managements' control over people and action at the lower organizational level. Organizations are described as though they were individuals (see Chapter 5 for a detailed discussion of this point). It is the task of management to strive to fulfil these descriptions. Most managements would find it difficult to claim the opposite, i.e. that they were striving to achieve inconsistency, or trying to avoid action and control.

However, organizations tend not to live up to these descriptions. The literature describing actual organizational processes tells us that organizations are commonly characterized by a higher degree of inconsistency, by greater difficulty in mobilizing action, and by a lesser degree of top-down control than is ever described in organizational presentations or desired by management (Cohen *et al.* 1972; Meyer and Rowan 1977; Weick 1979). But the tension between presentations and intentions on the one hand and experiences of actual behaviour on the other provides an incentive for reform.

Even in organizations which achieve successful results, the tension between presentable ideas and actual behaviour may be strong. Thus even in successful organizations there can be widespread feeling that the organization is not working as it should, and that reforms are needed. For instance, good results do not preclude perceptions of poor control; even in successful organizations management may see major problems of control. Success may depend on an organization's capacity to adapt rapidly to changing circumstances in its environment, i.e. on its flexibility. But it has been suggested that organizational characteristics which lead to flexibility may also inhibit opportunities for manipulating the organization in a specific direction: 'changefulness' is not the same as 'changeability' (Brunsson 1985). A flexible organization may be successful in a changing environment, but it may also be particularly difficult to steer in the direction that its management desires.

Problems are a perceptual category. Some observers may perceive a situation as problematic, others not. Thus reformers may try to influence other people's perceptions of today's reality. But it may be easier to refer problems to an area in which we are not troubled by knowledge, namely the future. The future is especially important if things are going well now, so well-functioning, successful organizations need it more than others. The future provides particularly good arguments for reforms since reforms concern the future, not the present.

An organization's supply of problems is threatened in so far as it solves the problems. Therefore, the supply benefits from problems that cannot be solved. Organizations grapple with many problems that are insoluble in practice. These include those generated by conflicting demands, when it is impossible in practical terms to find any balance that could readily be regarded as exactly the right one. How, for example, can the organization strike a balance between the need for integration and the need for differentiation, between centralization and decentralization or between internal markets and hierarchies? Any solution concerning these opposing elements is open to criticism for failing to satisfy one or the other of the needs sufficiently – or indeed both. For instance, centralized organizations tend to generate complaints about insufficient consideration to local knowledge and local needs for specialization and adaptation, while decentralized organizations discover that they are not paying enough attention to the benefits of co-ordination and standardization. And organizations that have struck some sort of balance between centralization and decentralization may well face complaints from both sides. All these complaints can be used as arguments for reform.

Solutions

Problems are not in themselves enough to trigger administrative reforms. A supply of ideas for solutions is also needed: more specifically, ideas for administrative solutions which deal with organizational structures, processes and ideologies, and which differ from the current solutions. Solutions can exert an attraction on reformers and reformees. Like problems, solutions can provide incentives to reform (Cyert and March 1963; March 1981a). And like problems, solutions can be produced by those who wish to pursue reforms, though the task of the reformers is made easier if there is a supply of more or less ready-made solutions.

Organizational scholarship is an important source of solutions. There are many different theories and ideas from Fayol (1916) onwards which argue that organizational form is important to management control and performance, and which also specify the forms that are best in different situations (Woodward 1965; Burns and Stalker 1961; Williamson 1981). Such theories provide both ideas for reform and elaborate supporting arguments.

But in order to initiate reforms, a supply of solutions is not in itself enough. The solutions must also appear to be better than those currently in use. It is not difficult to find these better solutions when designing reforms: current practice seldom appears as attractive as novel solutions; unlike current solutions, reforms promise to overcome both current and future problems. And if current practices are rather one-sided owing to an earlier one-sided reform, then a new, equally one-sided but reverse reform may seem very promising. If current organizational practices are perceived as highly complex, inconsistent and difficult to understand, reform can offer greater simplicity and consistency and can be much easier to understand. The proposed reform solutions may bring the organization closer to the presentation model of the organization, to the way in which it is presented by its management and the way people think organizations should be. If we set a simple, clear and good reform idea against our knowledge of the current situation with all its slack, *ad hoc* solutions, its ambiguities, inconsistencies, conflicts, compromises and complex relationships, then there is a good chance that the proposed solution will be more attractive. Simple principles can more easily attract enthusiasm and support than can complex descriptions of reality (Jönsson and Lundin 1977).

For reforms to occur, it is important not only that solutions exist and that they are seen as improvements on current practices, but also that they exist in considerable diversity. If there were only one perfect solution to an administrative problem, there would be no need for reform once that solution had been installed.

A diversity of solutions is provided in several ways. Fashion, as to both appropriate solutions and problems, is something that both reduces and increases the variety of available solutions. Fashion reduces the number of acceptable problems and solutions at any one time, but over time it also fosters diversity and provides a strong incentive to vary the targeted problems and proposed solutions. The existence of strong fashions guarantees that the practices of an organization will at least sometimes appear old-fashioned and in need of reform.

Management consultants play their part in helping to spread fashions. They also provide some variety within particular fashionable practices. As one of their means of competition is to offer slightly different solutions, they will effectively create variety in the supply of both solutions and problems. To improve their competitiveness, less successful consultants at least may seek to update their product by defining new solutions. Administrative experts within organizations can assume a role similar to that of management consultants; their task is to reform.

The theories that describe the causal effects of organizational form on control and performance have two characteristics that are important in providing diversity: they do not agree with one another and they are not entirely true. Since they disagree, an individual organization can draw on different theories at different times which can thus motivate many reforms. Since empirically no conclusive relationship can be proven between organizational form on the one hand and control and performance on the other, we find successful organizations with different organizational forms. Consequently, if an organization wants to imitate other successful organizations, it can usually find a number of alternative solutions to choose from.

PROBLEMS AND SOLUTIONS IN INSTITUTIONAL ENVIRONMENTS

Theories about the relationship between organizational forms and outcomes are sources of norms for 'correct' form. As we indicated in Chapter 1, there are also a great many norms constructed in other ways, which led us to describe the environments of modern organizations as institutionalized. Institutionalized environments increase the supplies of both problems and solutions. If reformers themselves had to produce solutions for the problems they define, there would be a considerable risk of a shortage of solutions, which would make it more difficult to initiate reform.

If the only driving force behind reforms were the urge to improve performance we would risk a shortage of solutions. We generally know very little about the relationship between organizational form and performance; indeed there may often be little or no relationship. And if there were a close relation between forms and results, there would sometimes be few other organizations to learn from: the relation between forms and results would probably be specific for organizations with similar products, but organizations with similar products sometimes think of themselves as competitors and therefore have reason to conceal their forms that are successful.

Reform is far easier if ready-made standardized and general solutions are available, norms which directly prescribe appropriate forms for all, or a class of organizations. The supplies of both problems and solutions increase when organizational structures, processes and ideologies not only serve as means for improving performance but also take on independent values for the organizations' environments, and thus for organizations themselves. Even effective organizations with a consistently high demand for their products may find themselves in situations in which their structures, processes and ideologies fall foul of regulations or are seen as unjust, irrational or out of date. Successful products are no guarantee against pressure for administrative reform. Nor does a high degree of adaptation of structures, processes and ideologies to the relevant norms pose an enduring obstacle to reforms in environments where new norms are constantly being established and where changing fashion makes previous standards obsolete.

General and ready-made norms about proper organizational forms free reformers from the need to find the most suitable forms for their specific organizations: they imitate rather than innovate. Reformers conform to established norms or imitate other organizations which maintain or redefine norms. The task of identifying new norms to imitate is made easy by the eagerness of other organizations to show off their forms. Institutional environments also create a supply of problems: there are widely held beliefs about what problems organizations have or should have; fashionable problems are suited to the solutions that are in fashion.

In short, it is not necessary to brood about the effects of new forms because it is not the effects which make a reform important. Rather, the reform is important in itself: it is not the means to an end, but has a value of its own. Sometimes the consequences are considered in conjunction with forms, but often they are assumed to be standardized effects which automatically result from the form. They provide arguments for the reform. For example, decentralization may be embarked upon to achieve fuller market adaptation, but rarely is anyone given the task of evaluating whether reformed organizations have actually achieved greater market adaptation. Appropriate problems, solutions and effects tend to come in prefabricated packages.

As we mentioned in Chapter 1, the organizational forms presented externally by organizations are often not those which govern their practices or 'inner life': the external image may become decoupled from internal operations. This decoupling means that it is easier to reform the structures, processes and ideologies intended for external use, since it reduces the risk that changes will affect operations. If there is a wide gap between external and internal practices, even the most radical reforms need not disturb internal operations. During the radical reform at Swedish Rail described in Chapter 7, management thought that the reform being attempted was revolutionary and that it would result in near chaos, but the actual rail traffic was virtually undisrupted, punctuality improved, and many operational supervisors were unaffected by the reform and knew very little, if anything, about it. Thus, reformers need not feel intimidated by the possibility that they might disrupt or undermine the productive capacity of the organization. Moreover, such decoupling facilitates not only initiation but also other stages of reform: if there is no need to consider the demands created by actual operations, it is easier to determine the content of reforms; and if operations will not particularly be affected by reforms, they are less likely to meet opposition from operational departments. Introducing a new organizational structure in a well-decoupled organization is merely a matter of redrawing the organizational chart, which need not take long.

Inconsistent norms

The norms and demands confronted by organizations are sometimes difficult or impossible to reconcile one with another as they may be mutually contradictory or inconsistent. There may be logical, technical or resource reasons for this inconsistency. There may be concomitant norms stating that organizations are to be centralized and demanding that organizations are to be decentralized. Some groups may demand democratic management processes and others authoritarian ones. It may be technically impossible to reconcile customers' preferences with norms for environmental protection. And there may not be enough money available to satisfy all the groups that call upon an organization for financial contributions.

Inconsistent norms are difficult to deal with; it can be difficult to conform to them simultaneously, and they are difficult to reconcile with co-ordinated action. Organizations often react to inconsistent norms by reflecting these inconsistencies in their structures, processes and ideologies, which then also become inconsistent. Inconsistent norms produce conflict structures, problem-oriented processes and hypocrisy (Brunsson 1989). If it is important to reflect inconsistencies, conflict rather than consensus becomes the basis of organizational structure, and organizations will strive to recruit people who claim not to share the norms, values and opinions held by other members of the organization. Conflict is the structuring principle of parliaments, for instance, or of boards of directors on which trade unions are represented to meet the requirements of industrial democracy.

Inconsistent norms make it difficult to find solutions which satisfy everyone: solutions always run the risk of benefiting one party more than another. Many specific issues become problems simply because there are inconsistent norms involved. Discussions of the different aspects of a problem reflect different opinions. Organizations that confront inconsistent norms both have reasons to deal with difficult problems and are often forced to do so.

Organizations may also reflect norms ideologically, by producing talk and by taking decisions that are consistent with the norms. Inconsistent norms may be reflected in contradictory talk and decisions or by systematically constructing inconsistencies between talk, decisions and action, i.e. by producing hypocrisy. In such instances, talk may accord with one group of norms, decisions with another, and actions with yet a third. For instance, claiming that one of their ambitions is to save the environment is particularly important for a business or party whose operations create environmental problems.

When organizations respond to inconsistent norms with conflict, problem-orientation and hypocrisy, new reasons to reform arise. All these phenomena serve to uphold the belief that there is something better than the status quo, and satisfaction is avoided. It becomes clear that it is possible to do things differently or that they should be done differently; there are opponents who can point out that there are other solutions than the prevailing ones; they can claim that the existing problems should be solved; and they can argue that hypocrisy should be avoided – that promises should be kept, and that one should practice what one preaches. But as long as contradictory demands are being made on an organization, it will be impossible to banish hypocrisy: if the organization acts in a new way it will encounter criticisms from elsewhere and will need to talk in accordance with such criticisms to compensate for its new action. All of this can create a great deal of frustration, and as it helps neither to implement new actions nor to replace management, it is easy to blame the organizational form. The demand for administrative reform will therefore be close at hand.

Conflict, problem-orientation and hypocrisy are also qualities which conflict particularly sharply with established notions of how organizations should function. This gives rise to powerful incentives to attempt reforms aiming towards greater consensus, action-orientation and consistency. But such reforms cannot succeed without posing threats to the legitimacy of the organization in an environment with inconsistent norms, and thus there will be continuous reform proposals and attempted reforms.

THE SUPPLY OF ORGANIZATIONAL FORGETFULNESS

Administrative reforms are often repetitions of earlier reforms. The ideas they contain may be roughly the same as in the previous reform, perhaps because the previous reform did not close the gap between what was desired and what was achieved, between aspiration level and practice, and was therefore deemed unsuccessful. The reform process may also be repetitive because it is oscillatory. The ideas may be the reverse of those contained in the previous reform but identical to those of an earlier reform, whose shortcomings the most recent reform was designed to correct. In a study of organizational reforms at Swedish Rail over a 100-year period, for instance, it was shown that certain problems and solutions were repeated in a great many reforms. A problem recurring in all reforms was that top management dealt with too many detailed issues, and all reforms implied that they should not do so. Other issues turned up in roughly every second reform, so that reforms about centralization, for instance, were followed by others about decentralization, and so on (Brunsson *et al.* 1989).

Such repetitions may inhibit the initiation and pursuit of reforms. Proposing to reform an organization in the same way as on a previous occasion may encounter criticism: 'since we have to do it again, the earlier reform obviously did not succeed; and if the earlier reform did not succeed why should this one?' There may even be cynics in the organization who have experienced so many reforms that they have become sceptical about the very idea of reform itself as a means of solving problems or improving performance.

So reforms are facilitated not by learning but by forgetfulness, by mechanisms that cause the organization to forget previous reforms or at least those of a similar content. Reformers need a high degree of forgetfulness to avoid uncertainty as to whether their proposed reform is a good one. Forgetfulness also helps people to accept reforms. Reforms focus interest on the future rather than the present. Forgetfulness ensures that experience will not interfere with reform: it prevents the past from disturbing the future.

There are a number of mechanisms promoting such organizational forgetfulness, so clearing the path to reform. One such factor is high personnel turnover. Another is change among top management. A third is the use of management consultants: if they are fresh to an organization, consultants can easily repeat previous mistakes. Management consultants are generally expert at introducing reforms, but they are also normally too busy and too expensive to be involved in implementing them fully. When consultants are used in this way, they are systematically unlikely to learn that their reforms are not implemented and do not give the intended effects. They are therefore in a particularly good position for initiating and pursuing the same reform in new organizations with great enthusiasm and drive. Forgetfulness is their key competence.

REFORMS GENERATE REFORMS

Up to this point, we have argued that administrative reforms benefit from problems, solutions and forgetfulness, and that there tends to be a plentiful supply of these resources in modern organizations. Thus reforms tend to become common, indeed so common that in many organizations they virtually become routine. One further explanation of the frequency of reform is that reforms tend to generate new reforms. Reforms often result from previous reforms, and the outcome of reforms is often new reforms: reforms tend to be self-referential. The reason for this is that reforms tend to increase the supply of solutions, problems and forgetfulness.

Reforms may sometimes solve problems, but they may also trigger problems. This is true even of successful reforms. The successful implementation of a one-sided reform may well solve a particular problem while at the same time creating, reinforcing or drawing attention to other problems at which it was not aimed. For instance, successfully implemented reforms geared towards industrial democracy could produce new reforms aimed at increasing efficiency. Reform attempts aimed at addressing the insoluble problems mentioned above provide another set of examples: decentralizing a centralized organization, for instance, is a way of ensuring that the benefits of centralization will be discovered and sooner or later attended to. Reforms may therefore leave the organization oscillating between different solutions.

Reforms can also generate demands for further reforms aimed at the same problems and propagating the same solutions. This is the case when reforms generate more hope than they in fact fulfil, or even which they could ever fulfil. Reforms may be more productive in raising levels of aspiration than in achieving improvements. Reforms focus attention on the problems to be solved, and the process of promoting and trying to implement a reform can help to raise levels of aspiration, making people more eager to find solutions and to adopt higher standards about the kind of solutions they are prepared to accept. At the same time, it is often difficult to implement reforms. Or, even if one is implemented, in retrospect it may not be perceived as having been ambitious enough. For instance, a reform intended to promote democracy may be launched simply because the organization is extremely undemocratic. But that reform may lead to a considerably higher and more widespread appreciation of or preference for democracy, but only to a moderate increase in the actual level of democracy, thus making the lack of democracy and the need for further reform all the more evident.

In addition, reformers tend systematically to oversell what a reform can actually achieve (Baier *et al.* 1986). If overselling is an efficient technique in the acceptance and implementation of reforms, we can expect that reforms which have been accepted and implemented will also have been heavily oversold. And overselling may in turn help to raise aspiration levels even further.

Finally, reform constitutes a forgetfulness mechanism in itself. Reforms tend to be viewed very differently before and after the event, *ex ante* and *ex post*. At best, a reform proposal consists of a description of an expected future reality. Descriptions need to be simplified; and, as we have already noted, the descriptions associated with reforms tend to be greatly simplified. Reforms are often launched and sold in organizations mainly in the form of attractive principles. Simplicity *ex ante*, as mentioned above, is an important element in determining the likelihood of a reform being accepted. Reality *ex post,* when the reform has been implemented, tends not to be quite so simple. Opinions about the present are generally more complex than opinions about the future. Moreover, attempts to apply the simple principles to organizational realities in the course of reforms are usually characterized by a growing degree of complexity (see Chapter 7). As the level of complexity increases, difficulties, inconsistencies, conflicts and 'practical' problems become more evident. Attempts at implementing reforms tend to highlight these difficulties by making it obvious that the original ideas, which once seemed so attractive, no longer appear to be so simple, clear or precise; nor are they detailed enough for practical purposes, while making them practicable also makes them much less beautiful.

So just as comparison with today's chaotic reality makes the simple principles of a reform attractive, a reform which we have tried to implement will become less attractive than a reform that is new and still untried. A comparison between one reform *ex post* and another reform *ex ante* thus works to the advantage of the *ex ante* reform, even if the two reforms actually contain the same general ideas. Reforms tend not to deliver what they promise, but their promises are so good that people are easily persuaded to try again. As reforms lose their appeal over time, they become easy victims of proposals for new reforms.

So reforms can themselves be important suppliers of problems, solutions and forgetfulness, and thereby become important causes of new reforms. Reforms are both causes and effects of reforms. Reforms trigger new reforms, making the reform process a stable state.

AVOIDING REFORM

Reforms can be perceived as both positive and negative, from the point of view of both organizational insiders and external observers and stakeholders. They can be seen as important in encouraging repentance, hope and a tolerance of failure in a world where standards are and should be higher than it is possible to achieve in practice. They can also be regarded as futile and expensive attempts to achieve unrealistic goals.

Organizational legitimacy and survival may benefit from reforms, from maintaining belief in a future better than the present (March and Olsen 1983). If customers, financial institutions, state agencies or employees find the organization's present performance unsatisfactory, they may be persuaded not to withdraw their support by a reform that promises future improvement. But reforms are not a risk-free strategy from the point of view of organizational survival. We have argued here that reforms tend to be easy to initiate but more difficult to implement, so that they can focus attention on problems and increase levels of aspiration to a greater extent than improving performance. The main outcome is then that a reform reinforces the very perception of failure that was the initial reason for launching the reform. And since reforms are often directed to particularly problematic areas, they risk giving heightened importance to those very goals that an organization has greatest difficulty in achieving. While previous to a reform it might have been argued that the value to which the reform was geared was not very important or relevant to the organization, after the reform it may become an important criterion of evaluation. In some cases this can have a lethal effect on the organization.

For instance, an attempt to reform a railway company to become more business-like and profitable might succeed in establishing profitability as the main evaluation criterion, but without being able to change organizational behaviour enough to enable the organization to fulfil this criterion. This last would not be a surprising result, since profitability is the very criterion which railways have found most difficult to meet in the twentieth century. The overall outcome of reforms aiming at increasing profitability may therefore be to close down the reforming companies more quickly.

In this way the reform of individual organizations may be a way of introducing more modern forms, not by changing the organizations undergoing reform but by bringing a quicker demise to those which cannot meet modern standards, thus hastening the adoption of modern forms in the total population of organizations. From the point of view of the individual organization there is reason to avoid these effects, if survival is considered more important than the meeting of high standards.

Strategies against reforms

Organizations thus have reason not only to promote but also to avoid administrative reforms. The argument so far should encourage reformers: it seems to be fairly easy to initiate reforms. The task of those wanting to avoid reforms is more difficult, but there are a variety of threats to reform that can form the basis of their strategies. For instance, if problems or solutions or forgetfulness are lacking, reform is less likely.

It is difficult to imagine that a lack of problems could commonly form an obstacle to reforms in large organizations. However, one type of problem could actually block reform, namely problems that are acute. Since reforms take some time, they are more difficult to present as solutions to a threat of bankruptcy today than as solutions to future threat.

Reforms are threatened not only by a lack of problems, but also by alternative ways of responding to problems. Reforms imply a special approach to problems. They are aimed at action, change and problem-solving. Problems should be solved by doing something about them, i.e. changing the situation so that problems disappear. Another way of reacting to problems is to ignore them. For example, organizational managements may choose to delegate problems and let other units in the organization grapple with them, instead of intervening with reforms. Problems may also be dealt with by increasing organizational slack (Cyert and March 1963): instead of trying to solve problems by means of administrative reforms, an organization can try to increase its resources, perhaps by turning to more profitable products or improving its marketing.

Another way of dealing with problems is to administrate them, to live with them. People can analyse and discuss the problems without trying to find solutions in practice. Ignoring problems is difficult for a weak management unable to resist demands from lower levels of the organization for solutions to their problems. Living with problems instead of solving them is easier in organizations such as parliaments, which are judged more for their ability to provide a discussion of different opinions than for undertaking action.

A shortage of solutions may be experienced by a modern organization which has already introduced the latest structures, processes and ideologies. It is generally more difficult for innovators to find new solutions than it is for imitators. And if people have more than superficial knowledge of the solutions applied in other organizations they may find themselves in shortage of real solutions: a deep understanding of the detailed, practical problems involved in implementing fashionable solutions, as well as too much experience with their results, tends to make these solutions less attractive. People with such knowledge may become reluctant to propose or accept available reforms. Learning about others' reforms has similar effects as does learning about one's own.

If reforms can be facilitated by the mechanisms of organizational forget-fulness, they can also be prevented by the mechanisms of organizational learning. Efforts to keep an established management in power, avoiding new recruitment and refraining from the use of external people like consult-ants are all possible strategies for avoiding reform.

If reforms contribute to a tolerance of present failure and hope for a better future, they can also expect competition from other methods of achieving these things. One such method is to emphasize the good inten-tions of an organization or its management, at the expense of descriptions of results. Another method is to emphasize the future rather than the past, i.e. to promise improvement (Brunsson 1989). Goals describe both intentions and the future, and they can therefore produce both hope and tolerance. But all these methods may also lead to a demand for reform. Failure to fulfil intentions and goals is often blamed on administrative problems, and administrative problems in their turn provide arguments for administrative reform. And one way of increasing the credibility of refer-ences to a better future is to launch some reforms.

If reforms are much more attractive *ex ante* than *ex post*, attempts at implementing them will undermine their initial support. A relatively secure phase in the reform process is at the outset of implementing a reform, when it still looks promising. If reforms can remain at the stage where they have just been accepted but are still far from final implementation, they can survive for a long time. But if serious attempts are made to implement a reform, a stage may be reached where it is clear that the reform solution will not be so beautiful in practice, perhaps not even any better than the current practice. And if support falls off, perhaps the reform can be stopped.

So, paradoxically, attempts at implementing a specific reform may halt it. However, as we have seen, implementation can easily lead to a further reform with the same – or perhaps the opposite – characteristics. The same effect can arise from another important threat to reform: a proposal for another reform. Organizations cannot be expected to pursue several reforms in the same area at the same time. Proposing a reform to halt an existing one is most effective when the existing reform is at a weak stage in its life, when it has just been proposed and has not yet acquired too great a degree of commitment, or when it has gone far enough on the way to implementation for its less attractive *ex post* characteristics to have been revealed. It is then all too likely to be stopped by the proposal of a new reform presented in the more attractive *ex ante* version. Promising a new reform may even be the only practical way of halting one already under way.

Important strategies for anyone trying to stop reforms thus include providing arguments that easily lead to new reforms; further attempts to implement existing reforms; and proposing new reforms. The opponents of the reform following these strategies become reformers themselves! Even if it may be possible to put a stop to single reforms, it is difficult to stop the reforming process in general. So not only are reforms their own causes and effects, but attempts at avoiding reforms imply support for reform activities. Self-reference and opposition make routines of reforms.

The conclusion that may be drawn from our discussion up to this point is that it appears to be more difficult to resist administrative reforms than to initiate them. Generally, the difficulty lies not in persuading large organizations to reform but in preventing them from doing so. But it is one thing to initiate reforms and quite another to determine their content and succeed in implementing them. In the next three chapters we discuss how the contents of reform emerge. We demonstrate how ideas of modernity and rationality easily become the crucial elements of reforms, difficult to avoid for the reformers and difficult to resist for the reformees.

4 The modernization imperative[*]

* This chapter was contributed by Anders Forssell.

In 1950 there were 450 independent savings banks in Sweden. This number dropped slightly over the next decade, to 434 by the end of 1960, after which time a rapid process of mergers was initiated. During the 1960s many of the small savings banks merged with their nearest urban savings bank, with the result that by 1973 the number of savings banks had plummeted to 233. This process continued throughout the 1970s, when some of the urban savings banks also began to merge, resulting in larger banks covering whole counties or larger areas. By the end of the 1970s, the number of savings banks in Sweden had fallen to 175. The first merger between two large savings banks took place in 1982, when the Gothenburg and Stockholm banks combined to form what became Sweden's largest savings bank. This was followed by further large mergers in the 1980s, which changed the face of the savings bank map in Sweden. Instead of a large number of banks of a relatively even size, spread across Sweden, the savings bank movement of the late 1980s was dominated by a small number of regional and county banks. In 1987 there were still 115 savings banks in Sweden, but the twenty largest of these held roughly 80 per cent of the total deposits.

The process appeared to be moving in a unilateral direction – towards larger units with more resources – and in the autumn of 1989 a commission appointed by the Swedish Savings Bank Association proposed that the eleven largest savings banks merge to form a joint corporate group, the Swedish Savings Bank Group, Inc. All the remaining small and medium-sized banks would be associated with this group by agreements. The creation of the Savings Bank Group would be the culmination of a 30-year period of mergers.

These mergers were part of a larger process. During the twentieth century, most of the savings banks have been transformed from traditional institutions of savings and credit rooted in pre-industrial society and tied to the local economy, to business enterprises operating on the market with the same means and under the same conditions as other banks. The type of change the savings banks have undergone – mergers into larger units, the introduction of new technology, expansion of the product range, the appearance of a new 'business-like' mission, etc. – is one which many other organizations have also experienced over the same period. The transformation of the savings banks therefore serves as an example of a more general change in society. This process of change is often characterized by the people involved as modernization, and it often appears to them to be a natural, inevitable development. The issue addressed in this chapter is how this can be the case. How can a process which beyond any doubt is a social and political process, with proponents and opponents, be seen as having the attributes of a natural phenomenon?

THE EMERGENCE OF A MODERN ORGANIZATION

The first savings banks in Sweden were founded in the 1820s, prior to the advent of industrial capitalism, and long before the welfare state. Savings banks continued to be founded throughout the nineteenth and early twentieth centuries. Initially, the prototypes were savings banks in Great Britain and Germany. The savings bank was seen as an answer to the poverty and social misery that people began to perceive as a problem at the time. To quote from a brochure about the Savings Bank in the parish of Burs: 'The widespread social privation in our nation brought the first savings banks into being, as a kind of charitable institution, an attempt to assist people in overcoming adversities and hardships, and giving local communities some kind of economic backbone.'

Generally the initiative to found a savings bank was taken by wealthy members of the community. In Burs parish, the first board of directors, or Savings Bank Directorate as it was called, comprised the pastor, the schoolmaster and a few of the farmers. According to the founders, who were influenced by the philanthropic ideas of the times, savings would enable working-class people to provide themselves with some security in anticipation of illness or old age.

Thus the savings banks were a kind of public service institution. They were not business enterprises, did not operate on the free market, and did not aim to be profitable. But once operations had stabilized, savings banks often operated at a modest profit. These profits were used both to build up reserves and for charitable purposes, including contributions to churches and municipal chemists' shops.

In the beginning the entire emphasis was on savings. A savings bank was an organization for saving, and its modest amounts of capital were invested in fixed securities, primarily mortgages on property. In due course, however, with growing capital, credit for individual savers, for agriculture and for municipalities became important (Körberg 1990).

A savings bank usually limited its activities to one parish or municipality. Over time, the ties between a municipality and its savings bank were strengthened, so that the trustees of the bank, who initially were the founders themselves, came to be appointed by the local council. Not until the 1955 Savings Bank Act came into effect did the same rule begin to apply to all savings banks. According to this Act, half of the trustees were to be appointed by the council of 'the towns, villages and rural municipalities comprising the operating area of a savings bank, or of a county council (Körberg 1990). The remainder were then to be appointed by the trustees themselves. Some savings banks, particularly in those towns which were seats of county government, took the name 'County Savings Bank' quite early on, but savings banks covering entire counties did not actually emerge until well into the 1960s. It was the 1955 Act that also first allowed the savings banks to merge without prior liquidation. Thus it was not actually legally possible until after 1955 for a savings bank to break out of the geographical limitations of a local economy.

As volume increased, first the larger urban savings banks and later the rural banks extended their opening times beyond the occasional hours or days they had initially. The banks began to hire staff to work as tellers and bookkeepers. This was the beginning of the professionalization of operations, meaning that an administrative staff gradually took over all the day-to-day running of the bank, while the trustees and members of the board increasingly acted solely as decision-makers. This process began early in the large urban banks, while banking activities in the rural banks were run by the trustees well into this century, and a few still are to this day. Beginning in the 1960s, most of the savings banks hired more and more staff. From 1966 to 1987 the number of employees in the savings banks grew from about 6,000 to nearly 15,000. During this time most of the staff were given extended authority, and the need for specialists became evident as the range of operations broadened. Such specialists included trust staff, corporate credit staff and staff for advisory services, such as insurance and legal matters.

In conjunction with the growth of the savings banks and their increased importance in national and local community economies, a need arose for more regular and regulated co-operation between them. To meet this requirement, a number of joint organizations have been established during this century. The first was the Swedish Savings Bank Association, which was primarily a special-interest organization to interface with the state and state agencies, and a forum for debate and decision-making on issues of common interest. A number of service corporations have subsequently been established under the auspices of the Association dealing with a range of functions including promotion and marketing, data-processing and computer technology, the training of personnel, and real-estate. A central bank, the Savings Banks' Bank, was established in the 1940s, primarily as a joint clearing bank, but it has subsequently come to play a major role for the savings banks as a centre for foreign exchange trade and trade in securities, as a grantor, co-ordinator and source of large loans. Several credit institutions were also established for this latter purpose. However, until 1990 all Swedish savings banks remained independent units, and co-operation between them was voluntary.

In the savings banks of the 1950s, modern-minded bank directors had to combat considerable resistance to change. Reformers were to be found among a small group of younger directors, both in the Savings Bank Association and at some individual banks. They were influenced by changes in other spheres of society, and sought models beyond their own tradition.

But it was not until the early 1960s that the work of these reformers began to bear real fruit. One of the first major changes was the expansion of credit-giving services to allow depositors to apply for loans other than mortgage loans. Another was preparation for tougher competition, and the development of local and central marketing. In conjunction with this, the banks competed with commercial banks to be in charge of the payment of workers' wages and salaries. A third important change was the rapid introduction of state-of-the-art computer banking technology; and a fourth, towards the end of the decade, was a new interest in businesses as potential customers. There was also a parallel development of peripheral activities, which transformed savings banks into banks with all the regular banking services: sales of insurance policies, trust departments with securities trading and international transactions, corporate credit and legal advisory services.

However, not all the savings banks have implemented the changes described here and not all have merged. In 1987, 95 savings banks still only operated within an area of one or two municipalities or, in some cases, just one parish. These small savings banks have not always had sufficient resources to be able to offer as many services and products as their larger counterparts.

The development described above was facilitated by the amendment of the banking laws. In the past the operations of savings banks were tightly regulated and tied to the local economy. The new joint banking laws which came into effect in 1969 made all types of banking institutions – commercial banks, savings banks and agricultural societies – subject to the same rules with regard to their banking operations.

In the earlier system, savings banks had functioned mainly as collection points for individual depositors' savings and providers of credit to construction projects carried out by the municipalities and others. The agricultural societies had functioned as providers of credit to farmers, and corporate banks as the providers of credit to businesses. This previous strict division of banking operations into sectors, with specialized banking institutions in each, had now broken down, and the way was paved for the growth of a joint banking sector.

ARGUMENTS FOR AND AGAINST MERGERS

The kind of social and economic change described here could not have taken place if certain people in the savings banks had not worked to achieve reforms, i.e. reformulation and change. But there were also people who did not want change, or who wanted to change in different ways. Diverse interests and intentions were pulling in various directions. Let us examine how such a conflict of interests might have looked.

As we have seen, mergers are part of a more extensive process of transformation. They are interesting as such, not least because they often provide us with illustrations of the arguments for and against transformation as a whole. According to prevailing economic theories, mergers are forced into being by increasing competition, and are adopted because they lead to economies of scale, improve cost efficiency and thus make for greater competitive power. How was all this reflected in the history of the savings banks?

The main support for mergers came generally from the managements of the larger savings banks. Their main argument was that it was necessary to be equipped to confront tougher competition in the future. Other banks and financial institutions would be trying to attract clients away from the savings banks. Computer technology and a broadened product range would provide the means of competition. The savings banks could not stand passively by and observe a development that would threaten their existence. They had to keep up by developing their product ranges and improving their cost efficiency. But such developments required resources that would be available only to the large savings banks produced by the mergers. This explained the necessity of mergers.

The picture being painted was a threatening one, but little was said about profitability, as it was difficult to find compelling financial arguments for mergers. Often the profitability of the small savings banks was at least as good as that of the large ones, and they were better consolidated. There were reasons for this: small savings banks were usually inexpensive to administrate, had access to cheap deposit capital, and only took small risks with their lending, while large savings banks invested in new technology, in facilities and in staff, which resulted in heavy operating expenses and lower profits. Moreover, large banks often took greater risks in their lending, which put a strain on their equity.

Although the threatening picture did not convince everyone of the necessity to merge, it still seemed difficult to find powerful arguments against mergers that could be used in public. It was hard to argue that things were fine as they were. Such arguments were legitimate within small savings banks, but were far more difficult to assert in open negotiations with the larger banks. No-one wanted to appear reactionary. When those advocating mergers talked about future threats, they thereby also decided what issues were to be on the agenda, and determined the content of the discussion. The future could not be contradicted with descriptions of the past or even the present. For this reason, the negotiations were consistently 'won' by the reformers. But this did not mean that negotiations always resulted in mergers.

There was also a hidden debate, the main subjects of which were power and influence. Many representatives of small savings banks feared that a merger would mean that their own bank would be swallowed up by the larger one, and that they would completely lose control and influence in their own bank. When such arguments were used publicly, they were met with assurances of continued strong influence for the elected representatives of the smaller bank. But in the internal discussions of the local savings banks the representatives could use these counter-arguments, and some banks did decide to resist proposed mergers.

The reformers, too, were interested in power, but in the opposite way. Their public arguments were for greater competitive power and more influence for the merged banks. Implicitly, this greater influence also meant greater influence for the banks' managements, and a larger bank meant a wider field of operations. In addition, a larger bank with greater resources would be able to offer more in terms of career advancement, better salaries and other benefits for many bank employees. The foremost proponents of mergers – usually the managers and upper administrative staff of the larger savings banks – also had the most to gain by them.

These arguments, overt and covert, were used in relation to the type of mergers common in the 1960s and 1970s when all savings banks, even those referred to here as large, were still quite small. But, interestingly, the same main arguments were used in favour of the merger into a joint Savings Bank Group proposed in 1989. The anticipation of tougher future competition was still the prime argument; only the scale had increased. In the 1960s, the talk was of national competition, while in 1989 it was of competition on an international scale.

Mergers are the changes which appeared to be most charged with conflict, perhaps because they posed threats and offered potentials for new power relations, although this was not openly discussed. Other changes, such as the introduction of new technology or new products, received very little resistance. They were seen rather as neutral in relation to the various interest groups. The lack of resources was seen instead as the major obstacle to introducing such changes at the smaller savings banks. Many of the elements of modernization obviously required a larger scale of operations than that at which the small savings bank operates.

As mentioned above, tougher future competition, which would demand larger banks with greater resources, was the main argument for mergers throughout the entire period described here, from the 1960s to today. And although small and medium-sized savings banks on each occasion have proved to be as successful as large banks, developments have constantly attested to the strength of the argument: in practice, the savings banks have merged. As this argument was repeated time and time again, and as more and more mergers were completed, it became an accepted and important truth.

Irrespective of whether or not people were convinced of the necessity of establishing large savings banks, it was still possible to resist specific proposed mergers, but it was much more difficult to resist the idea of the necessity of mergers. Thus mergers ceased to appear as constructed social phenomena and seemed, instead, to be natural phenomena.

MERGERS AND MODERNIZATION

Up to this point we have stayed within the framework given by the savings banks and their mergers, and we have seen how mergers and the arguments for them were institutionalized within that framework. By extending the frame of reference to modern society, we can see mergers as part of the modernization of society.

It was impossible for savings banks to merge without mobilizing viable arguments. But the arguments for merging and for change were, as we have seen, often loosely related to the actual reality of the savings banks. The arguments were associated more with the future than with the present, and were of greater relevance in some contexts and to some savings banks than others.

Different kinds of savings banks with varying lines of products existed concomitantly. And rather than being about the present, the arguments of the reformers were about the future when, they claimed, competition would be overwhelming if mergers were not carried out now (Forssell 1992). Mergers would be forced into being by the conditions of the future. Thus the assumed causal relationship reversed the chronological order of events.

The effect – the merger – predated the cause – overwhelming competition. This is not consistent with formal models, which assume that causes precede effects. But if, instead of discussing actual events, we address people's ideas about reality, the logic becomes more consistent. If savings bank managers believed that the competition would be overwhelming in the future, it would be reasonable to anticipate this through merging. Thus it can be seen that people's ideas about the future, rather than factual knowledge about the present, had an impact on their actions.

Those savings banks which regarded the threats of the future as real and acute found it easier to merge than did others where the threats and the future were perceived as more distant and less real. There, mergers were more difficult to achieve. Different savings banks lived with different realities, and as some banks changed and others did not, the differences between them grew. What was feasible and correct for one type of bank became impossible and wrong for another.

People in the larger savings banks began to consider the traditional rural savings banks with one or two branch offices and limited opening hours and services to be anomalies: they were living museums and interesting curiosities, but entirely out of step with the times, and not viable in modern society. People in the small, traditional savings banks, on the other hand, acknowledged the existence of the large savings banks. At the same time, they were firmly convinced that the ways in which these banks operated could not possibly be applied in their own small savings banks. The people at the two types of savings banks not only had different ideas and represent- ations of their worlds and work, they also literally existed in different realities, with different conditions and values. But the modern savings banks had succeeded in establishing a clear, self-evident status, which the more traditional savings banks lacked.

One reason for this was that the reformers had grasped the concept of 'modern': mergers and other changes made at these savings banks could be characterized as 'modernization', and the savings banks which had under- gone these changes could be called 'modern'. This meant that the change and transformation could be directly linked with the ongoing process of modernization of society, i.e. with progress and development, two of the strongest values of modern society. By identifying themselves with modernization it was possible for the 'modern' savings banks to begin to perceive themselves as the only viable type of savings bank, despite the testimony of reality that this was not the case, and it was obvious that they would determine what was to be on the agenda in discussions with the traditional savings banks. By linking themselves with the modernization of society, the arguments for mergers and other 'modern' changes in the savings bank system were further reinforced.

Modernization is an empirical concept that lacks an unambiguous definition. It is often associated with industrialized society and the social changes which followed in its wake. Berger *et al.* (1973) define modernization as: 'the institutional concomitants of technologically-induced economic growth. This means that there is no such thing as a modern society plain and simple; there are only societies more or less advanced in a continuum of modernization' (Berger *et al.* 1973: 9). The 'primary carriers' of modernization are 'the institutions of technological production and bureaucracy' (ibid.). There are also 'secondary carriers', including the contemporary city and its socio-cultural pluralism. There are reciprocal causal relationships between them and other institutions. Berman (1983) extended the discussion by emphasizing modernism and modernization as a subversive power of constant change. Modernization is a movement which includes and transforms nearly all of society. Those who claim to modernize are thus part of a historical movement, while those who strive to maintain that which is no longer modern are working against history.

Yet, despite the revolutionization of society by modernization, there are still residues of a pre-modern society, particularly in the rural areas. And this is where we can still find those very small savings banks which have managed to hold out against mergers and other types of modernization. Here modernization has few active supporters, and the traditional way of life remains. Here, the idea of modernization as an inevitable natural process has far less support from the surrounding society, which also clings to the past.

INSTITUTIONALIZED MODELS

Modernization of the economy has brought with it strong expansion of the market and the state, at the expense of self-sufficiency and reciprocal forms of economic exchange (Polanyi 1968). This development means that the business enterprise and the public agency have become the most important forms of organization in modern society (Sjöstrand 1985). If this is the case, then the transformation of the savings banks into only one form, the business enterprise, cannot be explained strictly in terms of modernization; particularly not as there are examples of organizations with backgrounds similar to that of the savings banks which have been transformed into public organizations.

The Swedish health insurance fund represents one such organization. The public health insurance movement came into being in the nineteenth century and

> must be seen as a popular movement. Until 1955, the health insurance movement was a voluntary organization with a large number of

members and long-term objectives. It was strongly idealistic and dynamic. It was also indisputably close to the people. The health insurance movement was built up by 'equals for equals'.

(Fürth 1983: 166)

It was an example of an organization operating on a voluntary basis and rooted in the common interests of its members. What happened later was that the health insurance movement was incorporated into the body of nationalized public health social insurance schemes. The voluntary association thus became a public authority.

Why did this not happen to the savings banks? They had a similar origin and objective as support organizations, and they also had strong ties, if not to the state, then to the municipalities.

However, there was also an important difference between the savings banks and the health insurance movement. The savings banks considered themselves banks and part of the banking sector, while the health insurance movement and later the national health insurance fund saw themselves as part of the insurance sector. Each based its comparisons and models on the sector (Meyer and Scott 1983) or organizational field (DiMaggio and Powell 1983) to which it belonged. Neither the savings banks nor the health insurance fund defined themselves primarily as a public aid organization, nor was there a 'public aid organizations' sector. The national health insurance fund was compared with the other types of social insurance managed by the state, such as retirement insurance and occupational injury insurance, and this pointed to their organizational solution. From the 1950s onwards the savings banks, on the other hand, more and more began to compare themselves with other banks, particularly the commercial banks, which they began to perceive as the natural model for a banking organization.

Another difference between the savings banks and the national health insurance movement was that the latter was closely affiliated to the trade unions and the labour movement, which made it easy to associate them with the state once the Social Democrats had come to power and consolidated their position. The savings banks, on the other hand, due to their origin, were long viewed with some suspicion by the labour movement.

In order for the reformers to be able to start the process of change at the savings banks, they had to associate the arguments for change with the modernization of society. Once the resistance to mergers and other changes had been broken, and the process was under way, subsequent steps followed naturally. Distinct, complete models were to be found in the commercial banking sector. The savings banks sought to become modern, professional business enterprises. There was no need to invent the new form as it was already there. In fact it seemed that the reformers hardly needed to deliberate on how the problems were to be solved. Becoming modern business enterprises stood out as the obvious solution; indeed, it was so obvious that no-one proposed any alternative. Moreover, the reformers did not even have to discover or invent the problem: the idea of toughening competition and the risk of losing out neither originated with nor was specific to the savings banks. Generally speaking, such ideas will always be relevant in business and, more specifically, they will always be discussed throughout the banking sector, in all types of banks. For the savings banks, the transformation meant that the reformers borrowed a very common mode of thinking from business enterprises which contained ideas both about the problem and its solution. These ideas then shaped action taken within the organization: the design of its structure, the development of new products, the introduction of new technology, etc. Prefabricated ideas about reality already existed, and any given problem or problem formulation led to a given proposed solution.

A new definition of savings banks

Institutions such as markets, businesses, the state, administrations, local economies, shared interests and popular movements are social phenomena intertwined in special ways. Different types of institutions have evolved for different reasons and in different environments. The institutions and their environments give rise to institutional systems which follow different sets of rules and operate under different conditions. But the actors in the organizations do not always appear to realize this. We have seen how reformers in the savings banks gazed longingly at the market and applied its rules to their own organizations, which they also judged using the market's measuring rod. But as the savings bank was not originally constructed for the market, it was difficult for it to satisfy market demands. This enforced the reformers' arguments: the savings banks would have to be modernized, i.e. to be transformed into business corporations.

The savings banks were not originally part of the market. They arrived in the market from a different institutional context where the rules and conditions were different. The opponents of modernization did not fully realize that the traditional savings bank has little to do with the market, and they had no solution to propose. The savings bank reformers, on the other hand, supporting their arguments with the idea of the modernization of society as a whole, were able to establish their definition of the situation of the savings banks as self-evident, and from that definition there followed a ready-made solution: modern, merged savings banks.

But the world in which the modernizers of the savings banks live and for which they speak is a social construction (Berger and Luckmann 1966).

This does not imply that it is a false, unreal or imaginary world, only that it is a human creation and as such its laws are of a different type from natural laws. To use the terminology of Meyer and Scott (1983: 14), modern arguments as used in the Savings Banks case are 'rational myths' 'in the sense that they depend for their efficacy, for their reality, on the fact that they are widely shared, or are promulgated by individuals or groups that have been granted the right to determine such matters'. Thus modernization is not a natural phenomenon. It may be likened to a natural process, but it is not one. The modern world is one of many existing and potential worlds, one which is maintained because people believe in it and thus reproduce it.

5 Organizational individuality and rationality as reform content

In earlier chapters, we have argued that it is common to assume that formal organizations are clearly distinguishable from their environments, that they have identities of their own, can be governed from above, and are hierarchical and rational. The norm that they ought to have these characteristics is even more common. We have also argued that such assumptions frequently fail to correspond with reality, and that the norm is open to question. But identity, hierarchy and rationality are commonly the content of reforms. In this chapter and the next, we attempt to explain why this is often so. We argue that notions of identity, hierarchy and rationality are deeply rooted in our culture, and are based on the concept of the individual.

ORGANIZATIONS AS INDIVIDUALS

The idea of the individual has been an important concept in Western philosophy since the time of classical Greece. 'Individual' means 'indivisible', and the concept expresses the idea that human beings are unique units clearly distinguished from their environment, stable over time and in different situations. The concept of the individual stands in contrast with both older Greek ideas and ideas from non-Western cultures, where human beings are not seen as such clearly separate units, where human action is considered more a product of the situation than of 'personal characteristics', and where the human being is basically considered to be equivalent to his or her role in various contexts.

The concept of the individual is more than an idea, however. The individual is also one of the central institutions in Western culture, an institution which has given rise to a large number of formal and informal rules for behaviour. The individual is assumed, for instance, to have particular rights and obligations. Any behaviour too far removed from what is encompassed by the idea of the individual is considered deviant or even pathological. The institution of the individual is often attributed a great deal of value: people should be individuals. It is also a strong institution in the sense that many people confuse preconceptions with reality: people are often assumed to be individuals. It is symptomatic that Western-language dictionaries often treat 'human beings' and 'individuals' as synonymous.

Responsibility is one important consequence of the institution of the individual. In Western culture, the definition of responsibility is linked to the perception of influence (Aristotle, Book Three, ch. 1): the person who is seen as affecting actions or events is also responsible for them. Human beings are responsible for their actions precisely because they are assumed to be individuals; because their thoughts and values are assumed to govern their actions. Responsibility is an important cornerstone of the individual's rights and obligations. In order to assert them it must be possible to hold the individual responsible, for example by punishing someone who does not satisfy her or his obligations. The concept of the individual is also the basis for entire theories or models of the human being. It is fundamental to Christianity, which has (particularly in its Protestant version) produced some of the best-developed theories of the existential and moral consequences of the concept of the individual. The model of the individual includes an idea about consistency, not only in time and in different situations but also between people's thoughts and values and their actions. A lack of consistency between correct values and actions is defined as sin. And since the individual is considered something stable, responsibility for his sins can be attributed to him.

One important development of the individual model is the idea of rationality: that thought is to govern action. People will first think, and then act as they have thought. The idea of rationality is a kind of process equivalent to the hierarchy described in the model of the individual: the hierarchy of thought and action, soul and body. This hierarchy recurs in rational ideas about how thinking should be done, which are most explicit in the rules for how rational decisions should be made. These rules establish a hierarchy between the normative and the positive, between the decision maker and his or her preferences on the one hand and the surrounding world and its material terms and conditions on the other. The preferences are superior to action alternatives and consequences: preferences are to be used to assess consequences and select among alternatives.

In modern societies, the individual model is not only used to describe people. 'Individual' has become an important figure of thought elsewhere as well. Organizations are often assumed to be a kind of individual. They are presented as uniform, well-co-ordinated units, clearly separate both from their environments and from other organizations, relatively stable and with norms including ideological consistency and agreement between ideology and action. The actions of organizations are assumed to be governed by the thoughts and talk of their leaders. In light of the pictures of organizations we are generally presented with, it appears particularly natural to describe organizations using the same terms we use to describe people. Organizational charts depict organizations as a kind of overgrown human being, with the executive management like the head at the top, and vertical lines symbolizing the way in which signals are transferred to the various limbs, the divisions of the organization which, it is assumed, will perform the actions thought out by the headquarters.

The frequent use of the individual model in organizational presentations is not only attributable to its strong cultural roots. The model is also closely associated with popular ideas of what justifies the existence of organizations, of what makes it possible for them to generate resources and gain the support of their environments to survive and grow. It is widely held, not only in organization theory but also in economic theory, that organizations generate resources and external support through their products, by supplying the environment with the goods and services it demands. These products are the result of co-ordinated, organized action: the actions of organizational members are designed to achieve a joint end. Organizations are often even defined in this way, as systems for co-ordinated action.

The individual model goes well with the idea of action. An important means of achieving action is hierarchy: management tells the members of the organization what to do. Efficient organizational action is facilitated if conflicts can be avoided and consistency can be promoted. It is easy to argue that organizations wanting to produce forceful action should behave as individuals.

How, then, does the individual model and its rational specification differ from the way in which organizations tend to work in practice? Some differences have been described in previous chapters, but before we go on, let us examine them, and a few others, in greater detail.

INDIVIDUALITY, RATIONALITY AND ORGANIZATION

The idea of the individual implies assumptions about identity, hierarchy and rationality. When organizations are viewed as individuals, it is assumed that they have unique identities and are clearly distinguishable from their environments. For example, they are assumed to have specific business ideas or tasks. We have previously questioned these assumptions by describing organizations as both part of and as expressions of the wider institutions of society. Organizations are far from unique: they reflect more general norms and patterns of behaviour, and the boundary between an organization and its environment may be ambiguous. Organizational members have loyalties other than those to the organization, including loyalties to their professions or their trade unions.

The assumption of hierarchy

Both the assumption of hierarchy and the assumption of rationality build on the distinction between thought and action. There are leaders, and they do not participate directly in organizations' material activities – they do not produce or sell goods and services. Instead, leaders have specialized in thinking out desirable activities and how they should be performed while others, the led, carry them out. This division of labour is established in organization theory as well as in organizations' presentation of themselves and organizational practice. The division into the leaders and the led has even been used to define organizations. Organizations are said to be systems co-ordinating the actions of various actors through a hierarchy, as opposed to markets, for example, which have other mechanisms of co-ordination.

The assumption about hierarchy implies that there is interplay and influence between the leaders and the led. However, in many organizations the connection between the leaders and the led is loose. Contact between them may be sparse and sporadic, there may be relatively little knowledge of what the other party actually does, and there is often only poor consistency between what is said, what is decided and what is done. Sometimes the connection between the leaders and the led is so weak that they may be said to be isolated from one another. They become separate owing to the fact that their tasks are different: the leaders live in the world of ideas and the led in the world of action. The conditions applying in these two worlds are very different, and many things can be thought and desired in the world of ideas but cannot be implemented in practice.

As mentioned in previous chapters, it can also be argued that a decoupling between the leaders and the led may contribute to the survival of organizations. Organizations are often judged by the environment on the basis not only of their actions, resulting in products, but also on the basis of the talk and decisions they present. In situations in which organizations encounter inconsistent demands from their environments, it may be important or necessary to produce hypocrisy: to systematically satisfy certain demands and norms by talk and decisions and to confront others through action. Leaders' talk and decisions may compensate for the actions of the led, and vice versa.

The assumption of hierarchy not only presupposes that there is an association between the leaders and the led, but also that this relationship is in a definite direction, that the leaders control the led. In practice, organizational managements often encounter a number of obstacles to this control. The led may be unwilling to be controlled, or may find it difficult to perceive or understand the signals of the leaders. In addition, leaders are normally dependent on the knowledge of the led to know what action should be taken. But the effect of this dependence may easily be that the led influence what the leaders want, that the led control the leaders instead of the other way around (Brunsson and Jönsson 1979; Brunsson 1989).

Management talk and decisions may be in agreement with organizational actions, but rather than controlling those actions they may justify and defend them to the outside world. It is far from certain that organizations where management controls actions gain greater external support or have a better chance of survival than organizations in which management defends the actions of the led to the outside world. For this reason, the ability to describe and explain actions to the rest of the world in order for them to be accepted or appreciated is often an important management task. The led may be more successful in implementing difficult, complex organizational actions if they themselves determine the content of these actions. And the leaders do not necessarily have more information than the led as to what actions ought to be taken.

The assumption of rationality

The rational specification of the idea of the individual also encompasses an assumption that actions are controlled by statements about the future, such as decisions. A rational individual first decides what to do and then does it; in an organization the leaders decide that an action or state of affairs for the future is desirable, and it is up to the led to bring them to fulfilment. Control is proactive.

An alternative type of control is reaction, whether reacting to implemented actions or achieved states: action precedes judgement of the action and its results; and 'if at first we don't succeed, we'll try again'. We affect the actions of others by distributing rewards and sanctions after having judged the actions implemented and the results achieved.

Reactive management may be advantageous in comparison with proactive management: it may make it possible to achieve results that could hardly have been imagined, while planning may mean setting an unnecessarily low level of aspiration. It may also be extremely difficult to specify in advance which actions are best. Innovations – new actions – might be difficult to achieve by proactive control. (Children, fortunately, are not rational; if they were they would not be able to develop, moving from the satisfaction of simple needs to more advanced needs and preferences (March 1988).) There is also a risk that future-orientation will lead to too high a level of aspiration. If descriptions of the future are too unrealistic ever to be achievable, they doom the participants to perpetual dissatisfaction. So it is impossible to state generally which is more sensible, the rationalistic future orientation or its opposite. It is clear that both approaches are important for both people and organizations.

There are both rational and irrational ways to decide which actions are desirable. The rational model of decision-making specifies in great detail how decisions are to be made. In making a choice, decision-makers must establish what their future preferences will be, what alternative actions are possible and what future consequences the various action alternatives will have. Then they must compare their preferences with the consequences. The guiding principle is that preferences are superior to alternatives and consequences. Preferences determine which consequences are relevant, and how they are assessed, as well as affecting the choice of action alternative. The superiority of preferences guarantees that the genuine thought, the norm unsullied by material terms of action, is the ultimate force governing action. The only thing leaders can be assumed to know more about than the led is their own preferences, and, by making them their point of departure, they are assumed to control the led.

But in the real world actions may also influence preferences: acting leads us to discover what we prefer. In the absence of information on material states and alternative actions it is, in fact, extremely difficult to know what we prefer. It is easy to uphold very general desires, such as the happiness of all, or maximum profit for the company. But in order to describe these desires in detail, or to know how we would like to see them achieved, it is necessary to have knowledge of the states, needs and potentials in the world of practice. As described above, those who are closest to this world may have the advantage in terms of knowledge, and this may mean not only that they are better equipped than management to describe alternatives and calculate consequences, but also that they are able to substantially affect management's preferences.

Rationality also requires an exhaustive description of preferences, alternatives and consequences. It must be possible to weigh all the decision-makers' preferences against one another, to establish an order of preference in which the respective weights of the different preferences are clear. Decision-makers must take all potential alternative actions into consideration, as well as all the relevant consequences for their preferences. It is, of course, difficult to achieve this in practice, not least because it requires that decision-makers evaluate the future about which, as we know, the only thing we can know for certain is that we know nothing. It has also been demonstrated in experiments that when people are requested to estimate consequences or probabilities, and to weigh consequences, they use a number of rules of thumb which are incomplete and, in fact, faulty (Nisbett and Ross 1980). Such rules of thumb are difficult to eliminate through training. Furthermore, it cannot be proven that rational decision-making processes lead to better conclusions than irrational processes when future consequences and their probabilities are unknown, which is often the situation for organizational decisions.

In normative decision theories, the decision-makers are frequently characterized as being uncertain of consequences. If their decisions are about recurring events, they may be helped by knowing the probability of different consequences; there are normative models for decision-making stipulating how such probabilities should be applied. It is less commonly noted that decision-makers may be uncertain as to their alternatives: one method of bounded rationality for reducing the number of alternatives is known as 'satisficing', i.e. sifting alternatives until you find one you believe is satisfactory (Simon 1955). It is also seldom noted that decision-makers may be uncertain of their preferences and, as mentioned above, they may be interested in acting in order to discover them, or to feel more certain about them (March 1978).

Last but not least, rational decision processes may pose obstacles to action. When it comes to assessing future consequences of actions in unpredictable, complex social systems, rationality is an effective means of increasing the uncertainty experienced by decision-makers. Basing a judgement on one's own preferences, dealing with many alternatives, and assessing many consequences, both positive and negative, easily give rise to uncertainty as to which alternative one should choose and, in organizational contexts, also uncertainty as to which action will actually be implemented. This type of uncertainty tends to reduce the level of motivation for any given action, undermine expectations that it will really be implemented, and prevent the actors from committing themselves to it (Brunsson 1985). A desire to preserve the possibility of acting forcefully may be one important explanation of why individuals, groups and organizations avoid rationality in decision processes and often make decisions in systematically irrational ways. In the rational model it is assumed that the difficult and important thing is to think correctly, while in organizations the main difficulty is often to achieve co-ordinated organizational action. The ability to act forcefully is often more important to the survival and success of an organization than the ability to analyse successfully.

Thus, viewing organizations as individuals involves and gives rise to a number of assumptions. Organizations may sometimes behave in ways similar to one or more of these assumptions. But our description indicates that the situation is most commonly the reverse: normally organizations behave in ways that contradict the idea of the individual, at least rationality is anti-entropic (Etzioni 1988). What is even more important in this discussion is that, in many situations, it is impossible or unsuitable for organizations, as for individuals, to follow the ideal of the individual in thought and action. Thus it is not always sensible to be a rational individual.

INTENTION, RESULT AND REFORM

All these deviations from the idea of organizations as individuals are familiar ones to most people who have worked in or studied the behaviour of large organizations. The individual is often not a particularly true description of people, and it appears to be an even less satisfactory description of organizations. Fewer people have defended deviations from the individual and from rationality: the deviations belong more to descriptive theory than to normative theory. Although some organizational managements might describe their organizations as not quite functioning in accordance with the individual model, it would be difficult to imagine them arguing in favour of conflicts, inconsistencies, hypocrisy and poor control. Even if the individual model is not often a good one for organizations to apply in action, it is a good model for describing the intentions an organization should have. Similarly, rationality is a more common method for explaining and motivating decisions to the outside world than for making them.

So ideas concerning individuality and rationality are often components of organizations' presentations and intentions, but seldom traits in their behaviour. The tension between how organizations are presented and how they work, between intentions and results, creates a sense of failure. Managements fail to achieve the consistency between talk, decisions and actions they claim to be striving for, management influence is limited and there are problems of achieving efficient action. Discrepancies between presentation and results may explain why many people are often dissatisfied with the functioning and management of their organizations, even in organizations considered successful, for example, in terms of profitability. The failure produced by the discrepancy between presentation and results tends to produce repentance and reform. It is natural for leaders, convinced of their own good intentions, to try to improve organizational structures, processes and ideologies and bring them more into line with the individual model. These intentions clearly appear to be right, while there equally clearly seems to be something wrong with the organization which is to fulfil the intentions. Structures, processes and ideologies which do not express or benefit identity, unity, hierarchy, co-ordination, purposefulness and efficient action must be abolished: the organization must be trimmed and rationalized.

Presenting the organization in accordance with the individual model is also a means by which the management accepts responsibility. When it is seen as controlling, it is endowed with responsibility. Management responsibility is important in legislation regulating enforcement of responsibility for organizational actions. Responsibility is also important in all the ideas rooting organizations to their environments by means of various theories of control: for instance, doctrines claiming that the people control public organizations directly or indirectly by electing politicians as the ultimate leaders of these organizations, or that owners control companies by appointing boards of directors and managing directors. The idea of responsibility is also important as a way of understanding and explaining events: it implies that events are explained in light of human action. This is important in a secularized society where people prefer not to explain things in terms of chance, nature or God.

The ability of the individual model to produce responsibility is another important explanation of its popularity. The great significance of responsibility for organizations and their environments may explain why it is difficult, if not impossible, for organizations to avoid making use of the individual model when presenting themselves. It is, furthermore, natural for anyone in a position of responsibility to desire a position from which he is really able to control – it is not particularly surprising that managements want to implement reforms aimed at making their organizations controllable.

But if it is important for organizations not to work in accordance with the individual model, it is also important for reforms aiming at that model not to succeed. Luckily, they are not very likely to. The less like the individual model an organization is, the more difficult it is for it to mobilize the necessary consensus, control and ability to act to implement such an extensive reform.

March and Olsen (1983) pointed out that every new US president since World War II has launched administrative reforms, but with modest results, and very little interest in them. However, by promising reforms, by promising to improve in the future, an organization may spread hope: things are moving in the right direction after all. Launching reforms results in talk and decisions which compensate for present action. This provides a further example of hypocrisy.

The result of the idea of the individual, then, is not very different for organizations than it is for people. Individuals should have high values and good intentions, and they should strive to make these values and intentions characterize their actions as well. As they are considered able to govern their actions, they are also responsible for them. Where values and actions do not agree, hypocrisy and sin are to be found. The loftier the values, the more easily hypocrisy and sin arise. If the values demanded are high enough, the individual is automatically sinful. Without relinquishing his estimable values, the individual ought to realize his responsibility and strive for change, to bring thought and action better into line. The striving itself is the point; total success is an impossibility. The individual cannot redeem himself. When organizations are considered to be individuals, they reproduce patterns of action and thought otherwise reserved for individual people.

The individual as a recurring component of reform

The discussion above provides a very general answer to our initial question in this chapter: why do organizations try to reform in line with the individual model? If there is a strong norm stating that organizations should behave like rational individuals and, simultaneously, if organizations tend not to satisfy that norm, reform is needed.

This only explains one-time reforms, however. Why are individual-rational reforms repeated in different organizations or within the same one even if they constantly fail? This may result from the kind of organizational forgetfulness we described in Chapter 3. But sometimes people in organizations who have vast experience both of how organizations work in practice, and even of a number of previous failed individual-rational reforms, still go on trying to implement new reforms of the same kind. As reforms striving towards the individual model are also very common, knowledge of such reforms and their results should spread from one organization to another, thus working to deter new reforms.

There are three factors beyond organizational forgetfulness, which could stop continued reform. The first is a successful reform: if, through a reform, an organization were successfully and durably transformed into a rational individual, there would be no reason to launch a new individual-rational reform. If, moreover, such successes were common, individual-rational reforms would generally become rare. But, as described above, it is not only difficult or impossible to make organizations function in accordance with the individual model and its rational specification: this type of functioning would also pose a grave threat to the legitimacy and survival of organizations. In other words, reformed organizations would run the risk of putting themselves out of business.

A second threat to continued reform would be total isolation between the reformers and the reformees. If the reformers were entirely ignorant of how the reformees worked, they might think that they were already working according to the individual model, although they were not. This would mean that the reformers saw no need for reform, although the organization was not behaving like an individual. This undoubtedly happens occasionally. One situation in which it might be expected to be common would be just after a reform has been carried out: at least the reformers may then believe that the reformees will soon behave correctly. But in the long run it is probably rare for there to be total isolation between the reformers and the reformees. Even after reforms, management usually gradually discovers that the organization is not working quite as they had anticipated.

A third threat to continued reform is that the very norm, of individuality and rationality, has changed. It should be natural for those who, time and again, have tried but failed to carry out individual-rational reforms to question whether the idea is such a good one after all. Actually, reforms themselves should pose the greatest threat to the individual-rational model. As long as the norm is only being discussed at the normative level of thought, it is difficult to see how it would be threatened: as an idea the individual-rational model appears both attractive and sensible. The criticisms aimed at it, some of which we summarized above, mainly stem from questions of practicality: the impossibility and unsuitability of applying the idea in practice, not the value of the idea in itself. And reforms are, in fact, attempts to apply ideas in practice. It is during times of attempted reform, if ever, that reformers and others should discover that the idea is inappropriate, and be discouraged from trying again.

If that were so, the result of reforms should be abandonment of the individual as a model for how organizations should work, resulting in the gradual phasing-out of this type of reform. Although this effect is considered morally dubious with regard to people, we might not consider it a moral problem in relation to organizations.

The remainder of this chapter and all of Chapter 6 are devoted to the question of why, despite their failure, reforms with an individual-rational content do not result in undermining and abandonment of the individual-rational norm, but serve as a recurring point of departure for new reforms with the same contents. How does the norm come to be maintained although it does not govern practice and although it is confronted with practice in reforms? Why is such a fundamental part of our society as the individual-rational norm not threatened by experience, the only apparent potential threat? If we can answer this question, we will have part of the explanation of why the rational individual is, and will remain, such a powerful idea, model and institution in our society.

In this chapter and the next, we discuss these issues by examining two processes of reform aimed at individualizing and rationalizing organizations. We examine in detail what created the supply of and demand for these reforms. In this chapter we describe a reform that was the work of a Swedish Government Commission of Inquiry appointed to review the relationship between the government and state agencies in Sweden. The aim of this reform was increased hierarchy and rationality. In the next chapter we describe the introduction of a method of corporate strategic planning, a method aimed at both clarifying the company's identity and at increasing hierarchy and rationality. We illustrate how these reforms not only reproduced the individual-rational norm, but also even strengthened it.

In order to make the text easier to read, we henceforth refer to the conglomerate of ideas about the individual and its assumptions about identity, hierarchy and rationality as the 'rational model', and to attempts to transfer these ideas into organizational practices as attempted 'rationalizations'. These concepts, then, are used here to refer not only to the idea of rationality but also to the roots of that idea in the individual.

RATIONALIZATION IN PRACTICE

The Government Commission of Inquiry used as an example here was part of a process of renewal of the public sector, a popular theme in many countries in the early and mid-1980s. This commission was appointed to review the relationship between the government and the state agencies, and the forms by which the agencies were managed. In the government directives to the commission, a number of demands on state agencies were described. They were to serve as the tools for implementing the intentions of the parliament and the government, their operations were to be well-suited to the needs of the public, and they were to be able to adapt to new demands. 'Service' and 'efficiency' were two concepts which recurred in the directives. The commission was given a very broad mandate to study the management of the agencies and to recommend how they should be organized, and the directives mentioned many examples of different types of management for agencies. The desirability of diversified representation from many sectors of society on the boards of state agencies was emphasized. The commission staff consisted of a secretariat, headed by a chairman, and a decision-making committee composed almost exclusively of members of parliament from the majority and opposition parties.

In contrast to what was stipulated in the directives, the secretariat focused its work on control, in the sense of politicians' control of the agencies, a subject only mentioned explicitly once in the directives. This was the area the members of the commission and the people at the ministry who initiated the commission saw as the real problem area. Service and efficiency were not discussed by the commission.

The idea that good, improved political control of state agencies was desirable was the basis for the commission's work, on which they drew up their proposals. They launched the principle that the government should govern more, in the sense that it should state the objectives for operations more clearly, and should govern less, in the sense that it should not get involved in the details of how the agencies chose to achieve these objectives. The main proposals from the commission dealt with the budget process, the terms of employment of Director Generals, and the authorities' boards. The budget process was supposed to be a three-year one, which would give the agencies a better chance of providing the government with good information for decision-making, and would give the government more time to consider this material. Measures were proposed to improve the mobility of the office of Director General. When it came to the boards, the commission had two main proposals: some agencies should be managed by a Director General with an advisory council at his side, while others should have a board of politicians, which would also make the most important decisions.

Discussions in the meetings of the working committee focused mainly on the formulation of these proposed boards of politicians. The secretariat wanted most agencies to have no boards, while the majority of the committee members wanted considerably more boards. The compromise solution was a proposal with both advisory councils and boards, with various models being tried as pilot projects, after which a final decision as to the distribution of councils and boards of politicians among the agencies would be made.

Rationalization

This commission was a good example both of selling and buying ideas strongly characterized by the model of the individual and of rationality. The individual-rational traits were strong both in the proposals of the commission and in the reasoning and motivations it presented. All the elements of the rational model were represented in at least some main sections of the report, as will be described below. The whole idea of having the commission was based on the division between the leaders and the led. There were strong opinions asserting that the government and the agencies should be more closely related. The specific tradition of agencies being independent from the government no longer seemed relevant, at least if interpreted as the idea that it was not the task of government to control state agencies. Even if, according to the tradition and constitution, only the government as a whole could give (limited) orders to agencies, there had always been informal contacts between relevant ministries and agencies. But now these contacts were described in the report of the commission as vital to governing of agencies, as well as both natural and acceptable.

The idea of governing both more and less implied that control was to be limited to stating objectives for future operations: the controllers were no longer to have an impact on details as to the means to be used. Management by objectives was to replace governing by rule. The budgeting process was no longer to deal with unimportant issues but with important ones. Budgeting was presented as a rational decision-making process at government level, not as negotiations among various parties.

In the opinion of the commission, it was important for the agencies to provide the government with detailed factual information before a decision was made. Information given to the government by agencies normally becomes public, and will therefore be influenced by the agencies' tactical concerns. Also, politicians are normally attributed responsibility for bad results of the agencies, so they have strong reasons to suppress rather than publish such information. But the commission still viewed information as being unproblematic. This view also made it propose formal evaluations of the operations. The idea that more detailed facts from those who are to be controlled would improve rather than undermine the position of the controllers is well in agreement with the assumption of the rationalistic model that intentions are prior to and dominate over the analysis of alternatives and consequences, rather than the other way around.

The rational model was also an important aspect of three of the main proposals in the report of the commission: to change the role of the board of directors, to govern more and less, and to change the budget process. The ultimate proposal on the boards, however, was a compromise, in which the rationalist ideas were forced to give way to others to some extent. What made the commission's report so strongly characterized by rationality? Why were rational ideas launched by some actors, and why were these ideas so widely accepted by other actors?

Irrational methods of rationalization

It should first be noted that the commission did not propose increased rationality in a desire to force its own working methods upon others. On the contrary, as will be described below, it did its own work in a systematically irrational way, and several members also stated that they did not consider rationality to be a good way for them personally to work. So there was a sharp contrast between the proposals of the commission and its own working methods. Their proposals were characterized by rationality, their work by irrationality. The commission did not practise what it preached, and this actually enhanced its ability to propose rationalizations.

The original idea of undertaking an inquiry and of reforming did not emerge as a result of a rational analysis highlighting vital aspects of inadequate implementation of objectives. Nor were the directives written on this basis. The commission did not allow its work to be governed by the directives. Directives for commissions can be interpreted as efforts made by the principals behind the commission to control it. The directives are the one thing about a commission which the government can decide. In this case, it can be said that the directives satisfied at least one of the commission's ideas: they were not detailed instructions as to what the commission should do; they 'governed less'. The directives gave a more general sense of direction, serving as a kind of management by objectives. But the members of the commission, as described above, still did not allow themselves to be particularly controlled by the directives, and they did not analyse them in any great detail: they regarded their own particular ideas about what to propose as the self-evident ones.

Furthermore, the report focused on solutions rather than on objectives and principles. It did not begin by analysing objectives and then go on to determine how to achieve them. Instead, it brought up ideas for solutions, and the important process was imitation rather than analysis. The fact that the solutions already seemed to exist elsewhere was an important source of inspiration. Nevertheless, one member actually tried to work in a more rational way at the start of the work. He wrote a memorandum describing how control might actually be defined, and existing potential solutions to problems of control. His memorandum had very little impact on the inquiry and he soon resigned from the commission. The rational ideas proposed became norms in themselves, not means by which established objectives could be satisfied.

The politicians who comprised the committee gave priority to the highly concrete issues of the composition and duties of the authorities' boards, and displayed minimal interest in the more abstract issues. According to the model of management by objectives they should have done the opposite, establishing the general principles and allowing the civil servants at the secretariat to work with the concrete proposals.

In most cases the work and the report were structured so that no alternative solutions were considered – another non-rational feature. Most members found it difficult even to see any alternatives to the proposals in the report, with the possible exception of the status quo. The only exception was the discussion of the composition and duties of the boards, but not even this discussion took the form of a rational analysis based on established objectives.

Neither the commission members, the civil servants at the ministry who had written the directives, nor the politicians expressed any kind of surprise over or apology for their lack of rationality. On the contrary, most considered the commission to have worked in a natural and right way. Most of them had a high degree of awareness of the necessity of irrationality: 'when you've been in this field for a while you realize that the only way to achieve change is by muddling through', as someone put it. 'Muddling through' is Lindblom's (1959) term which describes the opposite of rational processes. As we have seen, however, the commission investigators did not think that the government should avail itself of this effective governing technique in the future.

Although the work of the commission was characterized by experience of the benefits of muddling through, its proposals were not. It was a distinguishing feature of the report of the commission that its proposals were not based on experience. The fact that earlier experiments with rationalistic budgeting – in the form of 'programme budgeting' – had failed did not stop them from making proposals that were, to a large extent, a repetition of those ideas. One member had been involved in implementing management by objectives in local government, where there had been major difficulties in the system being accepted and even greater problems in making it work. Yet he was prepared to propose the model once again. The reaction to past failures was to recommend more of the same medicine.

One general argument was that the solutions being suggested were in use elsewhere, and reforms had been made elsewhere, but the experience gained from these solutions and reforms was not referred to. The secretariat's urge to reform was also unaffected by their knowledge of the results of interviews which showed that the undersecretaries of state, who worked closely with the principals of the commission, were reasonably pleased with the status quo. And they were equally unaffected by their own experience with the politicians on the committee who obviously were not working in accordance with the proposed model.

The fact that the commission members themselves neither worked rationally themselves nor regarded rationality as a good working method for them seems sensible, on the basis of what we know about organizations. The fact that they avoided the rationality which they themselves suggested, and would not allow themselves to be brought down by negative experiences of their own ideas, was also an important prerequisite for their being able to produce rational proposals. If the commission had not followed these principles there is a serious risk – if it had ever been initiated – that it would not have drawn attention to control, that it would not have suggested any changes or suggested non-rational changes and, according to the actor cited above, that this would not have led to real change. This was nothing unique; in the next chapter we describe how a successful consultant, selling a highly rationalistic method for adapting organizations to customer needs, refused to adapt his own method to his customer needs, even when his customers requested such adaptation.

There are, however, several reasons why the commission put forth rationalistic proposals. As is pointed out in the next section, various kinds of clarity were more motivating to the members than their own personal, practical experience. The rational model offered explanations, and it both clarified and was self-evident.

Rationality as explanation

The commission's report dealt extensively with organizational control, that is how to influence future conditions. However, the real driving force behind its proposals was explanations which stated how to analyse existing conditions or past events. Explanation was more primary than change for many actors. Those initiating the commission and its leading members saw a major problem in the difficulty of explaining the nature of the relationship between government and agencies in Sweden. This had been a particular problem in the international context when they needed to describe 'the Swedish model' and Sweden's significant departures from the international norm. They met with difficulties when making presentations at international conferences or writing articles for international or foreign journals. Several of those who can be regarded as initiators of the commission made it clear that the need to be able to explain was the main reason they had wanted the commission appointed. They found most difficulty in explaining why state agencies in Sweden had boards. Although changes in reality might be necessary in order to solve this problem of explanation, change was not the main issue.

Furthermore, these direct statements with regard to the difficulties inherent in explanations to others were not the only evidence of why explanation became such an important task for the commission. The main complaints about the prevailing system were generally that it had not been sufficiently thought through, and that it was not characterized by a set of coherent ideas. The appointments of boards and the existence of different types of boards was not the result of planned activities but of ad hoc decisions. All this was thought to give an amateurish impression. These comments illustrate the commission belief that thought and actions should be interrelated. In addition, they involve an implicit criticism that the idea of rational planning had not been implemented, i.e. that thought should precede action.

The idea of planning was not strong enough, however, to eliminate its opposite, the idea that it is important to equip actions with thoughts retroactively. It had been possible to appoint boards without very much thought, or at least by not basing the appointments on consistent ideas. What was more difficult was to justify the existence of all these boards. This required one consistent idea and professionalism rather than amateurism. It was also the ambition of several members of the commission as well as those who had initiated the commission to prove that the Swedish model was a good one, and this made it necessary to be able to associate the model with a high-quality idea.

The discussion within the commission was also marked by the explanatory task. As mentioned above, it made no difference that key groups were quite satisfied with the status quo: this did not make the members of the commission satisfied with it. Neither the fact that the undersecretaries of state reported that they considered the prevailing order to be quite unproblematic in terms of control, nor the fact that the national politicians on the commission expressed opposition to change in the roles of the boards, in any way muffled the arguments for changes that would make the system easier to explain. Several of the actors also spoke more about politicians' responsibility than about control: like explanations, responsibility is a retrospective phenomenon, occurring as a result of explaining that someone has been in control.

It was also the opinion of many that the report should contain more proposals of principle than concrete proposals. They thought it should describe the principles of control, not give details as to how various instruments of control should be formulated. This fits very well with the explanatory approach; a principle is a coherent idea and coherent ideas are useful for explanation.

As long as the work of the commission remained at the level of principles, there was no difficulty achieving consensus. The conflicts arose when the ideas became concrete, and the commission needed to decide whether or not there should be boards of the old kind. The statement of principle of the commission as to hierarchy between the government and the agencies led logically to the idea that most of the boards should be abolished, but the majority of the politicians were against this. The final result in the proposals was the half-baked compromise most of the secretariat members considered to be the greatest shortcoming of the report: the proposal was 'illogical'.

But the politicians on the committee did not completely neglect the explanatory aspect. One leading politician stated that, although the work of the commission had not resulted in major changes, it had been useful to debate the issues in detail and to find that, at the end of the day, the Swedish model was good.

The flight from ambiguity

A strong interest in clarification is closely associated with the explanatory approach. To 'ex-plain' is to make things plain, but the work of the commission seems to have gone even further, elevating plain speaking and clarity as independent values.

The actors discussed the need for clarification both in the report itself and when they were interviewed by us, stating that they saw it as one of the important driving forces of the commission's work. They described the general task of the commission as 'getting things organized and sorted out'. In order to do so, things had to be simplified and made plain; a rational system was necessary, with 'rational' defined as simple rules and 'wide brush-strokes'. This striving for clarity led, for example, to a demand for the number of possible models for boards to be trimmed down to two, and to a distaste for compromise. According to the report, clarity has widespread effects: 'if our work can lead to a clarification of the relationship between the government and the state agencies, then the committee will have contributed to a desirable strengthening of popular governance in Sweden.'

Striving for clarity also affected the choice of subjects addressed by the commission worked on and the solutions they proposed. One area of ambiguity was how the Ministries informally controlled the agencies. This had the somewhat odd effect that this traditionally informal phenomenon was now subjected to formal treatment in an official Government Commission of Inquiry.

Striving for clarity also marked several of the proposals. One key concept was that the government should exert 'more precise control' without thereby becoming more involved in details. The politicians were supposed to describe their priorities in greater detail, and state clear objectives. The committee objected to the ambiguity they felt characterized the prevailing political governance. But their report did not exemplify what it considered clear objectives. One of the main reasons for examining the boards was precisely that their role was considered ambiguous. The report proposed two refined models for boards based on different principles, and it contrasted these to the prevailing mixture and confusion of principles and forms.

The self-evident nature of rationality

For most people involved, the rational ideas with which the commission was working were self-evident. When they were interviewed, the members of the commission found it difficult to justify these ideas or explain why they had chosen them. Most of them had not considered the fact that the government directives to the commission were more concerned with service and efficiency than with control; either it had not occurred to them or they had forgotten. When the commission members were interviewed, their justifications were that the wording about service and efficiency was not serious, but rather part of the general rhetoric used in commission directives, which were always worded as generally as that. It could not be meant to serve as a point of departure for the real work of the commission.

Those interviewed also found it difficult to justify the individual proposals. Questions such as what was so good about management by objectives appeared to take most of them by surprise, and they had difficulty mustering arguments. Instead, they presented arguments against the current situation: detailed governance is wrong, short-term budget work is wrong, and it is wrong for politicians to refrain from prioritizing. Many of them even said that they considered the present situation untenable. They knew it was important to get away from something, but appeared to have given far less thought to where they were going. In terms of the focus on control, the idea of management by objectives, and three-year budgeting, there was no discussion at all of concrete alternatives, except that two members submitted formal protests to the report. The opinion of most committee members was that they were doing the only possible thing. Several members of the commission also said they found it difficult to understand the objections of the two people who had protested to the report. No-one but these two people could recall any criticism being expressed at the meetings.

The proposals' high level of abstraction probably contributed to their appearing self-evident and not being compared with alternatives. They were proposals of principle, and it was not part of the assignment of the commission to formulate the different instruments of control in detail. Several of the members were unable to give one single example of an objective the politicians might use in controlling the agencies. The only concrete proposals were on the compositions of the boards, and in those cases alternatives were actually discussed.

Another cause of self-evidence was that many people considered the proposals to be norms in themselves rather than predictions about what might be expedient. To use the terms of the rational model itself, they were ends rather than means. It was a common norm that politicians are meant to control, that they should not control details, and that they should not be short-sighted. Both logic and rationality were also norms: it was a sufficient argument that the proposals were logical and rational; no further motivation of them was necessary. Refining the lines of command from the government to the agencies, which in most cases would mean doing away with the politicians on the boards, was presented as logical and thus of value in itself. Since the proposals were seen as norms, it is understandable that empirical experience was of little value when it came to assessing them. This was probably the reason why previous experience of the difficulty or even the impossibility of implementing identical or very similar ideas, for example of programme budgeting or of management by objectives, did not discourage the secretariat. They did not see how it could be wrong to try again, and considered optimism a virtue. Those who knew the difficulties of implementing management by objectives in practice did not think that therefore there was anything wrong with the idea, or that there was any reason not to propose it. Even the idea that the current situation was untenable was more an expression of a norm than of empirical facts; after all, the relationship between the state and the agencies had been as it was for decades, a time which was also very successful for the state, and the politicians had not been raising their voices in complaint.

Models and sources of inspiration

The general ideas the commission proposed were not new. They had not developed through any kind of internal brainstorming and problem solving in the committee, but had been taken from outside. The work of the commission had been to collect ideas and adapt and formulate them in greater detail. The fact that the ideas were not new was used by many of the members as an argument in their favour.

The general idea of public sector reform was in agreement with current developments in other countries as described in Chapter 2. Public sector reforms had been considered or implemented in most OECD states. The content of these reforms was also believed to be in agreement with the ideas being put forward by the commission; and they were also in line with what was understood to be the opinion of qualified sources within the public administration, such as staff members at the State Agency for Administrative Development. The idea of three-year budgeting had previously been presented in debates on control in public administration. It was also stated to be desirable by the Director Generals interviewed by the commission.

The ideas were also believed to be in agreement with what was happening in private industry, where developments were thought to be going in the same direction, according to the commission representative for trade and industry. The ideas were also described as 'the accepted truth within business administration', and thus as being what everyone knew should apply to companies and other organizations. The idea of management by objectives, long-term planning, and clear control and responsibility were in the air everywhere.

In other words, the secretariat mainly imitated presentation models of organizations, i.e. the images presented by organizations themselves or by others of how organizations work or should work. The commission made no independent analyses of how other organizations worked in practice, nor did they study or refer to practical experience, for example from previous attempts to use programme budgeting. There was one exception: the commission sent a questionnaire to members of the boards of directors of state agencies asking how they perceived their roles. The members of the secretariat thought that the answers revealed a 'messy' situation, with no uniformity of opinion and lots of 'peculiar' ideas. As argued earlier in this chapter, organizations are normally messier and more complex in practice than in presentation models, and comparisons between presentations and practices generally provide arguments for reform, as they did here.

The commission not only imitated models, but also had other sources of inspiration to support its ideas of control. When the commission was appointed, a government jurist 'discovered' that, according to the new Constitution, the government was actually meant to control the state agencies. This same idea was a central one in an examination of principles which preceded the commission's report. In this investigation, control by politicians was emphasized as an important link in the chain of democracy in which the people, ultimately, govern.

Thus the secretariat's argumentation took its main support from a kind of general argument: that the ideas it was promoting were applicable in many situations and environments, in fact virtually everywhere. They were also general in the sense that they had strong normative overtones: this was how one ought to behave. The politicians who opposed changes in the compositions of the boards used more specific models. They pointed out what made the 'Swedish model' special in terms of the relationship between the government and the agencies, and that the uniqueness of the national tradition made it difficult to learn from other countries. They placed greater emphasis on previous experience of this particular relationship than on external models, and spoke of developing current practices rather than referring to given norms.

Reception of the ideas: the inoffensive nature of the rational

The commission followed the Swedish tradition with regard to Government Commissions of Inquiry. The Chairman and the secretariat presented their ideas and proposed 'wordings' at the committee meetings. The role of the politicians in the committee was to examine them and express their opinions. The secretariat members were 'senders' of information and the politicians were the 'receivers' (Brunsson and Jönsson 1979). Most of what was ultimately written in the report was never discussed at the committee meetings, which were almost exclusively devoted to the composition of the boards. Most ideas and wordings were accepted by the committee without objection. However, this does not mean that the committee members personally accepted or supported the ideas. On the contrary, several members had many misgivings. For example, some thought that three-year budgeting might inhibit the ability of new governments to implement their ideas; that management by objectives was more easily said than done; that politicians actually should control details in the areas which they were supposed to be governing; that it was questionable to talk about government control, since most of the signals transmitted from 'the government' were actually just from civil servants in the government offices; that the reason for boards was that they could justify the work of the agencies to the outside world; and that logical order was not necessarily the best order. So there was no shortage of radically dissenting opinions though they were not voiced in the debate.

There were several explanations for the silence of the committee members. One was their striving for consensus: they did not want to rock the boat unnecessarily. Another was priorities: they were trying to concentrate on the important things, which were seen as the concrete proposals as to the boards, not the abstract ideas. Moreover, some of the members thought it was good to set one's sights high, although they knew that things could not work perfectly in reality. They saw the abstract ideas as norms for how things ought to be, and they thought there was nothing wrong with norms just because they could not be implemented completely in reality. They also thought that it must also be right, rather than wrong, to write about those norms – unless of course they had unsuitable practical consequences, as they clearly had in relation to the boards. Another similar argument for not protesting was that the ideas looked good on paper: ideas are attractive, but that doesn't mean that the corresponding practical results necessarily are.

Thus the rational ideas appeared inoffensive, as not worth fussing about, and they were also perceived as normatively and aesthetically good and undeserving of censure. This made the concrete ideas about the compositions of the boards all the more vexing: the rational ideas belonged to a different, more abstract world than the proposals about how the boards should be composed. If people's thoughts on more abstract phenomena are not in agreement with their opinions on more concrete phenomena, they run the risk of being accused of erroneous logic, and this is precisely what happened to the committee members. They had no alternative system of abstract ideas to associate with their counter-proposals, so they went directly to the concrete elements in their arguments. The members of the secretariat thought the committee members were behaving illogically, which they explained by saying that the committee members were not gifted enough or that, at the end of the day, they allowed themselves to be influenced by their egotistical group interests rather than concentrating on the best interests of the government administration as a whole. The civil servants found it more difficult than the politicians to distinguish between thoughts and actions, and they also found it difficult to take the politicians seriously.

But it would not necessarily have been particularly helpful for the politicians to protest unanimously against the abstract, rational ideas. Two people did, in fact, protest: they said that they criticized the basic ideas at the meetings and ultimately wrote statements of their own. But the civil servants at the secretariat did not understand them and complained that, in their opinions, the protesting politicians did not present their criticisms at the meetings, and that they were incomprehensible. According to the civil servants, the criticism was not articulated.

Strategic explanations

Up to this point, we have discussed qualities of the rational model which make it easy to propose and accept. But it does not necessarily mean that people find ideas and proposals valuable in themselves when they speak in favour of them or accept them. They may also do so because those ideas and proposals serve their own interests or hold some advantage for them in one or more respects. It is difficult to know to what extent this may have been the case in the committee, but in some respects there is agreement between action and interests which indicates that the actions may have been chosen strategically. One example is that the people at ministry level who initiated the commission thought they had, and were considered by others as having, the task of reforming the government administration. This was one reason they proposed the appointment of a commission of inquiry on reforms.

The conflicts in the work of the commission basically followed the line of demarcation between civil servants and politicians. The civil servants asked other civil servants, particularly Director Generals, what they thought, and emphasized those things. They were far less attentive to what the undersecretaries of state, who were the other parties in the governing relationship, might have thought. Although only the former, and not the latter, had been known to complain about the prevailing order of things, this was sufficient to initiate the commission of inquiry and to uphold it. Several of the ideas also seemed to favour the administration at the expense of the politicians: management by objectives was to give administrations greater freedom; the politicians were to set budget priorities (which experience has shown to facilitate expansion or at least save agencies from making un- pleasant decisions) (Wildavsky 1964; Brunsson and Rombach 1982); and the number of politicians who would be able to become involved in the operations of the agencies of the board was to be reduced.

Some members of the secretariat also saw the norms of rationality as so self-evident and important that it was difficult to distinguish them from their own interests. If a norm is held very strongly, it is similar to self-interest. Statements such as 'Politicians should not be able to wriggle out of having to establish priorities – it's their damned duty' or 'What has to be done is to force a new way of thinking through in the government offices' are signs of norms being a kind of interest.

One side of the attitude of the politicians can also be interpreted strategically. The politicians on the committee were members of parliament, not government politicians. Their defence of the boards of directors was a way of promoting an important role for MPs in the state agencies. One person expressed this interest in terms of the necessity of 'maintaining the self-respect of the politicians'.

Interests may also be equated with the different political views of the politicians. Some of the differences of opinion amongst the politicians can also be explained as differences of opinion between their parties. For example, some members felt that it was vital to defend the public sector and equip state agencies with strong boards which could defend their interests, while others thought that the boards just gave rise to too much political fracas, which disrupted the professional work of the agencies. The most striking thing, however, is the weakness of the political ideologies in relation to the rational ideology. First, identical political ideologies were found to lead to different conclusions: representatives of the same party sometimes had different opinions, for example with regard to the boards. This was in sharp contrast to the rational ideology, which led to general and strong consensus amongst the civil servants as to which proposals were natural and good. Second, in contrast with the rational ideology, political ideologies were not used in arguments at meetings or in the report itself. There may be many reasons for this: the same ideology's being able to lead to different conclusions did not make it an especially forceful argument. The political ideologies were also unsuitable in light of the desire of the politicians to avoid disagreements. The politicians may also have suspected that their ideologies would not have much clout in comparison with the rational ideas: 'in the long run only factual arguments hold water', as one civil servant expressed it.

In summary, our impression is that strategic considerations had relatively little significance. There were no strategic arguments at all in the discussions. Rational ideas dominated, and appear to have been so strong amongst the members of the secretariat that they became part of their self-interest. Rather, the strategy seems more to have been to promote the rationalist ideas themselves than to use them to further other interests. The rational model not only stood as a norm and a fixed pattern for how inquiries should be conducted, it also had spokesmen interested in its maintenance.

REFORMING TALK

The reform described above is one example of how the rational model can shape the content of a reform without being practised by the reformers themselves or being part of their practical experience. Experience and comprehension of how organizations work are thus not necessarily threats to the assertion of the rational model. Nor did the reform lead to any questioning of the rational model. On the contrary, it further strengthened the model: the work of the commission resulted in a text and further work which were propaganda for the model. The sections below offer some explanations of this development.

The first explanation is the fact that the reform was stated as a set of principles, rather than as a set of detailed, complex prescriptions of what to do. We have previously maintained that reforms are attempts to change practices by producing talk about them. What was characteristic of the work of the committee was that it focused more on changing the talk than changing the practices directly. Its work was 'in principle': it was assumed that practices would change gradually and indirectly once principles had been changed. The criteria and terms for the discussion were thus kept within the world of ideas rather than within the world of action: they consisted of principles rather than practices. And it is in the world of ideas that explanations and clarifications are important.

The rational model has far greater competitive power in the world of ideas than in the world of action. We have seen that it had such competitive power that many people took it for granted, and others found it difficult to argue against. This was true despite the fact that the same actors saw that the rational model had a number of weaknesses as a model for practice, and would not have voted for its being put into practice. Because the rational model was so obviously a matter of norms and ideas, practical experience was considered irrelevant, and the model met with virtually no opposition. One reason the model was easy to assert was that it was so readily accessible at the level of principles. It consisted of a fixed set of norms most people were familiar with from the outset. It could also be transferred by imitating other organizations: their principles were easily accessible (as opposed to their practices).

By separating the norm of rationality from practice, the reformers rescued it. But their work was not only a matter of principles. In some cases they, in fact, stipulated that changes in practice would be made. This should have brought questioning the norm closer to hand. But the commission members managed even so to avoid questioning it. They used two methods: future-orientation and confession.

As the report was so much about principles, many of the proposals were not meant to be introduced immediately. Instead, it was proposed that further inquiries should be carried out; for example, the details of management by objectives and budgeting should be determined by special projects. In other words, the proposals were to be implemented in practice, but not now and not without further consideration. In this way the commission postponed the final confrontation with practice, and did not need to make immediate decisions to change practices. They left the problematical transition from principle to practice to the future and, probably, to others. There is no reason to question a good norm until it is absolutely clear that it is not being observed; there is no reason either to justify or confess transgressions until they have been committed.

The one practical issue not postponed until the future was that of the composition of the boards. In this matter, the norm was in conflict with the opinions of most politicians on the committee as to what was desirable in practice. So the politicians rejected the secretariat's first proposal of eliminating MPs from the boards. But the important thing was that the politicians did not therefore question the norm: they still thought of it as correct, but allowed themselves to deviate from it. Those who argued for deviation from the norm in practice did not claim that there was anything wrong with the norm. On the contrary, they confessed that they were not observing a norm which, in itself, was good. One cannot always do the right thing. So they confessed that they sinned and were sinners; they did not try to justify their behaviour by changing the norms.

By keeping the discussion at the level of principle, by postponing practice until the future, and by confessing their sins, reformers can avoid confronting the rational norm with the demands of practice and can thus avoid questioning it. The reformers can, instead, promote and strengthen the norm.

There is also a good chance that continuing to try to implement the rational model would not pose a threat to it, even when it proved incapable of altering practices. Working at the level of principles in the commission meant that in most cases its rational proposals were less specific and far more general than in relation to the composition of the boards. In this way a great deal of behaviour could be described as consistent with the model, and the reformees would be able to assert that they are now behaving in accordance with the model without having to alter their behaviour in any respects that are important to them. For example, most politicians are probably able to state objectives in accordance with the model, but to phrase them so generally or in terms so similar to the means for achieving them that they actually contain the same message as their previous statements with other names, such as 'visions' or 'political programmes'.

So it is quite possible not only to launch, but also to implement reforms at the level of talk: the reform changes the way in which both reformers and reformees talk. Consistency between the talk of the reformers and the reformees makes the reform seem implemented: the picture of what practice ought to look like is in agreement with the picture of what it does look like. Implementation at the level of talk is not only a way of legitimatizing operations without needing to change them, but also a way of strengthening the rational model per se. It is presented not only as a norm, an unrealistic dream, but also as something which can really be fulfilled in practice and which moreover, at least in this case, permeates the practical work. The rational model becomes not only the norm but also the truth.

The launching and implementation of this type of reform may later serve as a pattern for other reformers in other organizations. Those can only imitate the aspects of reformed organizations that are presented to the outside world. Such patterns may be particularly important in rescuing the rational model in organizations which have actually discovered that they have not succeeded in implementing it in practice, in which it has not produced the desired results in terms of control, or in which it simply tends to be forgotten. This type of implementation process is the subject of the next chapter.

In the early part of this chapter, we attempted to show the strength of the idea, the model and the institution of the individual, and its main functions in organizational applications. We have used the case of the Government Commission of Inquiry to exemplify processes in which the idea of the individual and its rational specification are reproduced in reforms even if they are only minor features of organizational practices. The main explanation has been that reforms, by definition, are talk about desired states of affairs, and that such talk is adapted, for natural reasons, to the norms of how people should think and talk rather than to the world of practices. The individual and rationality are two strong norms of this type, and therefore often determine the content of reforms. Although individual-rational reforms do not often affect the world of practices, this does not mean that the norms are questioned. It may rather mean that they are further reinforced. The ideas of the individual and rationality appear robust in comparison with practice; they may be vulnerable only to criticism which is as normative and as much a matter of principle as the ideas themselves. In that case, we can predict that they will have a long if not eternal life, just like the individual person.

6 The reform principle, realities and mediating concepts*

* This chapter was contributed by Karin Fernler.

In the preceding chapter, we discussed how the individual-rational norm is preserved or reproduced, although it is difficult or inappropriate to implement in practice. We indicated that there are a number of mechanisms that help the norm survive. The four mechanisms we discussed were: the norm is kept at the level of principle; the actors confess that they are deviating from the norm in practice but not rejecting it as an ideal; implementation of the norm is postponed until the future; and reformees talk as if they were abiding by the norm, but their behaviour does not reflect this.

The preceding chapter included examples of the first three of these four methods of reproduction. In the present chapter, on the basis of a case study of an attempted major corporate reform, we exemplify the fourth method of reproduction. We describe an organization in which the reformees talked as if they were following a reform while acting differently.

The aim of the particular reform was to change the working processes in a large company in order to create a more market-orientated and rational organization. In practice, this meant that a planning and working procedure was introduced. We refer to this method as 'Stratplan'. The Stratplan method was developed by a management consultancy. Over the years the company sold the method to a very large number of different kinds of organizations. Discussions with 'Stratplan users' in different organizations indicated that it generally was considered a success.

This chapter is based on a study of people's reactions to the introduction of Stratplan. The study consisted of interviews with people at different organizational levels approximately one year after the method had been introduced. Just before our study of the reform began, a journalist wrote about the company and its Managing Director. Some of his statements referred to Stratplan, and he claimed that 'everyone he had spoken with was positive to the reform'. The results of our study confirm this: the company employees agreed unanimously that Stratplan was a good reform which the company badly needed. In addition to being positive about the reform, both the reformers and the reformees talked as if it were in the process of being implemented, or even as if it had already been successfully implemented. This rhetoric was so successful that it took some time for us to realize that, in this case as well, there was a discrepancy between idea and reality, between talk and action.

ANOTHER RATIONALISTIC REFORM

Reforms may be changes in structures, processes, or ideologies. Stratplan was an attempt to reform organizational processes and ideologies. Stratplan was marketed as a tool for increased market orientation. The reform consisted of several parts. Its core was a method constructed so that the company mission and business strategies would govern operations. The method consisted of a number of steps or items to be gone through. The first step, establishing the company mission (or objective, as it was also called), was meant to clarify who the company's customers really were and what needs they had. The next step was the setting up of strategies, deciding what the organization would do to satisfy their customers' needs. Concrete actions were then derived from the objective and the strategies, for instance what activities were to be carried out and what reporting routines the company required. Other important steps in the method included prediction of potential problems, setting up quantifiable short- and long-term goals, and thinking out alternatives if forecasts proved inaccurate.

The method was to be taught to the staff in the organization in hierarchical order, beginning with the executive management. It was taught to groups consisting of people who worked together on an everyday basis. Each group would work together to draw up an operating plan for their own areas of responsibility. An 'executive management' plan was set up for the whole organization. Each subsidiary, division and business area would then set up plans for their own operations, moving progressively downward to lower levels of the corporate hierarchy.

The underlying idea of working in this hierarchical order was that the plans would successively be broken down. This would bind the whole organization together, so that all its units were working to achieve the same objectives. As the strategies and objectives of the executive management were drawn up first, they would then permeate all operating plans as they were gradually set up at each level. The strategies of the division management would permeate all operating plans at the divisional level, and so on down the hierarchy. During the course of this work, it was possible to supplement the objectives and strategies with parallel, but not contradictory, ones. But the customers and their needs as defined by the executive management were always to be the basis for the discussion and action.

Plans were not the most important part of the Stratplan reform. Stratplan was intended to be a dynamic reform which the actors in the organization could use in their daily work, for instance when planning a project or a new set of facilities, or for reshaping their ordinary routines. The Stratplan method was meant to provide the corporation with a working process shared by all which, as it was based on the customer and customer needs, would create a customer-orientated culture. The method would also become a common corporate language, spoken and understood by all.

The consultants selling Stratplan claimed that in order to bind the organization together, achieve this shared language, and construct a customer-orientated culture, as many members of the organization as possible had to learn the method. At the company we studied, just over 5 per cent of the employees, both strategic and operative personnel, had been trained and had drawn up plans for their own sphere of operations. We define 'strategic personnel' here as people with independent, long-term, primarily planning assignments, such as individuals at staff level or in top management. By 'operative personnel' we mean employees with distinct, well-defined, regular work assignments, the performance of which was controlled by rules and routines; for example foremen of groups of five workers on the shop floor, or employees working with routine monthly planning.

The Stratplan reform required that large numbers of employees at the company learn the method. At the company studied, special Stratplan teachers were trained. Their task was not only to teach the method but to also serve as 'engines', and see to it that Stratplan was used in daily work, and did not just get filed away as plans.

The Stratplan reform may be seen as an attempt to create a greater degree of identity, hierarchy and rationality. The various steps in the method would encourage rational action by individuals. Defining the customer for the entire organization was a way of providing unity and identity for the organization. Setting up a company mission and strategies at executive management level and then bringing them down to even the smallest departments would ensure hierarchical coupling between the leaders and the led; and, ultimately, the entire organization would be associated with the highest value of all, the Customer and his Needs.

A well-known problem in attempts to create hierarchy is that management and its goals and values tend to be loosely coupled with the everyday, operational activities of the company. Advanced strategies and plans are drawn up at management level, but the effect at operational level is small. Models from the world of ideas seldom gain a foothold in practice. The Stratplan reform was interesting in this respect. Great emphasis was placed on disseminating the method throughout the organization, even to operative personnel. Its consistent design should have given Stratplan good potential for succeeding in increasing identity, hierarchy and rationality, particularly as the employees were very positive to the reform. However, as we implied initially, it soon appeared that most of this was talk, and separate from action. Let us go on to look in greater detail at how that separation occurred.

The idea: everyone moving in the same direction

I think the most important contribution Stratplan is making to the company is that we are all pulling in the same direction. Today, I think the main thing is that we all have goals for our operations, so we all have something to work for, which we haven't had in the past. The top part of the company has had goals, but how could the fellow down in the shop doing assembly work relate to that goal – for the company to make a billion kronor in profits – when he didn't know what it meant in his own area.

Well, the best thing about Stratplan isn't the name or the course, but that it's the same for everybody, from the top down. We've all been taught the same course and can all try to direct operations in the same direction . . . . Everybody's turned right instead of half being turned left and half right. We're trying to move in the same direction.

It was evident from the very early stages of this study how positive the employees were towards the Stratplan reform. The reform was praised because it was going to unify the company, concentrate its energy and focus on the customer. There was consensus at all levels that the company needed Stratplan. The employees pointed out that the organization had lacked unity, that by tradition there was a negative attitude towards managers, that the company was bureaucratic, self-centred and disinclined to change. The contrast between the current negative situation and the ideal state to be achieved with the help of the Stratplan reform was great. Instead of bureaucracy, inertia and self-centredness, the reform would bring about customer orientation, market adaptation, a shared language and a philosophy of 'everyone moving in the same direction'.

In the previous chapter, we indicated that the charm of reforms is that, as long as they remain at the idea stage, they are pure and beautiful, as compared with the 'ugly' and unstructured reality. One important characteristic of successful reforms is that they can credibly conjure up a picture of a future ideal state. When the actors described the effects of Stratplan, they painted an extremely powerful picture: an organization permeated by aims and strategies, focusing on the customer, and with everyone working together to satisfy the customer's needs.

It is a rule rather than an exception that reforms are beautiful at the conceptual stage. What was special about the actors' way of talking about Stratplan was that the reform seemed to create a firm belief that it would be implemented, or even that it already had been. Employees far down the organizational hierarchy had learned the method and drawn up operating plans. The existing plans and the large number of people who had attended the training course represented concrete, visible evidence that everyone spoke the same language and that the organization was bound together and united. Everyone spoke positively about the reform. It was only a matter of time before the effects would become visible. Implementation was built into Stratplan, in contrast with other reforms, where implementation was the stumbling block. The Stratplan reform meant everyone learning the method and drawing up plans; it consisted of concrete, tangible action rather than just talk and visions.

The positive attitude of the actors towards a reform which appeared both strong and dynamic was an unexpected result. Attempts to reform often encounter resistance when some of the actors discover that they dislike the intended change. What kept the Stratplan reform from falling into this pattern? It turned out that there were mechanisms to keep conflicts from arising.

THE ART OF DISTINGUISHING IDEAS FROM PRACTICE: MEDIATING CONCEPTS

Customer focus, market orientation and coupling between the leaders and the led via objectives were among the fundamental principles of the Stratplan reform. Thought was to precede action, and the leaders were to lead the led. In order to transform these principles into practice, the employees were to follow the stepwise construction of the method. The customer and his needs, as defined by management, thus became the point of departure for the way in which the customer was defined by all the other employees. From this definition concrete work assignments were derived.

As we have shown, the members of the organization all agreed that Stratplan was good for the company. All those interviewed had both taken the training course in the Stratplan method and drawn up an operating plan, but we were surprised to find that they did not criticize the control the method so clearly implied. It was also difficult for us to understand why people with decades of experience in their jobs would be so enthusiastic about having to relearn things.

We found, however, that for most organization members relearning and control were not an issue. The reason was that they saw 'Stratplan as an idea' and 'Stratplan in practice' as two separate phenomena. Discussing

'Stratplan as an idea' refers to the idea that the entire company should be tightly coupled, the customer should be put into focus, and the organization should become more market and profit-orientated. 'Stratplan in practice' refers quite simply to the way in which employees answered the question: 'How do you use Stratplan?'

We can define the most commonly held attitude towards Stratplan as that of the pragmatist. This is a refinement of the patterns we found to be typical in our empirical material, not a description of the attitude of any given person.

The pragmatist

You're asking how I use Stratplan in my everyday situation? Well, concretely, it's a little . . . . We drew up the activities list, on which I am responsible for all sorts of items. No, I'd say I use it mentally – I've got it in mind, so to speak.

No, I don't think the practical side of my work has really changed. We had our established routines for getting things done. But maybe we think a bit more about this customer thing. Still, I wouldn't say that was really new for us, either. We'd done it before, too, of course.

The pragmatist thought the reform was an excellent idea and talked at length about the company's need of it. In spite of this, he (or she) in practice only used it very sparsely. In other words, the pragmatist separated Stratplan as an idea and Stratplan in practice. Pragmatists could be subdivided into two types: the operative pragmatist and the strategic pragmatist. The operative pragmatist worked in day-to-day operations, with a short planning horizon. There were fixed, clear rules and routines for how his work was to be done. He was often controlled by the immediate needs of others, such as direct contacts with customers or fellow workers.

If an operative pragmatist used Stratplan at all, it was to make what he had always done more efficient and to structure it better. The operative pragmatist liked alternative plans, as well as dividing activities into sub-activities and using deadlines. But in his own work he considered a definition of objectives and strategies absolutely pointless.

The strategic pragmatist was involved in long-term general planning work. In contrast to the operative pragmatist, he was often in touch with the Stratplan method. The agendas of the meetings he was constantly attending and the content of the centrally written reports that required his attention were drawn up in accordance with it. However, it appeared to have very little effect on the work of which the strategic pragmatist himself was in charge. A strategic pragmatist did as he had always done, applying his established form of logic. Possibly, he said, he kept the newly formulated business strategy at the back of his mind.

In the opinion of the strategic pragmatist, the Stratplan method was a logical, well-structured tool. He appreciated the objectives, the strategies and the customer most. Though he had known all along how important this was, the rest of the organization really needed to learn it.

It was difficult for us to understand how the pragmatist could speak so warmly for and support an idea without also trying to work in accordance with it. The pragmatist, however, did not consider this a problem. Unless it was clearly pointed out that there was a contradiction between opinion and action, he tended not to notice. Even then, he did not consider it to be a contradiction. With the aid of mediating concepts, he made his actions appear entirely consistent with the norm. By 'mediating concepts' we mean widely accepted but unproven beliefs which bridge the world of ideas with the world of practices (cf. Abravanel 1983). Mediating concepts show why an idea cannot or will not be transformed into practice, with the norm still not being rejected.

Three main types of mediating concepts were used by the pragmatist. First, he claimed that he was already using Stratplan. Second, he claimed that Stratplan was actually intended for others. Third, he referred to other important organizational principles that made it impossible to follow the Stratplan method.

We are already using Stratplan

How can I explain it? It was a way of, well, becoming more customer-orientated, which is what we have always had to be here, you know.

I mean, it's not hard for those of us who do this kind of work to realize that there is a connection between the work we do and satisfied customers.

The most common mediating concept was that the pragmatist already considered himself to be using Stratplan. By interpreting Stratplan in his own way, the pragmatist could easily bring his behaviour into line with the idea of the reform. One way of achieving this consistency was to establish that the aim of the Stratplan reform was to become more customer-orientated, which the pragmatist already considered himself to be. Both the strategic pragmatist, who worked with long-term projects and to whom the customer was statistical tables and questionnaire surveys, and the operative pragmatist, who worked closely with the actual customers, thought they had always been aware of the importance of satisfied customers.

Yes, we've been using the system, although we weren't aware it was called Stratplan. You know, the thing about alternative plans and such. We've had to have them long before we knew about Stratplan.

We laughed at it. Most of us who are in a management position have always structured our thinking, otherwise nothing would work. I entirely stick to my own logic, and it mostly works.

Another reason the pragmatist considered himself already to be working according to the reform ideas was the completeness of the Stratplan method. It covered both abstract concepts such as the objective and strategies and concrete factors such as lists of activities and problems. The pragmatist selected elements on the basis of which he could draw parallels to existing routines and practices or common sense and structured thinking. And so he considered himself to be using Stratplan already.

When I got back from that training course, everyone who came into the room, well – they aren't exactly our customers, but for me I thought . . . they . . . came in wanting information. Naturally you think of them as your customer – although they aren't customers, they are customers to me. They have problems and I try to solve them. Because if their attitude turns positive, they'll do a better job.

In addition to taking advantage of the potential for interpretation available in the Stratplan method, the pragmatist could also create more complex private theories. The clearest example was ideas of how to actually satisfy the customer. One of the main ideas in the Stratplan method was that the company as a whole had one shared customer: the external group defined by management. For the pragmatist whose work was to serve other departments or some immediate superior, this gave rise to a conflict: the people they considered to be customers were not actually customers by definition. The solution to the conflict was a mediating explanation that went like this: if an in-house interested party is satisfied, he will do a better job and, at the end of the day, this will benefit the customer.

Stratplan is intended for others

You know, in my current position I can't exactly make use of it (i.e. knowing who the customer is). But maybe the cashiers can . . . .

Many, many parts of this company have needed Stratplan, I must say. I think, for example, that if we had had Stratplan earlier we might still have kept division X. Because that decision was engineered by the company, in my opinion. I don't think the customer had a thing to say about it.

The pragmatist thought the company really needed the Stratplan reform. In particular, more customer-orientation was needed. However, the pragmatist himself did not need Stratplan, only 'others' did. When referring to 'others', the operative pragmatist meant the strategic personnel. The strategic pragmatist, on the other hand, considered 'others' to be the people working with operations. The pragmatist was happy to give examples of mistakes 'others' had made, owing to their lack of customer orientation. The operative pragmatist then indicated divisions and services which had been rationalized out of existence by the strategic staff, with no consideration for the desires of the customer. The strategic pragmatist thought the operative staff neglected some aspects of their work, because of ignorance of the needs of the customer.

For the operative pragmatists who worked at the front lines, the idea of defining the customer was absolutely ridiculous. He lived with daily reminders of who the customers were and what they needed. But he really understood why people who never saw the customers needed a reform like Stratplan. On the other hand, the operative pragmatist who did not meet the customer felt that customers and their needs had very little impact on his job. Of course, it was the front-line staff who needed the reform.

> I've always been in favour of planning, so this was nothing new to me. But others seemed really surprised, so you can imagine what things were like before.

In addition to customer orientation, the pragmatist frequently felt that there was a need for improved structure and more logic in the work of the organization. In this area, too, the pragmatist thought he or she had the necessary planning systems. Once more there were 'others' who were worse off.

> They tell us this is what we are supposed to do. It's still the same, we are told do this or that and then we have to get the staff, uniforms, facilities .... You can't draw up long-term and short-term goals down here .... We have to be more activity-orientated, to say this is what we need to do.

The operative pragmatist had a mediating concept which said that Stratplan was meant for the strategic personnel. The argument was that the operative world was highly controlled. Since an operative worker was told where, when, and how to do things, there was very little room for goals, strategies and objectives. The work needed to be done, and the procedures for doing it were not changed by goals and strategies. At most it was possible to select aspects of the Stratplan method to facilitate everyday work.

Stratplan isn't meant to be followed

In one way, of course, Stratplan is very bureaucratic, if you are to follow it to the letter. But of course we don't do that. You know, that's how things always work. We have lots of stipulations we are supposed to follow, statutes and things, but I think it's the same with them. You have to see it like this: if there's a different way of working, you do it, you know. You soften up the rules and regulations . . . .

The last mediating concept was different from the other two. It neither claimed that the pragmatist followed the norms or that others were supposed to. Yet it was still not an admission that the pragmatist deviated from the norm. The norm was there and was in principle observed, but it was subservient to reality and other important norms, such as the fact that rules and procedures can never be followed to the letter. In relation to this mediating concept, the pragmatist often referred to the trainers who had run the course on the method. They too had said that the method was to be applied with common sense.

Maintaining a norm

The Stratplan reform was a very good example of an attempt to create identity, hierarchy and rationality. Our study indicates that even this highly ambitious reform encountered difficulties when it came to implementation. The majority of the actors took a pragmatic stand, separating the idea of the reform from their daily practice. This separation could be maintained thanks to the mediating concepts, with the aid of which the staff could speak as if they were using the Stratplan method.

When we listened to the pragmatist, it was striking that he presented the mediating concepts as if they were self-evident. They were also difficult to argue against. How could anyone claim that you should focus on the customer if you were already doing so? Why should a foreman on the shop floor focus on the customer if it did not change and improve his performance or what he did? Management often asserts that 'Our staff is our most important resource': didn't this mean that staff satisfaction was important to the customer? Working to rule is termed a slow-down, an effective instrument of industrial action. So how could anyone claim that rules and procedures should be followed to the letter? If the pragmatist was already customer-orientated and working in a structured fashion, didn't that mean that he was already using Stratplan?

The ease with which the organization members appeared to create mediating concepts, and the difficulty of arguing against them, illustrates one of the problems encountered in attempts to reform organizations from above. Reforms are always based on principles, and principles have special features.

Principles are never complete and comprehensive. They can always be interpreted and developed with theories of one's own. The mediating concept that personnel job satisfaction is the best thing for the customer, for example, may very well have been correct. Despite its apparent conflict with the principle of focusing on the customer, it may have been consistent with the idea of Stratplan.

Principles are never absolute. As soon as we leave the clarity of the world of ideas and step into the complexity of reality, there will always be more factors to be taken into consideration. The norm of Stratplan, to follow the method, contrasted with norms indicating that there should be less bureaucracy, and that rules should not be followed to the letter. Even statements made by those who taught the Stratplan method could be used in support of this argument. But as soon as there is space for a second, somewhat contradictory principle, it becomes difficult to determine where the balance between these two principles will be, which of them will weigh most heavily.

Principles are also abstract, while actions are concrete. An abstract principle makes space for a number of different concrete actions. It was difficult to contradict the pragmatist's interpretation of his current actions as being customer-orientated and in accordance with the principles of Stratplan. It is doubtful whether even detailed surveys of the working methods of every employee would have made it possible to determine whether or not the opinion of the pragmatist was correct. Furthermore, what company would have the time and resources to invest in such surveys?

For those who strive for rational, hierarchical organizations, the fact that principles are such unreliable instruments of control presents a problem. From a traditional implementation perspective, it was unfortunate that the pragmatist in our study appeared to be so competent at interpreting the idea of Stratplan in his own way. His mediating concepts became obstacles to the implementation of the ideas of Stratplan; the organization did not become more customer-orientated, and no increased control or rationality were attained.

From another perspective, however, the mediating concepts were highly functional, and even vital to the survival of the reform and the norms of Stratplan. When the idea of a reform is to be implemented in reality, it always collides with routines, habits, and other accepted principles. Reformers then quickly discover that it is not easy to manipulate employees or operations. The existing, the habitual, the familiar are stronger than newly invented principles. Frequently, the effect is that the employees put up resistance, implementation is blocked, and the reform dies.

The Stratplan reform did not work this way. Thanks to the mediating concepts, the reform became voluntary. No one was forced to be affected by it if they chose not to. Its voluntary nature kept the idea of the reform alive. It not only left the norm unchanged, but the two first types of mediating concepts created the impression that the norm had really been implemented. The first, that Stratplan was already in use, was not a criticism of the norm, but might have become a threat to the reform. Why spend time, effort and money on creating a logical, customer-orientated organization if it were already there? Thanks to the second mediating concept, that Stratplan was meant for 'others', this problem vanished. 'Others' needed to become more customer-orientated and to learn to work logically. As everyone spoke well of the reform and appeared to consider it necessary, the natural conclusion was that the organization was actually changing, and that the others had begun to learn to work just as logically and with as much customer-orientation as the pragmatist himself. But, as we have seen, the pragmatist was more the rule than the exception. The majority of the actors considered themselves to be special cases. Still, the effect was that everyone could go on calmly working as usual, while talking as if the organization actually had been reformed. The rational norm was once again reproduced.

The first two types of mediating concepts, then, were not only harmless but actually promoted the survival of both the reform and the norm. The last type, on the other hand, should have posed a threat, since it meant the pragmatist saying outright that the ideas of the reform could not be followed. However, not even this mediating concept stood up as any real criticism. The pragmatist still considered himself to support and follow the ideas in principle, which was quite sufficient to be able to discuss them as if he were a staunch supporter of the reform.

We can speculate as to the extent to which it is true that the more room there is for mediating concepts, the greater chance of success a reform will have. Mediating concepts ensure that individual actors have no difficulty in supporting the ideas of a reform. This creates the impression that the organization has changed in a positive direction, and become more like the ideal picture painted by the norm. The norm lives on unchanged. In the long run, this may be more important to the well-being and functioning of the organization than everyone's following a given method.

During the course of our study, we received unexpected support for our hypothesis that the separation of an idea from daily practice may be functional. At the beginning of the study, we interviewed the management of the company which sells the Stratplan method. One of our questions was how the method had developed during the years it had been on the market. The answer was that the method had not developed at all. But in selling the method, the salesmen had begun to emphasize that if a company wanted to introduce Stratplan, its management had to give its 100 per cent support to the ideas underlying the method. If the customer would not accept the method, the Stratplan company's management was not interested! When customers wanted slight changes in the standard timing of the courses (e.g. top management was not prepared to attend the full course from beginning to end but wanted one part one week and the next another), they were given the alternatives of taking the standard programme or having nothing at all. Considering that the main message of Stratplan was the necessity of adaptation to the customer and his needs, this attitude was truly unexpected. Nevertheless, it was probably a sound one. During the past decade, the Stratplan method has been highly successful and has been introduced in a large number of private and public organizations. Thus, a separation of an idea from its practical implementation may be both successful and profitable!

THE PRINCIPLE AND REALITIES

Up to this point we have described an organization populated with pragmatists who avoided following the norm by separating idea from practice. However, the findings of our study were more complex than this. Some of the employees really extended themselves to relate the idea to their daily practice. We can describe a second attitude, which we refer to as 'the idealist'. While the pragmatist successfully distinguished principles from reality, the efforts of the idealist took him to one of two extremes. Either he became an overwhelmingly positive, highly puristic idealist, or the result was frustration and confusion. The direction seems to have been determined by the idealist's position in the hierarchy.

The pure idealist

> As soon as I am called to a meeting, I ask: 'What is the objective of this meeting?' And if I need to make a complicated phone call and bring something up with someone, I set down a few key points, and try to think them through.

> The first reaction when you're told to identify the customer is 'Oh, that's easy'. Then you get deeper into it and start moving in all kinds of directions and end up almost back where you started. But then you have analysed it straight through and you know: This is our customer.

The pure idealist both tried and succeeded in coupling ideas with practice. In his everyday work he functioned on the basis of the objective defined in the operating plan, and extended himself to see that his activities supported it. He could give concrete examples of how construction plans had been changed in order to be better suited to the needs of the customer, and of how he had cancelled meetings and not made phone calls which did not support the defined objective.

The purist's job duties were independent planning work, i.e. a strategic position as we have defined it. He had a staff position, and ran long-range projects, etc. Often he was a Stratplan teacher. He considered the teacher's role had encouraged him to use Stratplan. But you did not have to be a teacher to be a purist; there were other purists as well.

When the purist described Stratplan, the method took on existential and religious overtones. Prior to Stratplan there had been chaos. Instead of floating around without direction, there was now a goal to strive for. Instead of floundering in ignorance about what good one's work was doing, there was now the Customer to serve. Who the customer really was, was analysed inside out. Stratplan became a way of sanctioning one's activities. With Stratplan to fall back on, the purist knew that he was doing his work right. Major problems arose when the overall plans of the company were not in agreement with his daily practice. But Stratplan was also a highly prosaic way of making one's own work more efficient, avoiding unnecessary efforts, and gaining better control of one's time.

The frustrated idealist

I kept being told to ask 'Who is our customer?' But looking at my own work, I was asked the same question: 'Who is your customer here, I mean here, on this job?' And in answer to that, it is hard for me to put the end customer as my customer. Here, I'm a kind of consultant, and my customers are people here who have problems. But we aren't supposed to look at it that way. The fact that the end customer is the customer is everybody's problem. Well, I don't know.

I have to efface myself completely – the customer is always right. I guess I've never really got used to that, but at the same time I think we work quite close to that model already, and what I wanted was to do something completely different. It's hard to explain. We haven't made such really strict plans with dates and things, but otherwise we've always – like had alternative plans and stuff.

The frustrated idealist functioned at the operational level. In his opinion, the ideas of the reform were to be put into practice, and he wanted to implement the whole Stratplan method in his daily work: defining the customer, drawing up goals, and deriving actions from them. But he had trouble making the method work.

One of the first problems the frustrated idealist encountered was difficulty in seeing what was so brilliant and different about the method. He had always thought of his own division as working in accordance with the intentions of Stratplan, trying to satisfy the customer and having access to alternative solutions. What they hadn't had were written plans, but the question was what difference they would make.

Another complication was that the frustrated idealist had problems allowing himself to be controlled by plans. He was used to allowing what he was going to do to be determined by the customer he met every day or by acute problems to be solved. This was particularly difficult for the frustrated idealist who worked for other employees at the company. If he tried to work in relation to the customer as defined on paper, he just created confusion, since his real 'buyer' was a familiar, living human being: his supervisor or a colleague.

Two realities

One of the basic ideas behind the Stratplan reform was that change was to take place through the entire organization learning a new working method. As we have shown, one problem was that the majority of the actors took a highly pragmatic stand in relation to their own use of the method. Another problem was that when the strategic planning method was brought down to the level of the operative personnel, no-one in that group appeared to have the ability to use it, although some people tried. The result was confusion and frustration. This was in sharp contrast with the idealist working on the strategic level. What kept the idealist working on the operative level from being converted? Comparing the ways in which the strategic personnel and the operative personnel (including both idealists and pragmatists) described and interpreted the Stratplan method provided the first clues.

The Stratplan of the strategic personnel: a concrete tool focusing on aims and strategies

> These things – the business idea, strategies and goals – must be passed along to the whole staff at evening meetings . . . that's what it is all really about, and it cannot be repeated often enough.

> I have studied at university, but nothing this concrete.

The strategic personnel emphasized two aspects of the method. First, that the key aspect, of highest relevance, was focusing on the objective and strategies. In the opinion of the strategic staff, employees who were too far down on the hierarchy to be given the entire course of study had to at least be informed of the objective and strategies. Second, they thought of the method as a practical tool suitable for use in daily work. Although there was nothing new in the facts, the systematic, logical, irreproachable, comprehensive structure was new.

Stratplan was concrete. In contrast to university courses, it did not consist of abstract definitions you had to fill with contents yourself. The point was to go through certain steps.

Stratplan was general. As opposed, for instance, to methods for the formulation of market strategy, Stratplan was a tool suited to all kinds of problems dealing with structuring and planning.

Stratplan made a comprehensive system available. It covered all issues, from the objective and goals to what the activities and distribution of responsibility should be, to how to organize. If you answered every question, you would not miss a thing.

The Stratplan of the operative personnel: abstract with some concrete parts

> Of course, the operating plan dates what we do . . . . Well, before we knew that we had to do a certain thing by a certain date. Now we draw up an operating plan saying that this has to be done by this date and that has to be done by that date, and I guess it has its advantages.

> Often things are so rushed here that there isn't time to draw up goals, comprehensive goals. Our goal is mostly to get the goods delivered . . . so from the beginning we saw it as pretty self-evident, a way of making things kind of complicated.

The operative personnel was directly committed to making daily work function. Pragmatist and frustrated idealist alike thought of Stratplan in the same way. First, the main advantages of the method were considered to be its concrete aspects and results. Second, the operative personnel thought of the method as unnecessarily complicated.

The operative personnel thought that the positive thing about Stratplan was learning to structure your ordinary activities, draw up alternative plans, and look ahead at critical events. Many of them also appreciated the operating plans drawn up during the course week. In contrast with the strategic employees, however, the operative employees found it difficult to see Stratplan as a tool for everyday work. They had the very opposite impression!

Stratplan was abstract. Defining the customer and his needs was a way of making the obvious complicated. The idea was simple: working so that the customers you dealt with were satisfied.

Stratplan was specific. It could be used in highly special situations, but its method was hardly useful in everyday work, which was governed by rules, routines, habitual practices or emergency needs.

Stratplan was comprehensive, but once you had been told what you were expected to do, you didn't really need a comprehensive method. However, many people found the whole method applicable to their private lives, for example when planning for a long holiday.

Relationships between preconstructed and personally constructed realities

The idealist, the type of employee who actually tried to observe the norm, either became a purist or was frustrated, depending upon whether the kind of work he did was operative or strategic. There were differences between how operative and strategic personnel interpreted the method. The strategic staff described it as a concrete tool, the most central aspect of which was the establishment of objectives and strategies. The operative group, however, described the method as unnecessarily complicated and quite useless, with the exception of its most tangible components, such as activity lists and alternative plans. Paradoxically, people who appreciated abstractions considered the method concrete, while those who preferred the concrete experienced it as abstract. How could this be? This paradox arises out of the fact that the two groups reflected different relationships between prior constructions of reality and their personal ones.

The world around us is largely a social construction (Berger and Luckmann 1966). Even things considered indisputable fact are fundamentally intersubjective truths, i.e. opinions shared by a number of people. These intersubjective truths comprise a kind of prior construction of reality which, in any given situation, defines the boundaries and framework of our actions, determines how the situation can be interpreted and how we can act. We also develop our own prior constructions via habits and routines, for example. There is great variation in the degree of prior construction of different situations. At times we have a large scope of freedom of choice, and the problems we encounter are new and unfamiliar. We do not know how to interpret them, and we know even less about how to behave in them. In such situations, it is both possible and vital to choose a perspective, in other words to construct our own reality. At other times, the situation is so clear, so completely preconstructed, that we cannot choose or even consider choosing. We put the problem directly into the right cubby-hole, and apply the prevailing rules of behaviour. In reality, both these examples are rare cases. Existing intersubjective truths always control our interpretations and behaviour. For example, if you work as an economist, you will be expected to behave like one. And even clear situations require some degree of personal interpretation. Thus we can say that in different situations there are different relations between preconstructions of reality and situational personal ones (cf. Weick 1983).

Although Stratplan may be described as a method for structuring work, it was primarily (like all planning tools) a method for constructing reality (Smircich and Stubbart 1985). Different situations provide us with different amounts of space for and different needs to construct our world. This also applies to different work assignments. Compare, for example, a management group with a traditional shop floor worker in industry. The management group has to make its own decisions as to what the company will produce, for whom, how and where. One of the most important functions of management is exactly that: to create meaning and a context for the organizational reality (Smircich and Morgan 1982). For the manual worker in industry, on the other hand, most work assignments are relatively clear and well-defined, highly regulated and governed by routines and habits. The extreme case in point is the assembly line, where what is to be done is exactly specified.

At the company we studied, the work tasks of the operative staff were recurring ones. Their working days were routine. Their daily lives were preconstructed to a relatively great extent, both via regulations from above and through the distribution of work assignments, but also through experientially based knowledge which had led to the development of habits and routines for different problems. Thus there was very little space for the manual worker to construct his own reality. As we have seen, the majority of the operative employees took a pragmatic stance in relation to Stratplan, selecting the parts of the method which fitted into their prior constructions of reality. The purely constructive aspects of Stratplan, such as defining the customer on the other hand, left them cold. The operative idealist who tried to apply the whole method felt confused. No matter how the customer was defined on paper, the operative idealist's work was determined by the person on the other side of the till. Whatever his long-range strategies, his work consisted of concrete tasks he had been assigned from above, and which he carried out in accordance with certain predetermined habits and routines. His reality was too preconstructed to allow Stratplan to be useful to him.

In contrast to the operative personnel, the strategic staff had more freedom to plan their work. They often faced new problems, to which there were no ready-made solutions. They worked over the long term, and the results of their work were not often immediately visible. In this diffuse, vague situation, it was both possible and necessary for a member of the strategic staff to set his own bounds and to structure, or rather to construct, his reality. Defining the customer simplified his work considerably. It gave him a fixed, concrete point of departure. It was considerably easier to plan for how to satisfy a certain type of customer than to plan to satisfy all imaginable customers.

The pure idealist, who actually used the method, saw the benefits of the constructive features of Stratplan clearly. The purist moved from chaos to order. By using the Stratplan method zealously in his daily work, he knew that what he was doing was right. The purist had seen the light, comprehended the nature of the world. His reality was endowed with contours, a context and a pattern: it had been constructed.

Since Stratplan was primarily a method for structuring the world, whether or not an idealist was likely to succeed depended upon whether he was a member of the strategic or the operative employees. The condition on which the method worked was that there was room for one's own constructions. To the strategic personnel, Stratplan served as a practical tool for creating patterns and connections, and making reality more concrete and comprehensible. To the operative personnel, whose reality was already preconstructed and comprehensible, every effort to transform the Stratplan principles into practice became tautological, providing them with a construction superimposed on the existing one. Rather than giving them increasing clarity, it had the opposite effect. It is confusing to try to reconstruct a preconstructed world.

It is interesting to speculate as to why there were idealists and pragmatists at both operative and strategic levels. If our theories about the constructible nature of reality are correct, then all the strategic staff should have used the Stratplan method. The difference we established in our empirical material was that the strategic pragmatist had more experience of strategic positions than the pure idealist. He also appears to have been able to relate Stratplan to other similar methods. The frustrated idealist on the operative level expressed great dissatisfaction with his present working situation. He found it difficult to have time to do all his work, and was of the opinion that a change in routines was needed. The operative pragmatist, on the other hand, appears to have been quite satisfied with the status quo. However, these patterns were not sufficiently distinct to answer the question exhaustively, and so we must leave it open for future research.

Of course, the idea of the Stratplan reform was for operative personnel to use the method to change their habits and routines in order better to satisfy the needs of the customer. It is, however, far more difficult to change a deeply rooted habit than to use a new method to attack a previously unknown problem. Furthermore, the Stratplan reform itself was highly ambivalent in its efforts to give all organization members objectives of their own to strive for. If you want people to take responsibility for their work, and to draw up their own objectives and strategies, then you must also give them the freedom to do so. The Stratplan reform made no efforts to revolutionize the organizational hierarchy. On the contrary, activity plans were prepared from the top down, and no-one's objective, strategies and goals were allowed to contradict those of his or her supervisor. At the operative level, Stratplan actually turned out to be an expensive way of giving the orders which would have been given under any circumstances. This was probably the easiest way of doing things. If the Stratplan reform had actually meant the operative level's implementing comprehensive changes, it is difficult to know what the results would have been. Perhaps the existing routines and habits were not the optimum ones, but they worked. Who knows if any cars at all would be manufactured at Renault tomorrow if the Renault workers started trying to identify the customers' real needs?

A successful reform

In this and the previous chapter we have discussed the observation that the individual-rational norm has an impressive capacity to reproduce itself, although empirical facts have repeatedly indicated that the norm is unlikely to work in reality. In this chapter we have demonstrated one of the more sophisticated mechanisms of reproduction which makes this possible, i.e. talking as if the reform had been introduced while acting in another way.

The effect of this mechanism was that the norm was not questioned, and the organization appeared both more hierarchically controlled and more rational. The identity and unity of the organization were strengthened: people spoke the same language and claimed to be working for the same customers.

However, seen in terms of a traditional view of implementation, the results of our study are depressing. Instead of following the Stratplan method, the majority of actors used mediating concepts. Among the idealists, only those in strategic positions succeeded in their efforts to apply the method. It is tempting to see mediating concepts as harmful, and to see the major investments in teaching operative personnel as a waste of money. But if there had been efforts to do away with mediating concepts, it would only have become evident that the principles of the reform were on a collision course with habits, routines and rules, i.e. with the reality of the actors. It is doubtful whether the norm would have emerged victorious from that conflict. On a more fundamental level it could also be questioned whether the organizational idea underlying the entire Stratplan reform, that abstract principles can guide actions, is a very realistic one. It is hard to conceive of principles sufficiently comprehensive, complete and absolute that they would preclude the possibility of constructing mediating concepts; and it is difficult to control the work of the operative staff by abstract objectives and strategies. Reforms of the Stratplan type are often unable to reinforce a hierarchy, or to produce tight coupling between the leaders and the led.

Still, Stratplan was a highly successful reform. The majority of the actors were satisfied with the reform both from the organizational and personal perspectives. The image of the reform, both inside the company and outside it, was a picture of success. One of the main reasons for this was the visible investment in the operative personnel. The reform enabled most of the operative personnel to commit themselves to the organization's identity, hierarchy and rationality, the very points at which the reform was aimed. The reproduction of the individual-rational norm thus resulted in the reform's appearing right and successful! As long as the mechanisms of reproduction work, a reform with an individual-rational content is guaranteed to succeed. Paradoxically, the very fact that it remains unimplemented leads to its being considered a success. Since it is not implemented there is no information about the problems of getting it to work in practice.

The next five chapters contain further analyses of the implementation and effects of reforms. In the next chapter we point out some of the fundamental problems associated with the idea of reform implementation. We ask whether it is actually possible at all, under realistic conditions, to achieve agreement between ideas and practices with the aid of reforms.

7   Implementing reforms[*]

* This chapter was co-authored by Hans Winberg.

One February day in 1987, the board of directors of Swedish Rail (Statens
Järnvägar, SJ) met to consider a plan drawn up by an international consultancy company. The idea was to implement a radical reform, the 'New
SJ'. In spite of a series of earlier attempts at reform, SJ was again going
through some lean years with stagnating traffic and heavy losses. Both SJ's
management and its owners, represented by the Swedish Ministry of
Transport, were anxious to implement rapid changes for the better. The
consultancy company had been called in to think out these changes and help
to carry them through. The basic idea was to make the company more
business-like. SJ was to be run as a company and not as a government
service, and its corporate aim was to be a profitable business. SJ was to
become the best transport company in the world and one of the most
attractive workplaces in Sweden. According to the consultants' plans, this
was to be achieved through 'market orientation, adaptation of resources and
decentralization' including concentration on rail traffic, improved financial
control and decentralized responsibility for results. The building and maintenance of the track infrastructure was to be separated from SJ through the
creation of a state agency, the Swedish Rail Administration. SJ was to
concentrate on the main business concept, running a railway service.

This was not the first time SJ had been subjected to attempts at radical
reform (Brunsson et al. 1989), and the content of previous reforms had not
been all that different from the one now proposed. Reforms of SJ's
organization had been considered or attempted at roughly five- to ten-year
intervals since the organization was founded in 1869. Much of the core
content of the New SJ had also been an important part of earlier reforms.
The need to be more business-like and market orientated had been proclaimed in most reforms since 1893, including the latest one, VO 80, which
had been carried out between 1979 and 1982. Ever since 1906, voices had
been raised in favour of improving the company's business profile by
having representatives of Swedish trade and industry on the board. The

question of decentralization contra centralization had been discussed in all the previous reform programmes; the majority of the past reformers, like the reformers promoting the New SJ, considered decentralization a necessity. Decentralized responsibility for results was the main idea behind VO 80. The idea of separating the business side from the rail administration, forming one company-like organization and one state agency, represented a return to the organization used prior to 1888.

It is natural to ask is why the reformers promoting the New SJ proposed solutions which had already been tried several times and failed. One reason might be (and was) the supply of forgetfulness we described in Chapter 3. Another reason might have been that, although attempts had been made in earlier reform programmes to implement the same solutions, these attempts had not completely succeeded, and this made it seem necessary to try again. The general consensus about VO 80 was that it had never been implemented. SJ's history of reforms shows that it does not appear difficult to launch reforms, but that it is far more difficult to implement them. This chapter addresses the question of why reforms may be difficult to implement. We suggest that there are certain fundamental and common characteristics of administrative reforms which make them difficult to implement by nature, taking the implementation of the New SJ as our example.

THE NEW SJ

As it was presented in February 1987, the proposal for the New SJ reform was described in very general terms. It presented the ideas in principle, while leaving all the rest to those who were to formulate the more specific programmes; this was a deliberate strategy. The aim was to try to change the SJ culture, or people's ways of thinking, making more space for creativity and new ideas. The reformers thought that this would also make the employees behave differently and that the organization's performance would improve. The major internal changes would be prepared and effected through special projects. Market orientation in the organization would be increased through a change in attitude, with all employees learning to put business and profit first. There would be more efficient utilization of capital, and operations would be rationalized. To facilitate this, a decentralized and more flexible business organization was to be constructed.

Responsibility for both results and production would be delegated. This would be done by drawing up a new system for financial control, and by developing new procedures for planning, co-ordination and scheduling of trains, making the products the basis of operations. Each train would be seen as a product and a profit centre. Personnel with product responsibility would schedule and co-ordinate the trains on this basis. Finally, the whole corporate group would concentrate its operations on running the railway, selling off other operations.

In the autumn of 1988, it was declared that the New SJ had been implemented. However, it had had no major impact on behaviour in the organization. Many people at the operational level still did not know of the reform or did not know that it had been implemented. A new organizational chart was introduced, according to which the old matrix organization was replaced with a divisional organization, the number of market regions was reduced, and they were renamed 'business areas'. But no new control system was developed, nor was the scheduling and co-ordination of the trains decentralized. The idea of working out profits in terms of train units was abandoned, and the planning of train services remained centralized. The idea of limiting the group's activities to running the railway also disappeared with the accession of a new management which decided to retain profitable activities outside the railway area as well. And the year after the reform was implemented, SJ continued to operate at a loss.

What the reform did have was a considerable effect on the company's relations with its environment. When the Swedish Rail Administration was separated from SJ, a cost of 600 million kronor (£60 million) was removed from the group. The state gave SJ better working conditions: it was freer and more like a business enterprise. Last but not least, SJ succeeded in recruiting a new board and a new management, both with greater competence in doing business.

In the remainder of this chapter we use the New SJ as an example to discuss some problems of reform implementation. We examine the discrepancy between the simplicity of reforms and the complexity of reality. We describe how reform work can be organized in a way that isolates reform ideas from practice and vice versa, and how the time lag between the formulation of ideas and implementation means that a reform's ideas go on being developed, and new reforms launched, until it ultimately becomes unclear which ideas are actually meant to be implemented.

THE SIMPLICITY OF REFORMS AND THE COMPLEXITY OF REALITY

The most striking characteristic of the ideas launched in the New SJ was their simplicity. This was in contrast to most people's ideas about the present situation, which were characterized by complexity. Railway operations may appear to be extremely complex, and many people at SJ saw its operations that way. There are close technical links between what the various units do: at any point in time there are thousands of engines and carriages in hundreds of terminals or on different parts of the railway network, and their locations at that point in time determine what can be done next. Customers use thousands of different combinations of routes along the lines for their trips or for transportation of goods; less busy lines feed into busier ones which feed back into less busy ones again. Transport sold in one region gives rise to costs in others.

One important tool for handling this complexity was the annual train plan drawn up by the train planning department in an effort to optimize capital use. Train timetables were determined by this plan. For example, the plan scheduled extremely complex routes for engines: an engine might be on the move for weeks without returning to the station from which it departed. In addition to all this complexity, there was the complexity of the previous business concept, according to which SJ was both a business enterprise and a state agency: it was supposed both to be a profit-making business and to satisfy political requirements. All this complexity had led, among other things, to a number of different regional and functional organizational charts being tried over a century of reforms.

Simplification by reform

In contrast to the existing complexity, the New SJ offered many kinds of simplification. One basic simplification was that the company was to be coupled to only one of the two institutions of business enterprise and state agency. It was to be a business enterprise, and not subject to special political requirements. Another simplification was the idea that dealing with the railway tracks was to be separated and assigned to the Swedish Rail Administration. The reformers also wanted to make a clear distinction, in terms of personnel and accounting, between the passenger traffic division and the freight traffic division. As mentioned, operations not clearly related to rail traffic were to be sold off. When negotiating financing with the state, SJ had, for years, used highly simplified models of the railway network, divided into profitable and unprofitable lines. This idea of distinguishing between different lines was used in the New SJ to provide a foundation for structuring the organization. Each line was to be seen as a profit unit, for which a regional group was responsible. The reformers had the idea that the various regional groups would 'own' not only the individual lines, but also the rolling stock on their parts of the line. The regional groups were also to be further subdivided into even smaller profit centres. The idea was to decentralize profit responsibility as far as possible in the organization; when it came to passenger traffic this meant down to the level of each individual train.

This simplicity was contrasted with the prevailing situation, where both operations and the picture of them were complex. For instance, the accounting system reflected this complexity, which made it impossible to measure profits further down than at Director General level. The simplicity also contrasted with people's general conception of the previous reform. VO 80 was seen as having led to far too complex ideas, e.g. the idea of the matrix organization.

However, not all the simplifications in the New SJ actually held up to implementation. It became apparent, for example, that the delegation of responsibility for material and personnel down to unit levels would lead to a far greater need for materials than under the old system. The idea of making each individual train a profit unit was also abandoned. Profitable operations unrelated to the railway were retained.

Thus simplifying ideas did not result in corresponding simplifications in action. But by the time that was clear, the simplicity of the ideas had probably accomplished their task. This type of simplification strategy is common in conjunction with reforms. Reforms are attempts to organize afresh, to give organizations new forms. When, or for as long as, reforms are ideological, they take place in thoughts, not in action or in material operations. It is a matter of constructing the organization in one's head, of organizing an image. In some respects there is greater freedom in the world of ideas than in the world of action. Many material restrictions can be neglected. This makes it possible to organize one's picture according to the principle of simplicity, despite the complexities of reality. So reformers have the freedom to simplify, but it can also be argued that there is good reason for them to make use of this freedom.

One argument is that simplification is an attempt to gain control. Having control of something tangible means being able to govern it; having control over an existing organization means being able to steer it in the desired direction. It is often very difficult to exercise this control, and this is an important reason for proposing reforms, reforms that will change an organization so as to make it more governable. And one main cause of a lack of control is exactly that the complexity is too great, i.e. so great that control also becomes far too complex, or so great that it becomes impossible to see how governance might even be carried out, what strings to pull to direct the organization. The essence of the concept of 'organizing' may even be said to be reduction of complexity. And thus simplifying reality in accordance with a simplified picture offers the hope of future control. We might say that reforms which simplify are aimed at changing organizations so they become easier to govern, and consequently easier to reform, in the future.

Another related reason for reformers' interest in simplification is the need for understanding, as discussed in Chapter 5. It is difficult to understand complex organizations and how they function. Reformers have the advantage of being able to change organizations, and strictly speaking all they need is to understand the new organization. The new organization only exists in their own minds: what they have to understand is their own image of the organization, and the simpler the picture is, the easier that will be. It is also easier to communicate a simple picture and make it comprehensible to others.

The substantial simplification of the ideas in the New SJ was facilitated by two of their other characteristics: their vagueness and their being rooted in a familiar institution. Although the ideas were simple and clear, they were not particularly precise. The most precise definition of being business-like was 'more in than out'. Although it was quite clear what this meant on a general level, what it would imply for action was not specified from the outset. The principle was clear, its impact was not spelled out. Vagueness is the term we use to describe such clear principles with ambiguous consequences. Vagueness was an important way of keeping the ideas simple: possible criticism that they were too simple or too general could easily be met by saying that they would be developed and specified in closer contact with the specific SJ reality.

As the ideas were part of a familiar institution (the business enterprise), and since market orientation and decentralization were in fashion at the moment, it was easy (rightly or wrongly) to get the impression that the same principles had been successfully applied in other organizations. This made it difficult to see why the ideas would not work in the context of SJ. There was no reason to demand information immediately about what was really meant. In addition, an institution such as the business enterprise consists of a package of ideas and requires consideration of the whole package, not individual details in it. The question was whether to accept the general idea of becoming a true business enterprise. 'I believe in the entirety,' was how one leading reformer expressed it.

Vagueness and institutional links, combined with simplicity, also made it easier for the reformers and those around them to establish a firm conviction that the reform was right. Vagueness enabled some wishful thinking and optimism about the potential for good detailed solutions in the future. Since the principles were derived from a well-known institution they had a semblance of general good sense. It seemed unnecessary to consider other alternative reforms or to forecast the consequences of the reforms in any detail at an early stage. Moreover, what was being held up for comparison was the current management strategy, which was strikingly inconsistent, unclear and incapable of achieving satisfactory results. Presenting more alternatives or detailed impact assessments might have created uncertainty as to whether the reform was a good one or the best possible one, or whether the reform was really going to be implemented, and this might threaten its support base. Avoiding detailed analysis reduces uncertainty and facilitates action; it is an expression of 'action rationality' (Brunsson 1985).

There was such firm conviction that it was even possible to officially state how much the reform was expected to yield in financial terms – 1,000 million kronor (£100 million) – without analysing how this was to be achieved. There was less certainty about this sum in private conversation, but people still considered it obvious that the reform should have the proposed content. Action rationality was also an expressed policy of the consultancy firm: their main idea was to invest in what they called rapid implementation rather than in long analyses.

Action rationality meant that the reform projects were easily and rapidly initiated. However, it proved more difficult to implement the reform ideas in practice. Their simplicity and vagueness made the ideas useless or difficult to use in the complex production process. Many of the people who worked with the day-to-day running of SJ's activities complained that they were not given any information: they did not realize there was no meaningful information to be given. Management and the reformers issued a great deal of information which was meaningful to themselves, but not to other people in the organization.

In conclusion, the New SJ exemplifies how administrative reforms are facilitated because they are about the future. Since reforms concern the future, they can long be maintained at the level of ideas, where it is possible to accomplish greater and more clearly positive things than can normally be achieved in practice. Thus they easily gain the support of many, and this support results in their being initiated. However, the same simplicity which acquires support also creates difficulties in implementation. Simplicity and complexity pose a dilemma for reformers: simple reforms gain support easily, but are difficult to implement, while reforms complex enough to reflect reality are more suited to being carried out, but more difficult to secure support for.

Separating ideas and practice

A project organization was created to implement the New SJ. The idea was to use a number of projects to investigate how the ideas were to be transformed into practice, and also to initiate their implementation. The project groups represented a sort of new organization parallel to the ordinary one. The terms and conditions applying to the project work differed from those applying to ordinary operations, as they were related to the world of ideas and were concerned with the future, and thus were able to neglect the prevailing complex reality. The project groups were partly composed of SJ employees and partly of consultants. The project members identified strongly with their roles in the reform work. They saw their roles as being quite different from that of operative personnel. In earlier reforms, many of these had been in operative positions themselves: 'I was on a different level then, so I didn't really notice the reforms' was a typical statement. Only project members or leaders were considered to be working with reforms.

The temporary organization created in this way meant that ordinary operations were decoupled from the ideas. The project members worked with ideas. Their mission was to articulate ideas for future practices, to distinguish them from prevailing practices, and thus to endow future operations with meaning. In the project, it seemed to be not only meaningful but also vital to work in abstract: the ideas had to be reformulated and left to mature before they could influence the practices of the future. Meanwhile, the operative personnel worked according to their daily routines and 'did as we'd always done'. They could easily proceed with their old routines, since no-one was asking them to make their present work meaningful: since a reform was being worked out, things were certain to change soon, and for the better. It was not necessary to justify present operations by connecting them to good ideas, so present actions and actors were not disturbed by lofty ideas and ideologies.

So the ideas were liberated from the complex operations which, in turn, were liberated from the abstract ideas, so difficult to associate with daily routines. The isolation between the reform project and operations made it possible to keep ideas on the agenda which would otherwise have been seen as impossible, and hence abandoned. The isolation also made it possible to use the reform organization as a buffer in time between ideas and practices, since the projects took, and were intended to take, time. Reforms must necessarily take time if the project members are to implement their work. This lag in time complicates the implementation of reforms considerably, as the next section elucidates.

The difficult time

Launching a reform is like making a decision. At a given time, the people whose ideas are expected to be implemented in practice announce which ideas are to be carried out. They commit themselves and others to ideas they have at the moment of launching the reform or making the decision. Ideas are constantly evolving, but in order to endow the operation with some backbone, certain ideas must be held static, at least for some time. Often, such ideas are put on paper, where they do not change. But it is difficult for reformers and decision-makers to decide to stop thinking, and so there is always the 'risk' that they will develop newer, better or more thought-through ideas, and thereby come to consider their old ideas as bad. And of course this risk increases over time. As mentioned above, during the first year of the New SJ, project groups worked with the aim of making each moving train, i.e. each departure, a separate profit unit. During the course of the project, this was changed to apply to each individual stretch of railway line. When the new management was appointed, this profit-centre idea was altered again, as it was considered unnecessary to measure the results for such small units. Consequently, during the two years of project work, no system of profit-centre measurement at these levels was established.

Ideas also change as a result of the reactions they provoke, both inside and outside the organization, when they are presented. One example of how ideas develop as a result of outside reactions was the idea of the business enterprise. When the initial thinking about the New SJ reform took shape and was approved by management and the owners' representatives, there was a strong belief that SJ should be given the same terms as any business enterprise. All parties considered this necessary if it were to be possible to run SJ as such. The old idea of making the former public utility into a joint stock company was relaunched; but it was rejected internally at a relatively early stage since it was considered unrealistic. It was reformulated in terms of far-reaching and specific demands for financial independence and discretion, albeit within the confines of the public utility. Reactions from the owners and other groups, not least the trade unions, however, made it necessary to modify these demands, and less far-reaching changes were accepted. One example was the size of investment decisions which SJ could make itself, where the compromise agreed upon was 20 million kronor (£2 million), instead of an unlimited sum.

Operative personnel also reacted to the proposed ideas for change. The project members sometimes had to look for support from operative personnel in formulating specific action plans. When that happened, the ideas were sometimes changed radically in the process, and sometimes even rejected altogether; albeit only occasionally, since ideas about change were often so general and future-oriented that they left room for many conclusions. Another way in which ideas were changed was when people in the organization were replaced, for instance when the new director was appointed. New people also reacted to the reform ideas.

The first situation, when the operative personnel reacted, was experienced in relation to the train plan project. Originally, the reformers and project members had intended the entire train planning work, i.e. work with plans for directing all traffic on the railways, to be decentralized. In their opinion, the train plan had come to govern all the work too much, and had come to stand as an obstacle to flexibility. However, there was such strong resistance to the decentralization of this planning work that nothing radical was actually done in the new organizational structure. It was said that more information was to be sent from local officials responsible for products, and that there would be shorter time lags between the original impulse and a change in the timetable, but there was no real decentralization.

There were two changes of management during the course of the reform, and this meant that the ideas changed. The information function provides a clear example of how signals were altered rapidly and radically. The original idea was to delegate responsibility for information throughout the organization. In order to ensure that all employees could be reached when necessary, people were to learn to take more independent initiatives and sometimes cut across the traditional hierarchy. The new management reversed this strategy, and held to the opinion that information needed to be uniform, and that it should therefore always emanate from the central information staff.

New reforms

Another difficulty in implementing reforms is that they sometimes give rise to new reforms even before they have been implemented. New reforms either can result from slowness in implementing the old ones, or it may take time to implement the old ones because ideas for new ones come up, or both conditions may apply. VO 80 had not been completed when the New SJ was launched, nor was the New SJ completely implemented before new reforms were launched. But in both cases the reform work was declared complete by the management as soon as the new organizational structure had been introduced.

One of the reforms after the New SJ consisted of a new method of strategic planning which, with respect to its simplicity, was extremely reminiscent of the early versions of the New SJ. Another was the establishment of new business plans for the various divisions, where it was specified what was to be accomplished, rather than how things were to be organized. The business plans stated objectives and how they were to be achieved, for instance which groups of customers to invest in and how to adapt products to suit them. VO 80 was seen by many people to be too complex and therefore not sufficiently attractive. Management complained that it was difficult for them to put across the message of VO 80. For this reason, they hired the consultants, but they reached the conclusion that there was nothing wrong with the information; rather a new reform was needed. Thus management's attempt to better implement the old reform led to a new one.

Similarly, the New SJ led to the recruitment of new management, and this new management naturally had ideas that were somewhat different from those of the consultants. Implementation of the new organization had, furthermore, been delayed, and if profitability were to be achieved it was high time to start taking measures in practice; there was no time to wait until the new organization was ready. Interest in the new organization faded rapidly, and management finally announced that the new organization was now implemented. Nothing much remained of the forceful slogans from the New SJs' initial launch about all the positive effects the new organization would have. The announcement that the reform could be considered complete also suggests that the management wished to wash its hands of responsibility for the more complex ideas of the later stages of the reform. And the reform no longer offered improved understanding.

PRESENTATION AND RESULTS

The New SJ was presented like many other reforms. Three ways in which it was described were particularly important. First, it was presented as a way of changing the organization itself: the audience was the SJ employees, they were the ones who were supposed to listen to the reformers and then change their behaviour. Second, the ultimate aim of the reform was presented as being to change operations at the technological core of the organization, to change its ways of producing and selling transport. Finally, the effects of the reform were presented as being in the future. A great deal of work in 'implementing' the reform, of organizing things differently and of getting people to change their behaviour, remained to be done. The reformers said that the effects of the reforms would not be apparent for five to ten years. It is difficult to say what the reformers' innermost intentions were, but we gained the impression that the way they presented the reform reflected their own objectives and convictions. Seemingly they both wanted the effects to be these and believed that they would be.

All these ways of presenting the reform proved to be at odds with how it worked in practice. The reform did have an internal audience, but the effects on the external audience proved much more important. The major changes brought about by the reform – including the new rules for relations with the state, the division into a business enterprise and the Swedish Rail Administration, writing off of capital, and recruitment of a new board and management – were all effects of changes in attitude and behaviour in persons outside the organization.

Although the reformers spoke a great deal about operations, they mostly worked with ideology and structure, with describing how people should think and which organizational structures would be useful. They did not devote themselves to changing the products, but to changing what they thought of as the structural and ideological prerequisites for the products to change.

The future effects of the New SJ were what the reformers talked about, but these were very uncertain, particularly as the reform was soon said to be complete and was replaced with new ideas. The New SJ reform was declared complete when many employees in the organization had not received any concrete information about what the reform was going to involve, what changes would affect them or what demands for changes in behaviour were being placed on them. It is hard to see that their future actions would be affected.

So instead of affecting future internal operations, the reform had fairly dramatic effects on SJ's external relations and its management's work while the reform was in progress. Rather than changing products and production the reform influenced external parties' ideas about SJ, and it forced management to work with ideological issues rather than with production.

One interpretation of the difference between the presentation and the results is that the New SJ failed: it did not achieve, and could not reasonably have been expected to achieve, what the reformers had promised. But another interpretation is that the reform was extremely successful, albeit not in the manner that had been predicted. The reform had major ideological external effects at the time it was ongoing, and if reforms generally have their greatest effects at the start of their existence, when they are sold to the organization and initiated, it may be a good thing if they later fail according to their own criteria: if they are seen as failing, this may give rise to arguments for new reforms which in turn quickly produce new effects.

The objectives stated by the reformers may not always be followed by the desired results; good objectives may have other effects. Precisely because SJ's production and results still did not improve, it was important to disseminate the hope that production and results would improve: interested parties both inside and outside the company would then be willing to wait for the future effects. The important effect of the reform was not improved operations, but the hope of improved operations. And to spread this hope the reform had to be presented as aiming at improved operations.

IMPLEMENTING REFORMS: A MODEL

The case of the New SJ presents a series of complications and difficulties both when it comes to implementing reforms and to defining what are good ways of implementing them, and even in generally defining implementation. In this final section we summarize the discussion with a simple model of implementation, which can deal with some complications.

Time as a complication

Implementation can be defined as a process by which reformers' ideas are put into practice. If the reformers' ideas control and permeate operations in the organization, the reform is implemented, i.e. there is consistency between idea and practice. Our study of the New SJ, however, demonstrates that this model for implementation is too simple and needs to be made somewhat more complex in order to be realistic. What distinguishes reforms is that it takes some time to implement them; ideas are not transformed into practice immediately. This is why we talk about a specific implementation process.

If the reformers' ideas remain stable over time, the delay between ideas and new practice does not represent a problem for our definitions of implementation and implemented. But if the reformers' ideas change over time the model becomes more complicated. Which ideas should characterize practices, the ones the reformers have when the reform commences or the ones they have when the reform is completed? If implementation means that the original ideas govern practice, even when the reformers' ideas have changed, it also means that the reformers are doomed to feel dissatisfied in a world where their reforms are implemented; neither at the start of the reforms nor at their conclusion will practices be consistent with the reformers' ideas. This implies that the implementation of reforms does not do away with the tension between idea and practice which gives rise to reforms, rather that its existence is upheld. If, instead, implementation is taken to have occurred when the reformees behave as the reformers want them to at that same point in time, the implementation process must be characterized by the reformees not having adapted to the ideas presented by the reformers when they launched the reforms. If reformers' ideas develop over time, implementation cannot possibly both mean that the original reform ideas control practice and that the reformers are content.

As we have tried to illustrate with the case of the New SJ, there are many reasons to expect that reformers' ideas do develop over time. Announcing an idea for reform can be seen as an attempt to stop thinking, to 'decide' that these ideas will prevail for some future period. But ideas are so easy to reshape and renew that it may be difficult for the reformers themselves to abide by their decision. Nor does it seem to be particularly intelligent to stop thinking, or to become as slow at thinking as the organization is slow at moving.

In the New SJ, we saw that one reason for ideas developing was that reforms led to new reforms long before they had been implemented. Ideas easily give rise to new ideas, without the first ideas being tested in practice. Experimenting is not the only way to learn. If we think we are wrong, there is good reason to think again before it is too late, rather than waiting for the practical results of each new thought.

The reform ideas may also be changed quite simply by the reformers' disappearance, because the people who launched a reform are replaced by new people and therefore do not evaluate it. This may sometimes happen quite shortly after the reform has been launched. This is a typical course of events when professional reformers, such as consultants, are called in. They are experts in launching reforms rather than implementing them. In the case of SJ, one important result of the reform was that the management was replaced and that the new management hired new consultants.

If the implementation process contains the complications described here, this will affect how implementation is achieved. It will be impossible to both implement the original ideas of the reform and to ensure that practice at a certain point in time corresponds with the reformers' ideas. If reformees want to invest in the first alternative, implementation of the original intentions of the reform, they should register the ideas in detail and then try to implement them without having any contact with the reformers; contact with the reformers' new ideas may confuse them. If this rule is followed, the reforms will be implemented more easily, but implementation means that the reformers will not be satisfied.

If reformees want to carry through the second alternative, there are several strategies they can adopt. The most fundamental thing for them is not to follow the ideas presented by the reformers when they launch the reform. This slightly increases the chances that some of the reformers' ideas will correspond with practice when the reform has been implemented. Reformers sometimes complain that it is difficult and lengthy to persuade the reformees to change their behaviour in practice according to the reformers' desires. But as demonstrated here, this type of resistance seems sensible even from the reformers' point of view since it increases their chances of experiencing the reform as successful.

In order to further increase the chances of implementation according to the second definition, the reformees could try to predict the reformers' future ideas and develop their practices in line with their predictions, that is the ideas to which they suppose the present thoughts of the reformers will lead. In order to do this, the reformees need to be able to think as strategically as the reformers.

The most effective means of achieving consistency between the reformers' ideas and practice is for the reformees to control the reformers instead of the other way round. If the reformees can convince the reformers that the right ideas are the ones reflected in current practice, then ideas and practice will correspond. Practice will be implemented in the world of ideas rather than vice versa. The reason for this being a more effective implementation strategy is quite simply the difference in the speed of adaptation between ideas and practice we have assumed. If ideas can be adapted to practice momentarily, or at very short notice, but not the other way round, consistency will, of course, most easily be reached through changing the ideas. The most satisfied reformers are those who launch reforms which describe the present and unchanging state of practices or the state in which practices are inevitably moving; such reforms create ideologies about, explain and justify what is being done in practice, or what those in operative positions want to do.

The assumed difference in speed between the development of ideas and the development of practices may also have another effect on the content of reforms. It may be tempting for reformers to try reforming things that can be changed quickly, for example redrawing an organizational chart rather than changing attitudes, installing ready-made, standardized accounting systems rather than developing systems of their own, even if the latter would have a better chance of affecting behaviour within their organization. It may also be tempting to launch ideas which can be assumed to be more stable than others. Ideas which are parts of institutions, for instance ideas which relate to traditional, accepted thinking about what a company is, may be assumed to be more enduring than the reformers' own innovations and therefore more attractive. And some reformers might expect their more abstract desires, such as making the organization more like a business enterprise, to last longer than more detailed ideas on how these desires should be put into practice, for instance ideas for a new budgeting system.

Ambiguity and implementation

We have assumed up to this point that it is easy to decide what the reformers' ideas are and what things look like in practice. Let us now add another complication, ambiguity. At the time when the reforms are considered to have been implemented it may not be clear what the reformers' original ideas really were; the ideas may have been ambiguous ever since the reforms were launched or they may be unclear because time has passed. Decisions about reforms are sometimes ambiguous, for instance when they are the result of compromises (Baier *et al.* 1986) or when reform ideas are vague, as in the New SJ. This type of ambiguity can be exploited for retrospective rationalization: when the reforms are considered to have been implemented, the original ideas for reform are interpreted and presented so as to match practice at that point in time.

What goes on in practice may also be ambiguous; it may be difficult to know what is really happening and how to describe it (Sahlin-Andersson 1989b), and this makes it difficult to decide whether it matches the reform ideas or not. It may be particularly difficult for the reformers, who are at a certain distance from practice, to decide this. Reformees who want to satisfy reformers can choose to respond to the reformers' ideology with repeating the same ideology and to describe practices so that they seem to correspond to the reformers' ideas.

Ambiguity about the original ideas of the reform is the most forceful kind of ambiguity. It may efface difficulties that the earlier complications gave rise to. In other words, ambiguity may contribute to implementation in both the senses we have referred to: practice may appear to correspond both to the earlier ideas of the reform and the current ones, since they appear to be the same.

Reforming the environment

Finally, let us introduce a further complication into our model. Up until now, the model has described two parties, the reformers and the reformees. But if we are to believe many reformers, including those at SJ, these are not the only relevant parties. The reformers want to change the reformees, but the ultimate purpose of doing so is often to improve the organization's relationship with its environment. SJ was to become more like a business enterprise in order to make more money in its contacts with customers, the financial sector, the government and other important groups in the world around the organization. Thus the environments of the reformers and the reformees are expected to react to the modified practices of the reformees.

If the ultimate purpose of the reformers in advocating a particular reform is to influence the organization's environment, the definition of implementation as changes in practice is too limited. Instead, a reform has really only been implemented when it has impacted on the environment.

Effects on the environment can be the result of changes in practice, but they can also occur as a direct result of the reformers presenting their ideas. When people outside the organization listen to the talk of the reformers, they may believe that practices are going to change, and already begin to adapt themselves, in relation to their picture of future practices. But they may also feel that the reformers' ideas are important in themselves, for example that they correspond better with their own views of how an organization should be controlled and function. In the case of SJ, we have seen that the reformers' ideas had a direct impact on the financiers and on recruitment on top managers, and this meant better business.

If the ultimate effects of the reforms are to be on outsiders' views of the organization, the problems we have discussed with regard to implementation and time delays disappear, or at least diminish. In principle, there is nothing to prevent ideas about the organization that are current in the environment from changing as rapidly as the reformers' ideas. In order to be satisfied with the results, reformers simply have to adhere to their ideas for as long as it takes to convince the environment of them.

Of course, the reformers may have higher ambitions than only to influence the opinions of the environment. They may also want these new opinions held by outside interests to influence those people's actions. The same problem may then arise in the external interests' organizations as in the reformers': it may take time to change practices. However, within the company, the reformers want administrative changes that often take a long time to implement, but the changes in the environment's practices they want to achieve may materialize more quickly – as the New SJ again exemplifies. At SJ, the reformers wanted to achieve complicated organizational and behavioural changes within the organization, but when it came to external interests, they simply wanted to see more money come into the company, and they wanted competent personnel to apply for employment with SJ. These last two changes were changes which could, and did, take place rapidly. By changing external interests' view of the company, SJ rapidly gained more money and a highly qualified management.

When reformers strive to influence the organization's environment directly through reform ideas, and not through the practices of the reformees, they have less reason to be interested in these practices. The practices can then develop in their own way, separate from the reformers' ideas. And the reformers can develop their ideas, separate from organizational practice. This gives a completely different mechanism for reforming than the difference between ideas and practice. Reformers can be expected to launch reforms irrespective of what the current practices are. Reforms become attempts to influence outsiders via ideas, and as soon as outside interest in the organization cools off, or its values about what the organization should be change, it is time to launch a new reform. Whether or not earlier reforms have been implemented in internal practice makes no difference. The reformers' satisfaction or dissatisfaction, and their reforms, are independent of whether or not their ideas are consistent with practices in the organization. Also, the content of reform becomes independent of the content of current practice. A reform may contain suggestions for new ways in which practice can function, or it could just as well have the same content as present practice. The reformers may propose a practice that is already in place, since they are unaware of current practice; or sometimes even for the very reason that they are aware of it and think it is consistent with outsiders' views of how organizations should work. People at the operational level in large organizations will recognize this type of reform.

Implementation strategies

We have argued that implementation of reforms in practice may encounter a number of complications. The complications we have discussed are that reforms take time to implement, that reformers' ideas are not stable, that there may be a difference in pace between the development of ideas and the development of practices, that ideas and practices are ambiguous, and that the reactions of the environment are more important than the reactions of the organization. Given these complications, there are four main ways of implementing reforms. From a normative point of view, they all have pros and cons.

The first type of implementation – implementing the reformers' original ideas – creates both dissatisfaction and a good starting point for new reforms, which in turn may create even more reforms. What we think of this result will depend on how we value reforms. Reforms may represent development, the desire for improvement and a struggle for higher values than we normally achieve in our daily activities; but reforms can also been seen as unrealistic projects and a waste of resources.

The second implementation strategy is that the reformees try to guess what the reformers' future ideas will be, and try to adapt to them. This seems to be a completely sensible method, but only if we ignore the uncertainty of those guesses.

The third implementation strategy is to adapt ideas to practice, which can be simplified by, but does not presuppose, ambiguity in ideas and practice. This strategy is more prone to create satisfaction and the peace and quiet required to get work done. But adapting ideas to practice may squeeze the goodness, justice and beauty common in reform ideas out of the picture. This development is seen in many contexts to be morally dubious: good morality presupposes the existence of sin, of peoples' values being so grand that they are unable to translate them into action. This method of implementation may also inhibit the intellect, making people think more slowly than is necessary.

The final strategy is to isolate reforms from operations, by, for example, reforming the environment rather than the organization itself. This type of isolation preserves beautiful ideas and the right to go on thinking. However, these effects are achieved not by people constantly striving for new goals in action but by creating the illusion of always treading the path of virtue. This may be a pleasant illusion, but it is also too close to hubris not to give rise to moral complications.

8 Implementation and institutional identity*

* This chapter was contributed by Marit Wærnes.

After the general discussion in the previous chapter, we turn to some more specific aspects of reform implementation in this chapter and the next three. In this chapter we discuss the extent to which the characteristics of the organizations which are to be reformed influence the chances of implementing a reform, and its effects. In Chapter 9 we illustrate how implementation may also be dependent on the contents of the reform itself. Both chapters demonstrate how reforms tend to have other effects than those presented by the reformers as their intentions. This theme is further developed in Chapter 10. In Chapter 11 we discuss how the organizations to be reformed can influence the reform content.

The analysis in this chapter is based on a study of an attempt to introduce three-year budgeting into Swedish government administration. It was initiated in pilot project form in 1985, as one of a number of highly rationalistic administrative reforms aimed at improving the efficiency and effectiveness of public sector administration. The reform brought about some changes in the government administration, although perhaps not exactly the ones the reformers had intended. The reactions were different in different agencies, according to their institutional identity.

A BUDGET REFORM

As part of its 'new administrative policy' of the 1980s, the government decided to gradually try out three-year budgeting principles in all public state agencies. The Ministries of Public Administration and Finance were to formulate and implement the decision. They decided to run a pilot project with roughly ten agencies of varying sizes and with different activities and work assignments. Specific planning directives were issued to each agency by the government. Each agency was required to account for its previous results, and for its efficiency and effectiveness over the last five years, as well as to indicate the proposed direction of activities and the resources needed for the next three years. On the basis of this in-depth analysis of activities and resources, each agency was to write a special report on its own organization, future objectives, programmes and planned results. These reports were to be submitted to the appropriate ministry six months before the agency's three-year budget request. The budget request was also to be based on a three-year planning perspective, drawn up in depth and directly related to activities in the agency, so as to provide a comprehensive, result-orientated set of facts and figures as a basis for analysis of the request.

The point of this new budget documentation was to make the agencies' resource planning more reasonable, rational and long-term. All activity plans and budget requests were to be related to previous results, and all new needs were to be justified and documented in a long-term, result-orientated manner. General demands were also placed upon the agencies to try out performance and productivity measurements, and to use better information and accounting systems. Then changes were thought to increase the agencies' efficiency.

Context, organization and objectives

Long-term budgeting had long been 'in the air' in connection with modernization of government management systems, and a three-year budgeting process had been proposed on several other occasions. The final proposal was initiated in the report of the Commission of Inquiry described in Chapter 5. The commission suggested that the division of roles between state ministries and agencies should be clearer. It was said that the government should increase its management capability; the government should issue policies and assess results, and the agencies should be given freedom to find the most effective means of implementing government policy. Three-year budgeting was a part of this management idea. Support groups were established for each agency involved in the pilot reform project. These groups included representatives of the government's staff agencies, the agency in question, and the Ministries of Public Administration and Finance. Each support group was meant to serve both as a pressure group for implementation of some kind of productivity or efficiency measurement system in the agency and as a support for developing such a system.

As three-year planning and budgeting were to be widened to more agencies and to become part of a total administrative management policy, different objectives of the reform were highlighted one by one:

- Agencies would become better at saving on costs. Instead of the incremental annual cost cutbacks, it would now be possible to spread out larger savings over several years. In-depth analysis of activities carried out in conjunction with the budget process and longer-term planning of efficiency measures and cutbacks would give each agency better control of its own productivity and efficiency. This would make it easier for each agency to set up priorities of its own and decide where and when to implement savings.

- Political control would increase with a three-year budget system. The government would carry out an exhaustive review of the agency every third year, following up all activities, resources and opportunities to increase efficiency. In the years between the reviews, the agency would make a performance evaluation, related to the three-year plan and resources. The detailed political control which had long been criticized would be reduced.
- The commission had agreed that three-year budgeting would lead to: 'the government defining more clearly what the agencies should accomplish in terms of results'. The government, and particularly the Ministry of Finance, emphasized that the agencies would have to co-ordinate their own decisions on improving efficiency into a coherent, long-term savings plan. Plans for a new accounting system, personnel planning and analysis of income possibilities were to be included in the three-year resource plan. The budget dialogue would now become more result-orientated, focusing on the qualitative, long-term effects of state agencies' activities. If the agencies could succeed in doing all this, they would be awarded a three-year spending authorization and agency-tailored performance directives in the budget process.
- The reform contained various rewards. It promised the agencies greater freedom. A three-year decision on plans and resources would simplify the annual budget work. The agencies would also have the opportunity to transfer some of their administrative costs between years, which would benefit their resource planning and simplify administrative adaptations. The agency-tailored directives from the government would be issued specifically for each agency's results and activities in general rather than details. This would make the budget process an attractive part of the new administrative policy.
- Both the management committee and the Ministry of Finance emphasized that the purpose of the new budget method was to improve efficiency: 'generally speaking, the productivity demands are high for all agencies' (Draft bill 1986/87: 99, p. 87). Therefore, the budget reform was formulated centrally and decided by politicians, and could be seen as a general demand on all agencies to 'carry out given tasks more efficiently', as the commission put it.

Ideology and management myth

The aim of three-year budget reform was to introduce in a concrete management process an 'ideal' role distribution between the parliament, the government and the state agencies. The reform assumed that a clear difference exists between political bodies managing by objectives and interested in general budget information, and state agencies interested in supplying this information. The belief in such a distinction made the reformers claim that political control could be reconciled with increased freedom for various agencies in the budget process. It was assumed that there is an unambiguous difference between politics and administration.

In this respect the three-year budget reform rested, as had all previous major state budget reforms, on a given myth: that rational models of management by objectives and distinct planning rules would solve most problems of political control, would get things in order (Brunsson 1986a). Implementation problems were considered to be problems of knowledge and information instead of problems of values, interests or politics. Political control was assumed to increase through increased information about administrative activities, goals and results, via better measuring and following up of activities and resources.

A valid question is what kind of chance such a reform can have in practice. Previous state budget reforms in many countries have emphasized general budget techniques for control and efficiency, and many have failed. Many state agencies or areas of state activity have hardly been affected at all. The staff responsible for the budget have gone on working as before, using old methods, without understanding or accepting the implications of the new budget demands. Alternatively, the budget reforms have had an effect: the agencies have accepted new techniques and methods for the planning system. But this has led to an increased administrative workload, an increasingly technically orientated budget process and, in the end, less political control of resource development and administrative results (Wildavsky 1964; Downs and Larkey 1986; Brunsson 1988; Back and Lane 1988). After pilot reform periods, things have often reverted to the traditional 'intricacies' and more familiar incremental budgeting methods, and faith has been lost in the new management techniques and budgeting methods.

Yet the new three-year budget reform was intended to be more than a rationalistic budget reform. It was part of the general modernization programme for the public sector, aimed at making state agencies more market-like, more management-orientated and more 'modern'. Throughout the 1980s, attempts were made to radically change the functioning of the state administration. Agencies were supposed to gain better control of their own economies, and to take more responsibility for their development and results. They were encouraged to provide more services and be more 'customer-orientated', irrespective of their activities, spending authorization forms or rule systems. Priorities and priority problems were to be delegated to lower agency levels, and more control for funds and transfers were in the long run to be delegated to the local levels. The government and the parliament were expected to make a more retrospective review in the form of 'reading whether results are in agreement with expectations' (Draft bill 1986/87: 99, p.35).

The three-year reform was to give the agencies the opportunity to take greater responsibility for public activities and results, even when facing cutbacks. Seen in this context, the reactions of the agencies in the pilot project more than answer the question of whether they are willing to learn, accept and master the techniques and methods of the new budget system. The reactions are responses to the opportunity of taking greater control of and responsibility for public resources in a time of cutbacks. Each agency signals its level of confidence in the ability to become more efficient. Their reactions can give us information as to the effects of the entire political 'modernization' of the public sector of which this reform was one part.

INSTRUMENTAL AND INSTITUTIONAL EXPLANATIONS

In Chapter 1 we distinguished between two ways of understanding reform, an instrumental and an institutional one. Here we contrast these when explaining how the agencies reacted to the budget reform. In an instrumental perspective, the agencies are expected to accept reforms that are useful for their own survival and prosperity. We expect them to adopt reforms which promise more resources and higher legitimacy and which are easy to implement.

But the reactions of the agencies can also be explained by particular institutional qualities of each agency. If we think of the agencies as institutionalized, as described in Chapter 2, each agency's activities, history, formal and informal rules, routines, norms and values are decisive for the actual implementation of reforms coming from the outside (Weber 1971; Crozier 1964; Eckhoff and Jacobsen 1960; Olsen 1978, 1988d, 1989). Let us now examine the agencies in relation to both the instrumental and the institutional perspectives.

Instrumental explanations

From an instrumental perspective, we can assume that all the agencies would accept the reform's strong orientation towards efficiency and its

simple model of political control of performance results. As state government bodies, all agencies are dependent on resources and legitimation from
the central government. At the time of the reform, the agencies had long
been competing for scarce administrative resources. The three-year budget
framework seemed to offer a long-term guarantee of resources and greater
freedom to take advantage of those resources. On the basis of relatively
simple rationalistic criteria, and seen from a typical administrative-
economic point of view, the new system seemed profitable.

Most recent administrative reforms had been characterized by the same
'efficiency' view of administration (Lindé 1982). This view dominated the
political climate at the time of the three-year reform. Almost everywhere,
agencies were valued as first and foremost executive instruments of
politics, evaluated on their ability to implement political objectives through
economically effective planning and performance. This view spoke in
favour of the new budget system's obtaining general acceptance by all
agencies.

The reform process also appeared to be relatively well organized. The
agencies were promised access to methodological help and expertise. The
three-year agency-specific budget directives were drawn up in general
agreement between both the ministries in question and the agency itself.
The new planning demands had also been developed from an earlier system
with programme budgeting. The whole system built on previous demands
for general reductions of administrative costs. Various methods for
performance measurements and in-depth resource requests had also been
developed by staff agencies supporting the pilot project.

Three-year budgeting might be understood as a reform emanating from
the agencies themselves. Previously, similar budget reforms had been
extensively agency controlled (Back and Lane 1988). There had been a
strong tradition of reform and administrative renewal in Swedish agencies
(Czarniawska-Joerges and Jacobsson 1989), and they were accustomed to
rationalistic reforms. Many agencies were technically very competent at
carrying out performance reviews, and at developing new structures and
methodologies in a short time. Furthermore, the agencies had a formal
responsibility to renew and develop their own administrative activities
(SFS 1965: 500).The ideas of the reform were popular ones in several
countries, and in most sectors of society, and no-one was really inclined to
question whether the timing of the reform was appropriate.

Different institutional identities

Thus, from an instrumental perspective, a great deal of evidence suggested
that the reactions of the pilot project agencies would be quite similar and

positive. But from an institutional perspective we would expect the pilot project to be far more difficult to implement and to be accepted to different degrees by different agencies.

Three-year budgeting was to be implemented by different state agencies, each one with a different institutional identity and part of a separate political and cultural system. State agencies have always had different traditions, activities, goals and operations, different rule systems, norms, practical tasks, personal contacts and relations to the actual political system, as well as different budgeting and planning habits. Each agency might be more or less adapted to the new demands, ideas, techniques and objectives of the budget reform. The myth of rationalism was more or less appropriate. Both administratively and operationally, the reform could be anticipated to affect each agency differently.

Seen from this perspective, the agencies could be expected to have varying capacities to take advantage of the reform and to live up to its demands. In many cases, the reform would not suit the existing operations, the traditional way of thinking or the planning norms. Each agency might have its own understanding of political control, leadership and organization of the public sector.

In addition to typical demands for efficiency, some agencies had a duty to safeguard the legal security of the citizens, some others to be sensitive to the opinions of different political groups and to take the different views of interested parties seriously. Swedish agencies are bearers of different norms with regard to independence, neutrality and equality, regardless of political fluctuations. These claims on neutrality might stand in contrast to the demands of the three-year reform. Agencies with typical citizen-orientated functions might actually want entirely different administrative solutions than a governing system ruled by three-year planning and budgeting.

Swedish agencies have a strong tradition of maintaining autonomy. Political control over the implementation of reforms has permeated political theory and discussion as a constant problem (Heckscher 1952; Söderlind and Petersson 1986; Jacobsson 1984; Brunsson 1986a; Rothstein 1986). The three-year budget reform was a typical attempt to achieve better government control, but each agency might have had its own view and interpretation of what would be the most important political tasks in the future, and this might have prevented their co-operating with the reform.

Depending on size, activities, tradition and culture, each agency faced different conditions during the reform process. The agencies would be able to develop their own defence and reinterpretation mechanisms during the process. This would easily mean that the reform could fail.

Thus from an institutional perspective we can assume that the agencies' reactions to the reform would be determined by the degree of fit between the reform and the agency itself. Agencies which might have reacted negatively towards the budget change were those bound up by laws and rules, or for example the smaller highly informal agencies which had a shortage of planning, administrative and accounting resources. Also, agencies with their own strong norms in terms of expertise, neutrality and learning from practice, and with a strong sense of bureaucratic 'ethics', would find the budget reform to be too uniform, economistic, rationalistic, irrelevant or threatening to their own competence and activities.

The pilot agencies were also in different phases of administrative modernization regarding performance measurement and money-saving techniques. The three-year reform built on certain practical techniques, analyses and methods. Some of the agencies had already started implementing these, while others were absolutely opposed to the new demands. The pilot project agencies also had widely varying resources and personnel to learn the new budget methods.

From an institutional perspective, positive reactions towards the reform could be expected from agencies whose characteristics fitted the administrative 'production' philosophy, the ideal of management by objectives and 'modern' budgeting routines. Negative reactions could be expected from older agencies with typical bureaucratic cultures, agencies which reacted negatively towards any change or agencies where operating norms were in competition with the main ideas and management model of the three-year reform.

THE REACTIONS: RESISTANCE, INERTIA AND ADAPTATION

So what then were the reactions of the different agencies taking part in the government's pilot project?

We studied the first three-year budget process at five different agencies: the Swedish Customs Agency, the National Judicial Board for Public Lands and Funds, the Swedish Board of Trade, the Imports Promotion Office for Products for Developing Countries (IMPOD) and Statistics Sweden. The Customs Agency is a large hierarchical, traditional state agency with several regional and local organizations, much on-the-job training, internal recruitment, and a registered 'income' of its own in the national budget. Customs activities are also strongly controlled by rules. The agency's own planning is limited. The Board for Public Lands and Funds is the oldest administrative agency in Sweden. It is a relatively small board with various legal experts performing traditional national administrative duties in relation to acquisition of national property, taxation and subsidies. The Board of Trade is also an old, small administrative agency whose work concerns investigative, advisory and regulatory means in the field of foreign trade. This agency has traditionally concentrated on Sweden's national interests in matters of trade with other nations. It has kept a close eye on weights and measures and comparative statistics and product quality measurements in relation to the products of other nations. It has some strong expert norms. IMPOD is quite a new, very small, non-traditional administrative agency, more like a service office for trade and commerce with developing countries. Its main task is to promote imports from developing countries. The office has a total staff of twelve, and administrative resources are limited. Planning is quite easy. Statistics Sweden is an enormous, firmly established monopoly expert which produces agency statistics in all areas of the public sector. It has strong traditions of independence, emphasizing neutrality and objectivity from political control. The Board of Statistics Sweden includes representatives from most of the big organizations on the labour market, and the agency deals with information for all types of social planning.

Initially, none of these five agencies accepted the reform unequivocally. Their reactions differed, as had been expected, depending on different institutional identities. But gradually, and especially after the first planning reports and in-depth budget requests had been submitted to the government, all five agencies seemed to have moved further towards implementing the reform. Slowly, all the agencies were willing to try out a three-year budget system, to carry out in-depth budget planning, do more activity analysis and performance measurements. From this point on, all the pilot agencies went on adjusting to the reform in a positive spirit, irrespective of what their first reactions had been. Let us – as an example of the dynamics of the reform process – study the pilot project in the Swedish Customs Agency.

The Customs Agency

The Customs Agency has traditional legitimacy as a central state agency with a monopoly of activity and high status. It is well known and follows a traditional state policy. Its activities are largely controlled by laws and regulations. The amount of work is governed by external factors such as international trade and changes in traffic. The agency is characterized by strong internal norms on keeping up with legal security and upholding fairness in relation to customs clearance and statements of content of shipments. The organization of the Customs Agency is a complex one, with a long 'catalogue' of duties, a large operative staff, and traditional 'group spirit'. It is a traditionally hierarchical, rule-governed organization. This is reflected in both internal and external budgeting and in planning systems. The Customs Agency appeared to have very limited freedom of action and the management ideal of more market orientation seemed foreign. The three-year reform management model seemed poorly suited to the traditional principles of control at the Swedish Customs Agency.

At the same time, the Customs Agency has always been an important state fiscal organization. Much of its activity may be seen as being economically profitable in itself, as the Agency takes in customs duty, taxes and large sums of money. The Agency could have a definition of efficiency different to that of the reform.

Initially, the Customs Agency also pointed out that they considered administrative reforms in general a disruption of their own more practical activities. The agency had also just adopted a new policy of its own, and the primary need was to act on this. Long-term resource planning was considered problematical in this situation. There was a growing awareness in the agency of the crisis in the imbalance between what they were expected to do and the resources they were allocated for doing it, an imbalance they considered to be caused by the cutbacks of recent years. The Customs Agency saw the three-year budget reform as another effort on the part of the Ministry of Finance to cut resources. In defence of their own activities, they were unwilling to accept further cutbacks, and certainly unwilling to plan themselves for such cutbacks for the next three years.

Institutional factors indicated that the Customs Agency would rather defend the traditional budget process and question all changes which emphasized economic performance measurements, more market-orientation and private management ideas as a policy for renewal. The agency also had great enough autonomy for its resistance to adjusting to win through.

The pilot project

The Customs Agency did not allow itself to be deeply affected by the general budget demands to begin with. They made their own future plans, drew up their traditional annual resource plans, and claimed that they were going to need increased resources in the future. The Agency used its own traditional measurements of performance, which were not expressed in terms of costs, quality of productivity. It completely opposed the demands to plan a 5 per cent cutback over three years. The administrative staff gave no special priority to the reform, and put little resources into the project. The trade union members' generally negative attitude towards cutbacks was now used from the managers' side to defend the traditional way of thinking, planning and requesting resources in the Agency.

The complexity of the organization, its size and effectiveness in collecting customs duties was used as an excuse for a negative, stand-offish attitude towards the whole project. The Agency issued a statement in the budget process that it did not wish to 'end up as a loser', and so 'preferred to wait and see' what would happen with the new budget system. These signals were all indicative of the Agency having strong institutional qualities that worked against the reform. The Agency was not about to let its planning activities and budget process be affected. The Agency pursued its 'own way' and its traditional budget was kept intact. But the Agency also missed the reward of a three-year administrative budget. The government refused to plan for a long-term resource framework for the Agency.

One year later

The following year, the Customs Agency received a directive from the Ministry of Finance to develop a whole new system of performance measurement and management controls in order to introduce three-year budgeting in the future. The new control system was developed and completed in February 1988, only two years after the Agency had become part of the pilot project, and the system was in use as of 1 January 1989.

The new management and budget system soon came to replace the existing traditional statistics and budget planning within the Agency. It provided information on all sorts of activities both to the Director General and the head of the Agency and to the government, making possible better comparison of resources, achievements and results in different divisions for different services. Subsequent performance analyses led to new priorities, alterations in the internal distribution of resources, and a new level of administrative ambition in the Agency. The new control and budget system appeared to be a way to achieve a 'modern' result-orientated state agency, which would make it possible for the Agency to compete with other state agencies for resources.

Gradually, a logic of service production, performance management and efficiency was introduced at the Customs Agency. Traditional work assignments were now classified in a completely new way, using the concepts of productivity and efficiency. Time studies were to be carried out in all parts of the agency, including the operative level to enable evaluation of all performance related to administrative costs. After one year it had become clear to the Director General and the promoters of the reform that 'we are going to get one of those programme budgets now and funding for three years . . . we want a three-year budget starting in 1990/91'. They realized that 'programme budgeting was back in people's good books'. Customs officials were now going to change their way of planning, budgeting and evaluating resources and results as time passed.

Thus, although at the initial stage the Swedish Customs Agency did not succumb to the reform at all or even allow itself to be controlled by its requirements, it adjusted to the budget reform in the next round, and adapted more of the new techniques than we would have expected from its typical institutional qualities. The joint modernization context of the reform, the pressure placed on the agency by its environment, the new wave of economic reforms, the political climate for in-depth assessments of productivity and efficiency probably all operated to the benefit of the reform. The Customs Agency surprisingly 'went modern' in the reform's terms, changed to cope with measuring and demonstrating its own productivity and efficiency, to show market orientation and cost consciousness and to produce results, all the way down to the smallest local customs office.

Other agencies' reactions

Statistics Sweden is an especially skilled agency when it comes to all sorts of information and performance measurement systems, as its own operating activities consist of making statistical measurements of public sector results, and developing micromodels for studying the social effects of public services. There is a also a growing market for the agency's services. Before the pilot project, Statistics Sweden had already developed extensive consultancy services, and its own competence in the type of rationalization that was required by the reform was quite good. The ideas of three-year budgeting could suit the general direction and activities of this agency quite well.

Statistics Sweden from the beginning not only produced a 'flawless' three-year budget plan but also invested enormous efforts in planning for the next three years of activity, resources and effects. The agency used the three-year perspective which had been foisted upon it as an opportunity to propose its own new statistical models, a new departmental computerization, and the need for increased statistical competence from its own customers, i.e. other agencies and ministries. The agency's response to the reform was almost overdone, including producing planning books with extensive three-year plans, detailed assessments of the agency's potential for increased effectivity in different activities, and a number of new arguments with regard to increased resources. The institutional identity of Statistics Sweden supported the agency in following up the reform, and it made the agency into a more than competent pilot agency.

The three other agencies in the pilot project were less able to affect the process in any special way. These are small state agencies, with scanty resources for planning, weak institutional identities, politically more vulnerable activities and, at the time of the reform, uncertain futures as state agencies. But the reform process in these agencies still shows that some of their institutional features influenced their reactions.

The Swedish Board of Trade used its special insights as an advisory body to foreign trade in its own long-term planning, giving priority to 'popular' international activities when requesting resources for the next three years.

The Board for Public Lands and Funds proposed a change with the objective of becoming a service institution, financed by income from other agencies. Its keen awareness of being in a deep crisis influenced its reactions. The agency was trying to uphold all its previous activities, norms and values, but by adapting their rhetoric they could prevent interference form above!

IMPOD had no administrative resources whatsoever to plan and report on performance at the technical level of the budget reform. But the agency made extensive efforts, in relation to size, to account for efficiency, results and service towards its own customers. It used its own brief history as an argument for why its own expansive plans should be accepted, which would mean more resources. The whole pilot project was seen as an opportunity for IMPOD to build up competence, efficiency and administrative expertise. The three-year resource request was turned into an attempt to gain more administrative resources, which would guarantee IMPOD's survival.

In other words, institutional variations among the agencies led to different pilot projects. There were many new interpretations of the meaning of new budget system. The pilot project triggered different defence mechanisms at the different agencies. The traditional 'watchman' identity of the Swedish Customs Agency led to inertia and slow-downs of the new budget process. The traditional statistical identity and well-developed rationalization routines of Statistics Sweden were suited to its own extended planning and it produced even more administrative statistics on results. The role of the Swedish Board of Trade as an export body led to a relatively pragmatic adaptation to the new administrative demands, well in line with its own future and planning resources. Since IMPOD was a completely new and small agency it tried to use the pilot project to obtain more administrative resources.

None of these reactions can, in any simple, straightforward way, be said to further the objectives of the reform that were to increase political control, to guarantee implementation of political objectives and to ensure economic efficiency in the state agencies.

The dynamics

To a large extent, the agencies' reactions to the reform were also characterized by a joint context of modernization. For all five agencies, the new planning process became more uniform and better adapted to the ideas and demands of the three-year reform than we could have predicted on the basis of the institutional characteristics of each of the agencies. All the agencies gradually incorporated the new budget demands and even completely new kinds of management techniques and performance measurements. Statistics Sweden increased its consultancy services, and began marketing its services much more widely than it had done previously to earn more money. It gradually ceased to see its 'independence' as an obstacle to adaptation to the three-year reform. The Board of Trade lowered the level of ambition for some of its activities to give altogether higher priority to others, which would result in less total administrative resources. IMPOD began slowly carrying out the result analysis techniques which the managers initially considered so poorly suited to its activities. Because the budget reform posed a special challenge to the small IMPOD agency, it could even show a special, positive attitude towards the very complex budget techniques, as a way of attracting the attention of the outside world to itself as a small but important organization. The pilot project became a step towards becoming a 'proper' and established state agency.

During the pilot project process, all the promoters of the reform at the agencies, i.e. at the management and administrative levels, were convinced that the technical problems of implementation could be 'solved as we go along'. They claimed that, in principle, they were in favour of a three-year budgeting and result management system, and that their own agency would gradually gain competence in using the system. The three-year perspective was said to have been 'in the air' and it was familiar. The budget reform was considered as a part of management by objectives, programme budgeting or long-term planning of activities, which everyone had to consider as sensible techniques. Each agency decided to go on thinking in three-year terms. No agency thought it would ever revert to the earlier one-year budgeting problems.

The emergence of this positive attitude towards the three-year reform can be explained in terms of the reward mechanism that was built into the system. Agencies preferred to save 5 per cent over three years rather than having annual cutbacks. But there is another explanation as well, based on the ideology of renewal.

How could all agencies, despite their strong first objections to the budget system, and despite their specific and alternative planning logic, their insecure planning situations, their limited administrative resources, and all the other, bigger and more pressing duties they had to perform, consider three-year budgeting to be a 'simplification', a better way of thinking, and something that would give them a 'better grip of their own activity'? This reaction was more than rhetoric. Many administrative changes took place in the pilot project agencies. They changed their budget language, put greater emphasis on performance measurement, reduced some of their operative ambitions, and they delegated administrative duties internally in the organization. They were aware that the new system would cause practical problems and they saw the risks of method manipulation in the budget dialogue.

But in spite of all this, they shared the fundamental attitude that changing over to three-year budgeting would mean progress and increased rationality. This attitude towards change as progress smoothed over the practical problems, and the attitude proved to be far more institutionalized than the different efficiency norms or operational logic of the individual agencies. The idea of three-year budgeting suited some basic ideas about modernization that all the agencies shared. This sharing kept the reform from being associated with previous reforms which had failed, including programme budgeting and zero-base budgeting. The new budget system was expected, instead, to endow the agencies with both scientific rationality (through shared methods), aesthetic rationality (through the promises of simplification, three-year cycles and principles of balance), and ethical rationality (a measure against wastefulness). These rationality principles are three of the prime elements of our shared understanding of 'modernity'. In other words, in this respect all the agencies lived in the same institutional environment, as defined in Chapter 1; they shared a general, wide-spread and taken-for-granted understanding of organizations and change. This common element proved to be more important than the agencies' specific institutional identities. It made the three-year budgeting idea appear as impeccably rational, beautiful and right.

This abstract appeal to modernity led to acceptance of the reform but it does not exactly speak for its intended effects, increased political control and efficiency. Instead of leading to more result-orientated budget discussion and political debate on the development of the state administration and prioritizing of resources for particular areas, three-year budgeting may lead to any sort of priorities and resources being concealed under a common veil of modernity.

AMBIGUOUS RESULTS

A reform may succeed on at least three different levels. At the planning level, the three-year budgeting project led to a number of changes. When the pilot project was over, the agencies had started long-term planning, they had introduced measuring their own productivity and efficiency, and they were now ready to take more responsibility for internal priorities and distribution of resources amongst areas, staff operation techniques, and practices. The administrative staff had from now on to keep the agency within a tight budget.

At the rhetorical level, new words and phrases relating to renewal were introduced. Today all agencies speak in terms of products and productivity, economic efficiency, service, operational markets, competition and marketing. Government agencies have become preoccupied with learning new means of presentation and packaging, new terms, a new administrative style – no matter how little significance this may have for actual operations, production or services. The new broom of the budget reform swept clean.

But these changes will not necessarily make the agencies less expensive, make the results better or operations more efficient. Instead, three-year budgeting has brought into existence a new kind of legitimacy for the agencies in relation to the government. It may give them new kinds of arguments for increased resources: the administration is now actively implementing some new means to improve its own planning, control and evaluation system. The agencies can make more local priorities between 'invisible' activities and more measurable productive ones. This can lead to internal shifts in power, conflicts and priority problems. In the prevailing political climate, it will also make it easier for an agency to 'market modernity' externally through the new budget process. The agencies might work more like independent 'business enterprises', taking responsibility for their long-term finances and results, and setting their own long-term priorities in relation to resource analysis. This will give signals of administrative rationality, competitiveness and a will to change in a time when the administrative policies are emphasizing a need for 'rational, dynamic organizational forms'. The three-year budget reform may reinforce the agencies' own resource arguments in their negotiations with the government and the parliament, rather than increasing political control.

The three-year budget reform had effects on organizations with an institutional identity very different from that of the reform, but the effects were not necessarily those the reformers presented as their intentions. In the next chapter we describe a reform which was deemed unambiguously successful by reformers, reformees and external observers alike. We demonstrate how success can be guaranteed by the content of the reform rather than by the reformers or the reformees.

9 Success at the expense of control*

* This chapter was contributed by Björn Rombach.

The literature on organizational change can be roughly described as falling into two categories. Books by consultants describe how major changes should be made. These are optimistic books, but poorly anchored in reality. Then there are books written by scholars who have evaluated major changes, which virtually unanimously point out the difficulty of achieving the changes the reformers desire (cf. Rombach 1986).

In contrast to many research reports on reforms, this chapter deals with a long-lasting and successful one, considered positive by people both inside and outside the organization. We discuss what characterizes a successful reform, and what explains its success.

It is open to question who is most competent to judge whether or not a reform has been successful. A common approach is for external evaluators to use measuring instruments they consider to be general or objective. For example, they might compare the initial objectives of the reformers with the effects they are able to measure, and if they find agreement between aims and effects, they see this as indicative of the reform's success.

We have chosen a different means of measuring success. A successful reform is a reform that is considered to have succeeded. There are no objective or general measures. A reform cannot be unambiguously described: it is a social construction. The parties able to judge the success of a reform are the reformers, the reformees, and spectators from the external environment. In this chapter we describe such a successful reform, carried out at a Swedish county council.

A SUCCESSFUL REFORM

In Sweden a typical county council is a large organization with tens of thousands of employees. Its main activity is to provide all kinds of health care for the county's inhabitants. It is led by a political assembly, the Council, and a Standing Committee of leading politicians.

During the first half of 1987, a survey of opinions about quality in county councils was performed (Rombach 1989a). All the county councils in Sweden participated. The survey questions included: What is being or has been done to improve quality in the county councils? What models are there for county councils in their work with the concept of quality?

All the county councils described their work on quality by comparing it with that of other county councils. Most mentioned specific councils they considered models. The county council most often mentioned was the Bohus county council, a medium-sized county council in western Sweden with some 18,000 employees. The reform model referred to was the 'Active County Council' reform (ACC).

Data from subsequent interviews confirm that the reform carried out by the Bohus county council was considered by evaluators from other county councils to be the most successful one anywhere. The Bohus council was the most commonly cited prototype for other county councils. The Bohus council and its ACC reform also received a great deal of positive press coverage, but we have not examined this coverage in detail.

Respondents working at management level in Bohus county were also positive towards ACC, and felt that there was broad general support for the idea. It is difficult to provide concrete evidence of this positive attitude without costly opinion polls (Rombach 1989b), but it often came out very clearly in the interviews, in which the respondents expressed their positive attitudes spontaneously. They defended ACC, and described its advantages. Normally, a respondent described the idea in positive terms and listed positive effects.

According to the management respondents, the employees working with the reform at operative level were also positive towards it, although at one time the 'active' aspect of the name was something of an in-house joke, e.g. 'Oh, I see you're being active, too . . .'. Indications of a positive attitude on the part of the staff were described as including good participation in a number of activities, the enthusiasm shown by many in working with ACC, as well as the absence of complaints or protests from staff and the trade unions. The ACC reform had virtually no opponents, which distinguishes it from many other reforms.

THE REFORM IMAGE

It appeared early in the study that ACC was not a reform which could be described easily. It was frustratingly difficult to identify what ACC actually was. Initially, the problem appeared to be with the researcher and information recipient.

Those whose jobs included describing the reform also considered it complex. No-one seemed to think it strange that it took the County Council Director and the Chief Information Officer four hours in front of an overhead projector to give an introduction to the ACC reform. The difficulty in making a simple description, they claimed, was partly that ACC was not a reform in the traditional sense of the word. The management did not accept the description 'reform', nor did they want it referred to as a 'project' or any other simple classification. They also claimed that ACC was not a decision to be implemented. The county council management and several other respondents spoke of ACC as a way of working for change. However, at least on the surface, it falls into the category of 'reform' as it has been used in this book, and is therefore referred to as such.

After a number of interviews with politicians and administrators in management positions in the county council, we accepted one of the characteristics of ACC as being that it was a reform which defied simple description and categorization.

During the course of the interviews, three dimensions of description took shape, as they were used by the interviewees to organize their descriptions. Both the descriptions given below and the structure for organizing the descriptions were provided by the respondents themselves. The first descriptive dimension was associated with attitudes, i.e. it described the internal organizational climate and a way of thinking about people. According to the respondents, these variables provided the platform for work and the prerequisites for change. Associated questions included the rules of the game and the distribution of roles between politicians and local officials, and between the employers and the trade unions. In addition, there were the demands made on the leadership to subscribe to a leadership policy for the Bohus county council. This descriptive dimension is henceforth referred to as 'the ACC idea'.

The second descriptive dimension is 'the ACC process'. In their descriptions of ACC, the respondents referred to meetings, the establishment of groups, and a number of actions which took place in different contexts at different times. The process may be described as a development over time, i.e. along a time axis. Along the way, ideas were discussed and developed which may, in turn, have affected the course of the process.

The third dimension was the concrete effects achieved. According to several of the respondents, it was essential for the ACC reform to achieve concrete effects if the process of change was to continue. Implementation gave rise to feedback for future work. Most of the results of ACC came out in the early interviews with the main local officials, and were supplemented throughout the study.

We have made a thorough survey of how the respondents viewed these results. We have endeavoured to visualize and document the respondents' pictures of reality. One might ask whether it would have been possible to collect some other type of data in order to describe the ACC reform. Would there have been some way to achieve a clearer and more objective description of what an 'Active County Council' really was? As far as we can see, this type of description is impossible. An ambiguous, unstable phenomenon or occurrence which is a construction produced by its participants and observers can only be described by using the logic of those very people. The ACC reform can only be an image of that reform.

The 'active county council' idea

In 1983, the Bohus county council presented a detailed description of its operating philosophy. In the 1984 action plan the ACC idea was formulated as follows:

> The Bohus county spirit will help us to make efficient operations even better; to give the people living under the jurisdiction of this county council even more thorough and personal health and medical care and service; and to give the staff more professional pride, job satisfaction and personal responsibility.

The Bohus county spirit was described as the 'putty holding the organization together', establishing basic attitudes and values. It provided an attitude to working for change and a platform for the work itself. In some interviews, the Bohus county spirit was referred to as a tangible corporate culture. The respondents and the programme documentation provided the following comprehensive definition of that spirit:

> The Bohus county spirit represents a consenting climate – a working environment where we think of one another as adults, and create space to grow and develop in.

- We shall work to strengthen group commitment.
- We shall feel that 'We are the Bohus county council'.
- We stand united for good work, and we represent successful activities.
- We shall be open – as an organization and in relation to one another.
- We shall learn to see the potential of our work and of our contact with one another.

Another way of describing the Bohus county spirit was to compare working methods of the past with those of the present. In the interviews, it was emphasized that the consenting climate referred to administrative errors, but not to errors in medical treatment.

'Past'	'Present'
• wait for orders	• test, experiment, suggest
• cover oneself against errors	• act – take risks
• punish whoever was responsible	• reward whoever takes responsibility
• mind your own business	• feel involved
• protect territory	• see the whole
• get detailed information	• share objectives.

It takes several years to develop a new working climate. The process is facilitated if there are sufficient resources to provide incentives. One of the factors motivating the implementation of ACC was the need for cutbacks. For this reason, management was not able to make extra resources available to facilitate working towards change. It is difficult to see how far down into the organization the spirit of Bohus county reached. Some comments indicate that it was mainly a change at management level, among the various management strata.

The rules of the game and the distribution of roles and leadership were approached through the watchword: 'success through confidence'. Work in the Bohus county council had been subject to a strict distribution of roles. The division of politicians versus officials was one of control and management: 'The politicians control operations and the officials manage them'. The Bohus council standing committee of leading politicians was therefore referred to as the Board, while the administrative management, carried out by the local officials, was referred to as the council management. The Chairman phrased it in the following way:

As a politician I say:
I know what needs to be done.
You know how to get it done.
We'll do it together.

It became evident from the interviews that this role distribution was sometimes a difficult one for the politicians, particularly the local politicians, who ran the risk of falling into executive roles. Politicians in a more central position found it easier to distinguish between their roles. Politicians considered themselves subject to two sets of demands, which were also the 'only' demands they felt could be made on a politician: 'from the people – that the politician represent them; and from the organization – that the politician can tell them what the people want'. The demands the politicians placed on the officials were summarized in 1983 by the new Chairman of the Board, and in the 1984 action plan. The Chairman created the headline: 'A positive obligation to provide information'.

The text read:

1 Civil servants are obliged to facilitate the work of the politicians in collecting the information on which they base their decisions.
2 Civil servants are obliged to work positively for the presentation of sufficient information on which to base decisions . . . .
3 Civil servants are obliged to follow changes attentively, even if they are beyond the direct scope of their job assignments, and to notify the politicians when they consider that the justification for their job assignments has been substantially altered.
4 Civil servants are obliged to keep the politicians informed of all eventualities, and this obligation increases in pace with seniority and specialization of the work. This obligation to keep the politicians informed of all eventualities is defined as follows: if, in conjunction with or subsequent to a decision, information comes up which substantially affects the problem, the alternatives for action or the consequences, the civil servant is to inform the politicians and present amendment proposals.
5 Civil servants are obliged to inform the politicians if it proves impossible to effect a decision at the right place, at the right time or using the right method. This information is to be given in sufficient time for the politicians to make supplementary decisions without having to change the target place, time and method.

The presentation of the Chairman's action plan focused on decision-making and the collection of information on which to base decisions. He described decision-making as the most important task of the politician. He also said, and illustrated (see figure 9.1): 'Decisions should be made as late as possible, and so as not to harm operations. Seen in time, planning should be three steps ahead, information should be two steps ahead, and decisions one step ahead.' This distribution of roles increased the responsibility of the officials, making the politicians the experts on politics. It meant that patients and the general public could still place demands on politicians with regard to administrative and medical issues, but that the role of the politicians in accordance with this new distribution was to mediate contacts and initiate changes through improved distribution of resources.

In these documents, co-operation between the top officials and the trade union was characterized by: a natural conflict of interests, mutual respect, an open attitude towards values and information, dialogue, and an attitude in which the trade unions were considered an asset. In 1983, the personnel delegation adopted a decision to draw up a policy for leadership. This policy included a statement of what it meant to have a

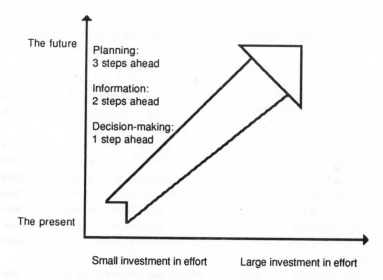

Figure 9.1 Planning and decision-making as described by the Chairman of the ACC Board

management position at the Bohus county council, what the council required of its executives, and what demands this implied for the employers.

In Sweden, definitions of leadership changed radically on two occasions over the last ten or fifteen years, from unilaterally patriarchal decision-making, via an ostensibly democratic leadership style in which the manager often turned things vaguely over to his colleagues to manage on their own, to today's definition. Today an individual in a management position has both the right and the obligation to make demands, but is also expected to delegate responsibility and discretion to his colleagues.

A management position at the county council means:

- ensuring that the work at your unit is done in accordance with previously set objectives
- seeing to it that the staff of your unit have a good working environment. This is defined as . . .
- ensuring that the staff of your unit have the opportunity to develop and advance . . .

- seeing to it that the head of the unit also develops, in order to be able to face and deal with change . . . .

The policy described leadership as seeing the whole picture and sharing it with the staff. The county council expected its executives to be holistic in their views and their leadership style, which meant:

- the ability to lead, develop and represent their operations
- the ability to communicate
- the ability to involve and enthuse their colleagues so that they take responsibility and feel free to act
- expertise in their own area of specialization . . .

This leadership policy marked the importance of the management's drawing up clearly defined fields of responsibility and authority. It was important that the management should be told the results of their work, and given the opportunity to discuss these results with their immediate superiors. The policy also required that sufficient resources be allocated for the tasks assigned, and for personal development for each executive.

At the same time as ACC was being implemented, work with a co-determination agreement was in progress, and was affected by the ACC reform. The co-determination agreement became an instrument in the work for change. Leadership, for example, which was a central concept in ACC, was incorporated into the co-determination agreement (see quotation below). The central co-determination agreement was signed in 1985. A few years later, local agreements had been adopted at every individual administrative unit. These agreements became part of the image of the Bohus county council.

> We need capable, involved executives who can lead our work, enthuse and motivate their colleagues, and carry through changes in work organization.

> The county council requires that its executives:

> - be able to envisage the work of the county council as a whole, and to realize the role of their own unit in that whole
> - be able to lead/develop and represent their unit and its activities
> - be able to communicate; their behaviour and their language must be adapted to every occasion so that their information is accessible and comprehensible
> - be able to involve and enthuse their colleagues, stimulate them to take responsibility, and encourage them to take action both in their everyday work and in the process towards change
> - have expertise in their own area of specialization except in fields in

which general knowledge and leadership ability are decisive (such as at directors' level).

The 'active county council' process

In the 1984 action plan for the ACC reform, the process was divided into four steps. Step one covered the period from 1983 until July 1985, and was to lead to a holistic view, attitude change and reinforced leadership functions. Step two ran into early 1984, and was to focus on concrete, local measures. In step three, from March 1984 until October 1985, marketing and image definition were to be addressed. Step four, which covered the rest of 1985, was intended to zoom in on external demands. During this period, demands from the outside world were to be encouraged. In reality, the process was extended, and the steps overlapped.

The first step in the ACC process was referred to as 'rallying the forces', and began in January 1983, when the new political leadership of the Bohus county council took over. The new Chairman of the Board was one of the Conservative members of the council. The results of the 1982 election were that the council distribution was 18 seats for the Conservatives, 7 for the Liberals, 11 for the Centre party, 32 for the Social Democrats and 3 for the Communist party. The leading politician of the county council thus only had the immediate backing of 18 of the 71 council seats, and in reality his position was even weaker. The Conservative party was considered extremist when it came to the council's main activities: health and medical care. Even if the Conservative party could get the Centre and Liberal parties to vote with them, a majority opinion in the county council often did not have much influence; unless the professionals (the physicians and nurses) supported a decision, it did not have much effect.

The new Chairman met all the executives and stated his view of the roles of the politicians and officials, as well as describing his expectations of them, on 2 February. The Chief Information Officer then began collecting information on the basis of which decisions could be made, in the light of current problems and this statement. On 17 February 1983, the Board was informed of the idea of the ACC reform. Less than a month later, the executive management was also informed.

An ACC group was established in mid-March, appointed by the Chairman and the Chief Information Officer. They included the people they considered important in reinforcing the development of ideas, thoughts and work. During the spring and early summer of 1983, the members of the ACC group presented their ideas to the administrative management and the trade unions. The Chairman presented these ideas to the leading politicians, who took them up with their respective party groups. During the same period, the ACC reform met with trade union resistance, when the blue-collar union stated that they reacted to the issues involved as being closely related to the policies of the Conservative party. They also stated that, in their opinion, the council employees were already active.

In June 1983, the assembly of the county council and the press were informed about the ACC reform, its ideas and proposals, but no decision was adopted. During the summer, the administrative management informed their colleagues. A flyer was written to present the basic information to all employees. In September, the Board adopted a unanimous decision to support ACC, and a corresponding decision was adopted by the county council assembly in November.

On 28 September 1983 an 'Active County Council' day was held, with the participation of politicians, the trade unions, representatives of county council operations, and the press. Each administrative unit was instructed to draw up an action plan. This represented the official inauguration of the ACC reform.

During the autumn of 1983, each administrative unit worked with the measures they had decided to adopt in accordance with their action plan. Work to bring about a change of attitude was carried out parallel with the local work of the administrative units. This work included 'service courses', leadership training, information about the ACC reform, and discussions on services and attitudes. Beginning in October 1983 and over roughly one year, all council employees were offered a two-day service course, arranged by 'Time Manager, Inc.'. The blue-collar union took a strong stand against these courses, and discouraged their members from participating. Participation was, nonetheless, widespread.

During 1983 a new top manager, the County Council Director, was appointed. The job specification was drawn up with ACC in mind. The ACC reform required more than just acceptance and the absence of opposition: it was necessary to have members in the organization who promoted and spread the reform. Many of the interviewees pointed out executive recruitment and management training as having played an important role. The County Council Director, the Head of Personnel and the Head of Finance were all examples of executive managers recruited to their positions because they were willing to espouse the idea of the ACC reform.

The new Director of the County Council presented an action plan to structure and consolidate ACC at the first group meeting for the executive management in early 1984. During the spring of 1984, he, the Chairman of the Standing Committee on Administration, and the Chief Information Officer visited all executive managers to discuss the action plan. A popularized version was also published in the personnel bulletin, where ACC received considerable coverage.

During 1984, a 'Corporate Leadership Group' was established. In 1986, this group was expanded, and its name changed to 'the County Council Leadership Group'. In 1984, the concept of ACC was toned down, and the reform renamed 'the Bohus spirit', to indicate the central importance of this spirit. Some of the respondents also claimed that this showed the ability of the County Council Director to deal with conflict. The name change meant that the support of previously hesitant parties was enlisted. Later, both names were used interchangeably to describe the reform.

A campaign, supported by the Social Democrats, helped reverse the attitude of the blue-collar union. Several of the interviewees indicated that the positive attitude of trade union members contributed to the upswing for ACC.

The local action plans were drawn up for the ACC day in September 1983. Local implementation of these plans comprised step two in the ACC process which was also characterized, according to some of the respondents, by general organization of the project work.

Step three was in progress when our study of the Bohus county council was carried out. This step was referred to as 'profiling and marketing', and the relevant measures included an open house showing the Bohus county council and some of its activities, and an ACC day in 1985. The change of name was considered an important measure with regard to identity development. A graphics programme was also closely associated with the name change. In 1985 the Board adopted a decision with regard to the graphic profile and identity of the county council. Graphic profile is defined as 'the model according to which all the forms, advertisements, printed matter, signs, etc. are drawn up with regard to typeface, design, colour, and so forth'. This was justified in a written communication from the county council offices as follows:

> The logotype . . . is to be a signal by which the county council is readily identifiable, giving us a unified outward front, and working as a co-ordinating link between different operations. The new graphic profile is one aspect of marketing the 'new' council, and symbolizes the spirit of openness, accessibility and caring for which we strive.

> In order to make the county council more outwardly distinct, and to give its profile greater impact, the names of the various units should also be consistent. Today, for example, there are no guidelines for naming neighbourhood health centres, or even for defining what they actually are. The names of many other units are awkward and unclear.

Although the name change appears to have had the undivided support of the organization members, there was some hesitance with regard to the graphics programme, which some people considered an unnecessary expense in a tight economic climate.

Making the changes visible was promoted as an important aspect of marketing. According to the respondents, the Bohus county council was making an effort to be visible in the public debate. The county council sent delegates to conferences and received study delegations. Representatives of most of the other councils had visited the Bohus council, and the council had actively reported on its reforms in many other counties and municipalities.

According to several of the respondents, spreading the message about the success of the reforms to others outside the Bohus council was instrumental in obtaining internal acceptance. External interest made the council executives feel that they had joined a winning team, and that supporting it would help in seeking advancement within the council. Interviewees stated that it was actually just a matter of saying you supported the reform, and you could do as you liked. People were willing to listen to the executives from the Bohus council describe their successful reform work, as long as they described it as associated with the ACC reform, and the structure of the reform made this easy to do. The Bohus county council became a winning organization, according to the leading politicians.

The exchange of ideas and experience, the reform work, and future developments were also presented and discussed at internal fairs and planning days, the first of which was held in 1984 (the first 'Experience Day'). There, enthusiasts and reformers from the Bohus county council presented and exhibited their projects and their reform work. The 1987 internal fair encouraged a couple of thousand employees to attend seminars and view their colleagues' exhibitions.

The effects of 'active county council'

When the respondents described the effects of ACC they mentioned objectives, service and attitudes, investments in personnel policy, executive training, restructuring of geriatric care, psychiatry and care of the mentally disabled, evaluation and control systems, what we have called the 'rules of the game' and roles and, finally, the flow of patients. Working with objectives was a central aspect of the change process at the Bohus council. The respondents described ACC as a way of getting started with the description of objectives necessary to instil management by objectives. With a few exceptions the work with objectives was still at an early stage at the time of our study.

The respondents considered service and attitudes towards patients a typical area in which quality work could be done. They mentioned a number of improvements that had been carried out, but were not sure whether these were really related to ACC. Many of the changes at the Bohus county council were related to personnel policy. For example, a twenty-five-week training course had been initiated as a paid, intensive course for nurses' aides who wanted to become assistant nurses. The 'Nursing Project' aimed to develop nursing norms to apply throughout the county council. 'Invisible Contracts' was a survey of the working atmosphere at the Bohus council. The 'thinking' groups reviewed the personnel policy programme. In a project on absenteeism, an effort was made to explain variations in absenteeism among units.

Work in the Bohus council was carried out via its leaders. The principles underlying the management training course correspond to the ideas behind ACC. According to several of the respondents, the programme had used methods which were quite upsetting to managers, in order to gain their support for ACC. These critical respondents, a minority of the interviewees, felt that they had been exposed to a kind of propaganda. Some of them mentioned the names of people at management level who had not been prepared to change, and who had thus not been able to remain employed at management level in the active county council.

The restructuring of geriatric care, psychiatry and care of the mentally disabled was seen to be associated with ACC to different extents by different respondents. The examples studied included the merging of management for social services and primary health care, the closing down of an old mental hospital, and the development of a democratic system for care of the mentally disabled.

The area of evaluation and control systems included projects for changes of various sizes and types. 'Project 90' was a project aiming at making future health care available on terms set by the inhabitants, and at better control of the production of health-care services and the expenses for medical care. It was a far-sighted project, and in many ways ran parallel with and extended the ACC reform. Links in the county council decentralization process included cost site and unit budgeting. A model was also drawn up for the distribution of resources in county medical care and primary care in order to improve the distribution of resources in a decentralized organization controlled by a budget function.

The work relating to rules of the game and roles clarified the lines of demarcation relating to decentralization of authority. Free patient flow meant that the inhabitants of the area covered by the Bohus county council and an adjacent county could go to the hospital of their choice, even if it were across the county border.

THE ROAD TO SUCCESS

ACC was judged a success by the reformers, the reformees and outside observers (other county councils and the press). Below, we describe some of the main aspects of this reform which contributed to its success.

The idea was difficult to pinpoint

The ACC reform was an idea, and one which was difficult to pinpoint. Different people described the idea differently, and even individual descriptions often contained contradictory information. The complexity of the ACC idea is surprising, in that it clearly contradicts the recipe for success cited in the management literature, and which usually requires a simple goal, preferably one which can be quantified.

The ACC idea was both new and old. The respondents who described the history of the Bohus county council divided it into three phases, the most recent of which was the one marked by the ACC idea. This was a time of major change for the council, and the very focus on change was what was new. During the previous phase, the policy had been marked by caution and stability, but there had been major changes prior to ACC as well.

The respondents were careful to indicate that not everything which had been done since the ACC concept was coined was new and noteworthy, that things were simply more clearly formulated and structured than in the past. However, they also thought there was a great deal that was new. The expansion and broadening of county council operations, for example, had been completed when ACC was initiated. Previous ideas in the Bohus county council had neither been presented nor sold as intensively as ACC. This way of working with an idea was something new.

The ACC idea was both ambiguous and clearly defined. One feature of the idea was to provide clarity. It was the intention of the leadership to be clear on a number of issues. At the same time, the ACC idea was definitely vague and abstract. The idea did not stipulate much as to what should be done or how. Instead, it dealt with prerequisites, attitudes, opinions, platforms, etc.

The ACC idea mainly affected the leaders, but it also mainly affected the employees. ACC was intended to work via the management, and management training was an important component. The basic description of this training programme corresponds to the ACC idea. The relationship between politicians and the top officials was also dealt with. At the same time, the idea was related to all employees, whose loyalty was considered the source of quality. The idea concerned their professional pride, job satisfaction and personal responsibility.

The ACC idea focused primarily on action and also on decision-making. It was described by the respondents as highly action-orientated, not allowing analyses and investigations to delay action. Local initiatives and an entrepreneurial spirit were encouraged, and making mistakes was permitted. At the same time, the role of the politicians was defined as decision-making. The politicians were in control via their decisions, which were to follow the plans.

The aim of the ACC idea was local adaptation and centrally controlled identity. The ACC idea encouraged the taking of local responsibility. People were encouraged to satisfy the needs of their own patients, to take risks and not feel they had to ask first. At the same time, the spirit of togetherness was strong, and shared norms were part of the ACC reform. A shared identity was important, and the demands made on the officials were tightened up.

The idea was open

In organizations, as in society, there is often competition between different ways of describing reality. In any given situation, the group whose description gains general acceptance has power. As soon as we perceive a situation in a certain way, we perceive certain problems. As soon as we have perceived the problems, a set of solutions appears.

It was surprising that ACC was such an open idea. No one seems to have owned the ACC idea. The different actors were able to endow it with the attributes of their choice. A number of different, somewhat contradictory elements were associated with the ACC idea, and even the associated ideas were permitted different interpretations.

In one isolated case, an unacceptable interpretation of the ACC idea was made. One of the trade unions interpreted it in a way which posed a threat to its survival. They associated the ACC idea solely with the Chairman of the Board, and thus with the Conservative party. This posed a threat to the entire idea: ACC was not to be seen as a Conservative manipulation of the health and medical care staff. On the other hand, the periodic jokes made about ACC by people within the organization were not considered a problem.

The reform changed with time

The description of the process behind ACC might have been expected to be a description of an implementation process. In that case, the picture of the ACC process would have reflected a process with the aid of which the leaders 'forced' the organization to carry out its plans. But the ACC reform was not a decision, and the process was not an implementation process.

Much of the process behind ACC dealt with the reform itself, i.e. the decisions that were made were about the reform, rather than its effects. The name of the reform was changed, as was its working organization. To some extent, the process was one of selling the reform, although the issue was not one of convincing in order to control. For example, the ACC idea was not made more concrete when it was presented throughout the organization. Instead, the sales pitch was aimed at making as many people as possible accept the reform in order to keep it alive.

The threats to the ACC reform were not directly dealt with in the process. Despite this, they affected that process. Many of the tactical considerations of the reformers in terms of presentations and the appointment of group members could be understood in the light of the perceived threats. The way in which the ACC reform was presented was affected by the risk that it would turn out to be Conservative politics. Changing the name and the management group of the reform were examples of measures associated with the threat to the reform.

Everything good was 'active county council'

The respondents devoted a great deal of the interview time to describing the effects of the reform. One question that arises is how far the stated effects actually were due to the ACC reform. To examine the issue, we must distinguish between two definitions of 'effect'. In research, it is common to define an effect as the consequence of something. Every effect should be attributable to at least one action, event, idea or the like, which predated it. This special type of effect is henceforth referred to as 'consequence'. Of course, 'effect' as used in everyday speech does not necessarily correspond to this definition.

In the following analysis, the question is how far the stated effects were consequences of ACC. However, it is not simple to analyse the association between ACC and its effects. Many of the respondents grew defensive when they were asked to concretize the controlling effects of the ACC idea. They were eager to state that ACC was an important factor, and that it had affected their own behaviour and that of other members of the organization. But they found it difficult to describe exactly how it had affected them. Despite these difficulties, we attempt to discuss the association between the idea and the stated effects, based primarily on the statements of the respondents.

We use a simple model to determine how far the effects of ACC had anything to do with the ACC process and the ACC idea. In table 9.1 the temporal correlations are headed 'in the air', 'during', and 'in the future'.

'In the air' designates an assessment of whether the same type of change

Table 9.1 Association between the idea and the process of ACC and its stated effects

Effects listed	In the air?	During?	In the future?
1 Work with objectives/ management by objectives	yes	yes	in progress
2 Service and attitudes	yes	previously	
3 Investments in personnel policy			
– 25-week course	?	yes?	
– nursing teams	yes	yes	pilot
– project on nursing norms			an idea in itself
– invisible contracts			evaluation
– thinking groups	?	yes	in progress
– absenteeism project			evaluation
4 Executive training	yes	yes	
5 Restructuring of			
– geriatric care	yes	previously	
– psychiatric care	yes	previously	
– care of the mentally disabled	yes	previously	
6 Follow-up and control systems			
– Project 90			an idea in itself
– cost site budgeting	?	yes	
– unit budgeting	?	yes	
– model for resource distribution			an idea in itself
7 Rules of the game and roles			
8 Free patient flow	yes	previously	

was also being carried out by other county councils at around the same time. If a change was in the air, then the probability decreases that it was a consequence of ACC. Also, other ideas seem to have had the same effect, but this is sometimes difficult to document on the basis of our data.

Under the heading 'During' we assess whether changes, described as effects, were initiated once the ACC process had begun or earlier. If the effect could be seen before the ACC process had begun, it was not a consequence of ACC.

'In the future' distinguishes whether the effects had already occurred when the interviews were made. If they were going to occur in the future, they were not yet a consequence either of the process or the idea of ACC.

The effects which could not be expected to occur as concrete changes are also noted here: some of the stated effects were ideas, others were new operational descriptions such as evaluations, etc.

The ACC idea was exactly that – an idea. It would therefore have been absurd to consider making a traditional implementation study of the ACC reform. It might have been possible to study the spread of the idea, but not whether or not the idea had been carried out. Basically, the ACC idea was expressed in terms which could not explicitly be carried out. The ACC process basically dealt with the survival of the reform. It was not an implementation process in which future effects were dealt with.

Table 9.1 above is a rough categorization of descriptions, in some cases based on insufficient data. Still, it indicates the general trend. The majority of the effects were independent of the ACC process or the idea. They would probably have occurred even if the Bohus county council had not been active. It is therefore difficult to assert that the stated effects of ACC were a consequence of the ACC reform. Instead, they must be seen as elements of a description of ACC. The effects were ACC in the same way as the ideas were 'Active County Council'.

Yet the reform's effects were decisive to its success. The ACC effects were open, in the same way as the idea was. A large number of phenomena considered positive could be reported as effects of ACC. This was supported by the fact that the respondents did not think that what they called the effects of ACC had to be what we have called consequences.

THE DESIRE FOR CONTROL: AN OBSTACLE TO SUCCESS

The idea of reform involves control and the desire for control can be assumed to motivate many reforms. Reformers often see themselves as agents of change, and wish to change the specific structures that apply to others. The reform idea expresses control in a narrow sense of the term; the reform is the means for the practical realization of reformers' ends.

It is often asserted that control requires a clear, simple idea. The idea or objective must be formulated by those in control and communicated throughout the organization. Those in control must own the idea, sell it, and protect it from misinterpretation. This means that a reform established in order to exercise control in the narrow sense must be different in various respects from the ACC reform.

A reform established to exercise control cannot be based on an open idea which is difficult to pinpoint. A reform established to exercise control cannot change with time, and it certainly cannot be changed by people other than those in control.

The success of a reform established to exercise control is determined by its measurable effects. But a reform established to exercise control can be expected to attract opposition. Competing interpretations of the idea behind the reform will conflict. If the environment changes, or conditions are not as they were meant to be, the reform may have to be adapted, and it may be difficult to gain acceptance for this. Problems of implementation make it easy to point out the absence of anticipated effects. Lack of success in a reform meant to control often results in its not surviving. Before the effects can be achieved, the reform is categorized as a failure.

In order to achieve success, then, the reformers may have to abandon their ambitions to be in control, as it is these very ambitions which prevent the reform from being formulated so as to be successful. In other words, it is difficult to control using a reform intended to control.

The leading reformer at the Bohus county council was in a weak political position. Moreover, he lacked the clear support of the professionals in health and medical care. In order for his reform to be accepted and successful, he had to satisfy the interests of all the other parties with regard to its idea and its rhetoric. It was also important that the reform did not offend the professionals. This openness also applied to the effects of the reform. Everything good was permitted to be an effect of ACC. It was possible for people to support the reform while describing it in different ways, and they attributed different effects to it. The reform was kept at a general level, and people were allowed to incorporate their personal hobby-horses into it. The fact that the Chief Information Officer at the county council was positive towards ACC and worked on describing the idea and its effects undoubtedly had some impact on the success of the reform. In order to keep the idea from gaining political dimensions, no concrete proposals were attached to it. Describing or concretizing the idea of ACC in detail could have threatened the reform. If the list of effects had been finalized, this might also have posed the same kind of danger to the reform.

Success allows some influence

The description given above may give the impression that the ACC reform was only popular in the organization and served as a model for other county councils. The reformers still appear to have failed, if they are supposed to have had any real desire for control. The reform appears to have resulted in a great deal of success but no control.

The respondents unilaterally asserted, however, that the ACC reform was not only successful but had also affected operations at the county council, although in a way that was difficult to describe in detail. One partial explanation is that the respondents defended the reform. Another explanation may be found in the difference between control and influence.

Control takes place in relation to a given objective, while influence simply guides things in an approximate direction. 'Influence', as defined here, means a limited type of control, or control in which precision is not required.

In the ACC reform, the leaders sacrificed their desire to exercise control. This made success possible, but it also left an opportunity to influence operations. The characteristics of the ACC reform were prerequisites for its success. But these characteristics did not entirely exclude the possibility of influencing the operations of the county council.

The Chairman could not count on many of his proposals being passed, nor were all of those which were passed implemented. Aware of this, he let the ACC balloon float freely. It became a focus, and an indicator of direction: this was his only hope for influencing the operations of the council. It is often maintained that large organizations, particularly if they are politically led, are difficult to control. The Chairman abandoned his ambitions to exercise control in order to be able, instead, to influence the general direction with the aid of a successful reform.

Although the ACC reform was ambiguous and open to interpretation, its interpretation was not entirely open. This provided the basis from which it could influence operations. For example, when there is a great deal of permissiveness, certain types of behaviour are also prohibited. When people are given freedom and responsibility, they are also expected to make use of it. Passivity, imitation, and strict adherence to bureaucratic regulations become behaviour which is no longer allowed. When people are allowed to try things and fail, they are expected to try. When change becomes the norm, it is difficult to use 'the done thing' in the operation to defend the prevailing order.

Chapter 10 goes on to discuss the effects of reforms the reformers tend not to talk about.

10 The implicit effects of reform*

* This chapter was contributed by Barbara Czarniawska-Joerges.

'Would you tell me, please, which way I ought to go from here?'
'That depends a good deal on where you want to get to,' said the Cat.
'I don't much care where –,' said Alice.
'then it does not matter which way you go,' said the Cat.
' – so long as I get *somewhere*,' Alice added as an explanation.
'Oh, you're sure to do that,' said the Cat, 'if only you walk long enough.'
(Carroll 1907)

This conversation, between Alice and the Cheshire Cat, could also have been a conversation between a consultant and a municipal politician or civil servant. Change begins when somebody has the idea that it would be good to change something. It is not necessary to spot a particular problem: every organization has plenty of unsolved problems. The will to change might originate in an ideology or, alternatively, may lead straight to decisions and plans for a change, with an ideology or an appropriate label coming later to make it possible to see the change in a context and interpret it. Then comes action: there is a great deal of talk, discussion and negotiation, decisions are made and amended, there are moves and counter-moves. In the midst of the inevitable confusion someone calls for an evaluation. Sooner or later some external forces are brought in (to give assistance or consultation, or to pose resistance), and the reform goes public. Now that the reform has become difficult to stop, some people abandon their resistance and begin trying to discover what can be gained from it. They may find that it can be redirected solve some problems, even ones at which it was not originally aimed. The power structure becomes visible, and can therefore be slightly reshuffled. With a little bit of luck everyone (or many people) may achieve a sense of renewal, be given new hope. If this is unsuccessful, chaos and frustration follow, and there is a rapid return to old forms and processes.

This picture of reforms is taken from a study of municipal reforms in local governments which have restructured into submunicipal committees.

DECENTRALIZATION

In the late 1960s and early 1970s, the key words in Swedish public administration included 'centralization' and 'economies of scale'. In one comprehensive reform, small municipalities were merged into large units.

The aim of the reforms of the 1960s and 1970s was to increase the economic efficiency of operations through concentration of resources. Critical voices pointed out that democracy was at risk. This criticism gave birth to new reforms. (Note, however, that associating current reforms with previous reforms is just one of many possible interpretations.)

At any rate, the end of the 1970s and the early 1980s brought a wave of pilot projects to the municipalities. Most of these focused on some kind of decentralization of political and administrative activities. This was conceivably the same wave which washed over most of private industry which, in line with the American model, also decided to decentralize at any price.

Soon there was also a legal framework to support these experiments. In 1977 the government called a meeting of the committee for local democracy, and in March 1979, the first draft bill on the subject was submitted to the Riksdag. But the municipality of Örebro had begun its own pilot project as early as 1977. Eskilstuna and Umeå went the same route in 1979. All three set up experiments with submunicipal committees, and these pilot projects attracted a great deal of attention when the Local Bodies Act gained legal force on 1 January 1980.

The initial pilot projects were imitated, and enthusiasm grew. The Stockholm morning newspaper *Dagens Nyheter* reported on 22 April 1985 that nineteen municipalities had introduced submunicipal committees, nearly the same number were just beginning to try them, and a further thirty municipalities were considering what organizational form to choose. This was the point in time at which our project began (Czarniawska-Joerges 1987).

In the autumn of 1985, we began an empirical study of the submunicipal committee reform. We have examined four municipalities, three of which were involved in the reform to varying extents and one which was not interested. We have also collected second-hand information from a fifth municipality. We have tried to understand why the municipalities introduced submunicipal committees or did not do so, and what the reform meant to those who took part in it. We have tried to achieve our objective by getting a picture of what the actors themselves thought of the reform. Selection, data collection and analysis were carried out in accordance with a 'grounded theory' approach (Glaser and Strauss 1974), a theory developed on the basis of the collected data. Our techniques were the semi-structured interview, observation, analysis of documentation and interpretation of newspaper articles.

We approached the municipalities with a picture of organizational change as it is presented in textbooks. This did not help us in our understanding of what was happening in the municipalities. We gradually came up with our own interpretation of the processes we had observed through the eyes of the actors. Below, we describe four of the main aspects of this interpretation: the power shift which takes place in a time of change; efforts to legitimize; education and training; and the effects of the reform on the well-being of the people involved.

THE POWER SHIFT

The reform revealed structures which are invisible in everyday life. We found the two worlds we have discussed in many chapters above in all the municipalities as well: the world of ideas or representations and the practical world.

The national politicians, who live in the world of representations, are not aware of any reality other than these idealized representations. They become the spokesmen of the most normative, but even when they describe things they can paint pictures of things which could exist.

We asked one politician to tell us about the results of the reform. 'I'll give you a very good example,' he said. 'The inhabitants of one sub-municipality did not want their sports field fenced in. So they went to the submunicipal committee and told them they wanted it open to all and not fenced in, and they got their way. In the past such decisions would have had to be made for the municipality as a whole, which was time and energy-consuming.' 'Fantastic,' we said, 'where was this?' He replied: 'It hasn't happened yet, but it could happen any time!'

The practical world is the world in which services are produced, in which actual problems arise, and real money is spent. The inhabitants of this world are the local civil servants, whose main assignment is to act. From their point of view, the world of representation is similar to television: you can be deeply affected by what you see there, but most of the time you keep it turned off because you have too much else to do.

There is a two-dimensional gap between the two worlds. One of the dimensions is *content*: ideas fill up the one world, actions fill up the other. Although the practical world also contains ideas, and the world of representations contains actions, neither the actions nor the ideas are the same. The two worlds can never meet, as the other dimension is time: the world of representations is in the future, while the practical world is now. To a politician, tomorrow is today.

On the outskirts are the people who have a better view of the second world: the local politicians, who are required to look at what is going on under their jurisdiction, at least occasionally, and the central civil servants, who have to consider the world of representations.

Everyone seems accustomed to this situation. It is there owing to the fact that a municipality is an organization which has to combine different spheres. But a reform makes the two worlds and the gap between them far more visible. Changes reveal hidden structures.

And where is the power? The reform was presented as decentralization, and this made it natural for us to examine what happened to power during the period of change.

Early in the reform period, it was said that top career civil servants in the hierarchy were gaining more power than was permissible under the democratic imperative, i.e. that power was too much concentrated in the hands of the central i.e. municipal public administration. The reform, then, was meant to reduce the power of central civil servants and politicians, and give more power, primarily to local (i.e. submunicipal) politicians and secondarily to local civil servants.

The word 'power' seldom occurred in our interviews. 'Power', as is generally the case (cf. McClelland 1907; Czarniawska-Joerges 1988d), was considered a negatively charged word. No-one talks about power if he or she can avoid it. But if it becomes necessary to discuss power, it is couched in terms which make it sound like a natural phenomenon, something which just goes on growing although no-one wants it, a dynamic substance not entirely subject to control – something like mould or dust.

The members of organizations try to influence one another. This is an entirely natural aspect of all collective action. In order to achieve shared goals, control and co-ordination, etc. become necessary. The result is that certain groups (rather than individuals) exercise greater influence than others. This may be referred to as 'power', and is natural but not positive.

According to the democratic imperative, some people represent the interests of others. They must see to it that the interests of their principals are protected, and transformed into action. But if influence accumulates in places where it does not belong, such as in the public administration, something is wrong. It begins to be referred to as power, and people say that power must be 'done away with', exactly as if it were mould or dust. This argument was asserted by our respondents.

> We also thought the power was really getting concentrated at the top in the municipalities, somehow, and of course this also made us critical of it, and we started thinking about what approach to use.
>
> (Central politician)

Did the central politicians actually want to give their influence away? Possibly, but we must recall that people work within routines. Politicians on government committees often forgot the main ideology of a reform in their daily work, acting in practice 'as if nothing had changed', even if they belonged to the party which had introduced the reform.

Moreover, they were not unaware that the local civil servants, who were also professionals, could easily begin controlling the local politicians. Many people expected central politicians and local civil servants ultimately to have more power than the local politicians.

> Sadly, politicians on a committee are often entirely in the hands of their civil servants. This means that they have neither the possibility nor the ability to go into things, bureaucracy being what it is, and question them. I mean, they often work as politicians on their free time. My advantage is that I am a full-time politician. In addition to which, as a member of the municipal council, I have some 'power', in inverted commas, a dirty word. But that power, in turn, means that I can question people about things. They don't generally dare to pull the wool over my eyes.
>
> (Central politician)

The local civil servants didn't think the problem was their own influence. They weren't the ones trying to hang onto their power – that was what the central civil servants were trying to do, at any price.

You might say that all three groups, the local politicians, the central politicians and the local civil servants, hoped to gain more influence. But they wanted more influence in order serve the citizens better. If there were personal gain to be had, no-one ever mentioned it.

Such attitudes are part of a deeply rooted culture in the Swedish public sector which permits no trace of cynicism. 'Of public benefit' is a value in the same category as 'democracy', and although to err is human, as is lack of information, malice aforethought is never suspected.

Similarly, coalitions between groups were inconceivable. They were constitutionally and culturally impossible. It made no difference what one group of representatives thought of another. No-one tried to take over or question anyone else's role. This explained how a situation in which three groups expected to win still did not give rise to power struggles, but instead led to the completion of the reform.

> I guess our civil servants are loyal, and so the fact that they are not absolutely enthralled with the division into submunicipal committees does not mean that they sabotage it at all. Rather, they do their jobs and make the best of the situation.
>
> (Central politician)

If power is like mould or dust, it cannot be shifted at will. It is not possible to 'give' or 'take' something that accumulates. But it is possible to distribute it and thus see to it that power does not accumulate in the wrong places. This also means that the results may surprise everyone, as was the case in several of the municipalities which were to be reformed. Quite out of the blue, the power began to accumulate in new places: the finance department, the administrative department . . . .

Was this accumulation of power in accordance or in conflict with the spirit of the reform? Those who thought that 'any decentralization requires a centralization' did not see the contradiction. These were usually national staff members, which comes as no surprise. But the course of events appeared to confuse people at the local level a mite.

At any rate, the central politicians learned, although not without some pain, that power cannot be 'redirected' according to plan. All anyone can do is to give it a nudge, with no guarantee as to the results.

LEGITIMATION

This study gives rise to two observations: first, that there were phenomena which might have posed obstacles to the reform, but did not do so; and, secondly, that the processes which were created by the reform did not appear to be new or specific to this particular reform. The latter observation appears to provide a good explanation of the former.

Not many opinions were universally shared, but one which was that submunicipal committees would be established. Everyone felt a strong sense of optimism as to the implementation of the reform, although there was clear hesitation about its effects. This was a bit surprising, since even the understanding of what the reform contained varied from person to person. Phenomena referred to as 'facts' appeared to be fairly relative: the actors were not agreed as to when the reform was begun, which individual or group had initiated it, how many submunicipal committees were going to be set up. And yet, if Murphy's law is that if something can go wrong it will, the law of municipal decentralization appeared to be worded: 'if something can succeed, it will'.

The most commonly held impression was that most of the actors were accustomed to reforms. No-one seemed surprised about what was happening, although no-one seemed to have a clear picture of why it was happening either. It was as if this were irrelevant, as if the reform were fated to be implemented.

There was a norm making organizational change a value unto itself. It also appeared as though, in order to play its role, a change had to have the characteristics of a reform, i.e. state in no uncertain terms what ill it was going to cure. No bottom-up organizational changes would be able to play that role.

And not trying to change these huge organizations all the time, make them into something you think is better, would be the worst thing that could happen. Though you might wish the pendulum didn't swing quite so far every time something happens . . . .

(Local civil servant)

The legitimacy of organizations lies in the congruence between organizational actions and the social values expressed in norms concerning organizational action (Dowling and Pfeffer 1975). Legitimation processes are, in turn, actions helping to prove or defend this kind of agreement (Richardson and Dowling 1986). Even the legitimation process itself always has to be in agreement with the prevailing definition of legitimacy. At the theoretical level, the question arises of whether symbolic legitimation is better suited to social norms than procedural legitimation (Richardson and Dowling 1986). The matter is simpler at the organizational level: some attempts at legitimation appear legitimate for some organizations but not for all.

What is an attempt at legitimation? It consists of making visible the fact that organizational actions correspond to relevant norms in society. To make it simple, political organizations reflect values in society, productive organizations manufacture products and profits, and administrative organizations must follow accepted rules and procedures (Brunsson 1986b). If an administrative organization begins to reflect values, loud protests issue from the politicians: the task of the administrator is to satisfy political will, not to dictate it. Today some administrations try to compete on the market with manufacturing organizations. As soon as they begin to run at a profit, everyone is upset. Public organizations are to apply procedures considered legitimate in the contemporary welfare state. But how are they supposed to show this?

The simplest way, in fact, is to use the recent invention of an 'open house'. Invite the general public in to see what you do. But that is not sufficient. Administrative organizations imitate some of the legitimacy efforts of others: they use contact with the mass media, annual reports and other methods when they can. In this way, they compete in the open market. One traditional means of legitimation in the public sector is the very act of *reforming*: showing that you are not only behaving correctly, but also that you are constantly improving.

Is reform a legitimate means of legitimation? The mass media tends to deny it: 'Reforms become symbolic actions, something to offer your inhabitants so that you do not have to make fundamental changes . . . ' (*Dagens Nyheter*, 22 April 1985). This statement can be interpreted as meaning: the newspaper denies that municipalities have the right to make symbolic attempts at legitimation. (Perhaps the media want to have the monopoly on symbolic action themselves?) Municipalities should devote themselves to procedural legitimation instead. On the other hand, it would be possible to assert that the mass media are the ones who are encouraging, even demanding, such symbolic legitimation. Municipalities are doing everything they can to fill the newspaper columns; it is lucky they have a little time left for their operations.

It is doubtful whether the journalist who made that comment would agree with our interpretation of it. Superficially, what the commentator is saying is that the symbolism no longer stands for anything but itself. Instead of demonstrating their actions, municipalities are demonstrating their attempts at legitimacy. Concrete actions vanish behind symbolic ones.

But is there really such a sharp line of demarcation between them? Anton (1967) discusses the same problem in relation to national expenditures, and concludes:

> Rationality derived Responsibility, Economy and Service are the principal symbols for which state actors compete and around which they organize their stylized behaviour. If the tangible outcome of such behaviour seldom corresponds to the symbols by which it is justified, nothing is lost, for it is not at all clear that tangible outcomes can be significantly influenced by anything done, or not done, by state actors. In this context, use of these symbols provides a net gain, for they reassure actors and their audiences that powerful figures are engaged in important activities, in a significant governmental context.
>
> (Anton 1967: 43)

The concrete and the symbolic are aspects of all actions, including political ones (Czarniawska-Joerges 1991). The mass media has no monopoly on the symbolic, nor do political organizations have a monopoly on politics. The material, the symbolic and the political recur in all actions in all organizations.

Another question is whether the content of actions are considered positive, desirable, etc., and by what person or people. With regard to reforms, symbolic actions have legitimatizing and educational functions. From a functional perspective, it then becomes possible to ask whether this is the least expensive or most suitable way of achieving these two aims. Would it not be better to allow legitimation to fend for itself and send people to 'charm schools' for their education? Municipalities don't think so.

EDUCATION AND IDEOLOGIES

March and Olsen (1983) studied public administration reforms in the United States, and concluded that reforms were a form of public education.

Similarly, it may be asserted that they are, perhaps primarily, a form of organizational education and training. Although the actors seldom discuss 'legitimation', they often refer to the education objectives of a reform.

> The idea is that when we introduce the submunicipal committees, they will have quite vaguely formulated aims and we will have a large measure of freedom. People are meant both to learn on their own and to be taught centrally . . . . This is not a change in the administration but a change in the point of view.
>
> (Central civil servant)

Thus ideologies are used as a link in an educational process.

An ideology is defined here as being a set of ideas describing how things are, how they should be, and how to achieve desired states (Czarniawska-Joerges 1988c). An ideology can be used to structure action, and to interpret ongoing actions. It is a shared structure, allowing co-ordinated, collective action (Brunsson 1982; Starbuck 1982). The co-ordination does not arise out of rules or a programme, but out of a shared way of thinking.

Although reforms are not always controlled by ideologies, they are always accompanied by ideologies. Studies of reforms in other countries (Argyriades 1965; Dente and Regonini 1980; Tolbert and Zucker 1983; March and Olsen 1983; DiTomaso 1985) have shown that there are at least three commonly recurring ideologies in the public sector: 'rationalization', 'power shift', and 'democratization'. Although the labels may vary slightly (Salamon 1981 calls them 'economy and effectivity', 'tactical advantage' and 'political effectivity'), the contents are virtually identical.

The submunicipal committee reform was marked by its interesting relationship between control and ideology. Ideologies may be both an ends of control (trying to affect things people believe in) and a means towards control (trying to affect things by introducing a new ideology). In the submunicipal committee reform, they served both functions. This made the reform dramatically different from previous ones, carried out in a typically 'bureaucratic' fashion, i.e. through directives and administrative decisions. Jönsson (1988), who refers to the reform of the 1970s as one 'gigantic rationalization', claims that since then a cultural revolution has taken place in Sweden. Recent events appear to confirm his theory: The Riksdag rejected the proposal of the Minister of Public Administration to introduce 'renewal programmes' in all municipalities. The result of this was that every municipality was free to decide whether and in what way to decentralize. This development is in good agreement with the assertion that adaptive learning will be the main model for action in the public administration (Olsen 1988a).

One of the sets of ideas used to control the submunicipal committee reform may be referred to as 'democracy through decentralization' (a variant of democratization; another familiar version is 'democracy through deregulation'). The ideology was formulated and applied at two levels: nationally (the Social Democratic Party and the government, particularly the Ministry of Public Administration) and at the local level (the municipalities).

The national level promoted its ideology by introducing it as a subject of public debate in the mass media, by initiating and studying research reports, and through internal information in the party. The Swedish Association of Local Authorities showed its support by organizing a seminar series in the city of Örebro on 'the model municipality' for all municipalities interested in the experiment. Foreign guests were invited to come to Örebro for a description of ongoing research on issues of decentralization.

As mentioned above, neither the Social Democratic Party nor the government 'ordered' the municipalities to try out submunicipal committees. What they did was more like transmitting a signal: 'We've got an idea here – are you interested?' Some of our respondents described 'riding the wave' or 'not missing the train', in the sense that right now the 'in' thing was submunicipal committees, 'free municipalities' and 'the municipality of the twenty-first century', and each municipality decided whether or not to go along for the ride.

Here is one local formulation of the ideology:

> Democracy is a question of our ability to be in on the decisions regarding the society we live in. Democracy is not given or once and for all: it has to be achieved anew by every generation. In municipalities, democratic principles can best be asserted in practice . . . the establishment of submunicipal committees facilitates contact between the voters and their elected representatives.

In comparison with charm schools (whose services were also enlisted) and management training courses, etc., reforms have one advantage: they are aimed at everyone who is involved in a given organization, and sometimes even at the observers of it. This total training programme can be more easily understood if we look back on the socialization process to which an individual entering an organization for the first time is subjected. He or she gradually learns to accept certain values and follow certain routines. The problem is that after some time both values and routines are taken for granted. This is good for routines, but nor for values. Reforms re-socialize, remind those involved of things they had forgotten in the monotony of everyday life: idealistic objectives, humanitarian values, the public good.

This also means that it is necessary to deal with deviators, both people and ideologies. In the submunicipal committee reform there was, for example, a competing ideology which maintained that the aim of the reform was not to increase democracy but to make financial cutbacks. The propaganda men behind the reform ('the holders of the ideology' according to Czarniawska-Joerges 1987: 74) energetically denied this interpretation:

> Faced with the current financial situation we could have come to a conclusion that concentration of resources was the important thing. This would of course provide just the opposite to an incentive to decentralize and distribute the resources to the municipalities. Very few municipalities are carrying out this decentralization process out of a conviction that it will make their bureaucracy less expensive . . . to decentralize.
>
> (Central civil servant)

But one really subversive ideology asserted that the decentralization process actually was a disguised return to the old type of municipalities. This allegation sounded particularly convincing owing to the fact that the first municipalities to attempt decentralization were the very ones which had resisted the municipal mergers most strongly. The submunicipal committees were often housed in the buildings where the old municipalities had had their offices. But this interpretation was denied in various ways, including sarcasm:

> More and more people are getting to experience how things used to be in the old municipalities, romanticizing. Well, things were a bit of a mess. There was no money to do anything with. But it was really idyllic in the old days.
>
> (Local civil servant)

How do you fight competing, subversive ideologies? How do you introduce new ideas? You create a relevant vocabulary – labels, metaphors and imagery – and you spread it around (Czarniawska-Joerges 1988a). When everyday language is permeated with the same words as public language, the course has been completed.

Reforms allow the opportunity for lessons in shared history, lectures on modernism and dreams of the future. The ideology of the submunicipal committee reform functioned as a pretext for an organizational debate on these three subjects. It also showed that the 'teachers' needed to learn just as much if not more than the 'pupils'. Civil servants took crash courses in municipal democracy, and politicians took crash courses in organizational change. What did they think of this?

REFORMS AS ROLLER-COASTERS

> There are people in organizations who are only happy during reform.
>
> (Local civil servant)

It has been pointed out that usually the same people spearheaded reforms, even consecutive and mutually opposed ones. Many people quite simply claimed that reforms were exciting, interesting, and brought pleasure to an otherwise dull life in an organization.

Not everyone enjoyed them, though. There were those who suffered during the reform, felt ill at ease and threatened. Some people at the central level were so firmly convinced of the ideology of reform that they decided to 'play missionary' at the local level where, when they called for assistance, they encountered a great deal of scepticism from below and indifference from above. Others discovered that there was no part for them to play. The managers at the national level were most hardly hit by the roller-coaster effects of the reform:

> Then I moved into a phase when I wondered whether there was actually any place for me at all in this type of organization, whether people like me were needed. And that has lasted for a couple of years now, though I'm starting to come out of it. It's been quite a serious thing, because I was both doubting myself in this context and thinking that if I left . . . . It's been an extremely frustrating experience.
>
> (Central civil servant)

The other strategy was deeply rooted in the culture of consensus which prefers compromise to conflict:

> Of course conflicts can arise at any point in a municipal organization . . . . But there is always a desire for agreement, which means you have to do the done thing here in Sweden – you compromise a bit.
>
> (Central civil servant)

Reforms are similar to roller-coasters: they make some people feel great and some people feel sick. But there is no denying that they are an important aspect of life in a municipality.

REFORMS AS SYMBOLIC ACCOMPLISHMENTS

This study and corroborating results from other studies reveal several important effects of reforms which are seldom mentioned in all the discussion of objectives and effects. These effects are primarily of a symbolic nature, but they may in turn have both material and political effects.

As Anton has put it: 'the consequences are real enough, but they are not the consequences we normally look for' (1967, p. 43). And we refrain from looking for them because they seem unimportant, if not actually deceptive. This can be attributed to our tendency to draw a sharp line of demarcation between 'the real' and 'the symbolic' (read: 'the unreal').

Reality is imagined as literal and objective, whereas symbols are seen as metaphoric and subjective. This distinction . . . clouds the awareness of an alternative view: that the realities to which symbols refer are also symbolic . . . human reality is experienced only with the mediation of symbols.

(Brown 1987: 118)

On the basis of this alternative perspective (referred to by Brown (1977) as 'symbolic realism') it is possible to gain new perspectives on the effects of reforms. Briefly, the effects may be described using the following claims:

Reforms reshuffle power: It may be difficult or impossible to redirect power precisely at will. But change reveals the power structures. This makes it easier, during a reform, to try to change these structures, and more difficult to keep the power intact. Organizational actors begin to discover the distribution of power and to talk about it, which is otherwise seldom the case in the everyday work situation.

Reforms re-legitimatize: When actions are initiated to show that organizations are constantly improving, the confidence which is a prerequisite of legitimate action is renewed.

Reforms educate: When people begin working in an organization they are educated, or rather re-socialized, with regard to the main norms, values and routines. The original message is gradually either lost or becomes obsolete. A reform is a way of retraining all the employees without sending them on a course. Ideologies are used as a means of education.

Reforms entertain and threaten: In addition to satisfying all the above-mentioned functions, reforms entertain certain actors and threaten others, and it is impossible to judge which is the more important. One suggestion is to deny the crude distinction between 'progressive' and 'conservative'. Everyone's role is important: the 'progressive' are important to renewal, the 'conservative' to the maintenance of tradition. A little more human respect would also be in order, even in terms of realization of the most noble ideals. This could be achieved through not being so quick to paste on labels: 'The ability to frustrate arbitrary intention . . . should not be confused with rigidity; nor should flexibility be confused with organizational effectiveness' (March 1981b: 564).

As we have said, administrative reforms are reminiscent of roller-coasters, like which they are neither good nor bad in themselves. They may create ample opportunities to learn new things, or give rise to many new problems: what is decisive is the ability to learn in an insecure situation.

11 Reform as a learning process*

* This chapter was contributed by Olov Olson.

In the three preceding chapters we discussed how reforms affect operations, how reformers affect the reformees; in other words, how norms affect procedures in practice. In this chapter we return to an idea we touched upon in Chapter 7: that operations, the reformees and procedures may also affect reforms, reformers and norms, and that the issue of implementation can therefore be broadened to include all the complex interaction between these two groups. We analyse change and learning in both the norm system and the procedural system, and how these learning processes interact, using the example of accounting reforms.

ACCOUNTING REFORM

Accounting is an important element of formal organizations. Normative rhetoric on accounting teaches us that the basic function of accounting is to reduce uncertainty in decision-making about future actions and to enforce responsibility for past actions (Mellemvik *et al.* 1988). This function has developed over centuries and has strongly influenced our way of thinking about and implementing economic activities. Accounting has developed into an important procedure for measuring the results of economic activities, and thus also into an important inter-organizational procedure for drawing lines of demarcation between organizations, or parts of an organization. In order to be considered legitimate, organizations are required to report their transactions with their environment. Accounting is a societal institution. Accounting today is therefore an institutionalized inter-organizational system.

An accounting system stands in relation to its environment, which, to varying extents, it reflects, affects and is affected by. Accounting and the environment in which it takes place form a context which differs according to the tasks carried out by the organization in question. Accounting therefore usually develops differently within industry, public administration and municipal administration. Since the environment in which the accounting takes place affects the accounting itself, the cultural and historical features of that environment will affect the way in which any given accounting system has developed. We can therefore expect the development of accounting systems to differ between countries, even when similar contexts are being studied.

This chapter deals with what happens when municipal accounting systems in Sweden and Norway are reformed. A comparative historical approach has been used in order to take into consideration the long-term effects of possible cultural and institutional differences on the reform processes being studied. The data on which this chapter is based were collected from historical studies by Bergevärn and Olson (1987, 1989b) and Bergevärn *et al.* (1989), and from two comprehensive action research projects carried out in the cities of Uppsala, Sweden and Bergen, Norway (Olson 1983, 1987; Högheim *et al.* 1989a).

Accounting as a partly regulated system

The accounting system involves at least two subsystems: a norm system and a procedural system. The task of the norm system is to formulate norms, such as laws and recommendations intended to regulate accounting procedure in organizations. The norms stipulate not only how the transactions are to be registered and reported, but also that the accounting procedures are to be audited. Because of the conceived relationship between the normative and supervisory aspects of the norm system and the procedural system's procedures, accounting is often referred to as a regulated system.

Accounting procedures are also affected by other factors. These effects can be observed primarily in conjunction with changes in economic activities. Changes which have had dramatic effects on the structure of accounting include the emergence of trade in the fifteenth century, the industrial revolution in the nineteenth century, and the foundation of major corporations in the early twentieth century. But changes in accounting are not necessarily directly linked to economic changes in the environment. The dispersion of power, the need for legitimization, ideologies and conflicts all affect, and are affected by, accounting (Mellemvik *et al.* 1988).

The results of accounting are the accounting reports produced, such as profit and loss statements. According to the normative rhetoric, these reports are intended to decrease uncertainty in decision-making and responsibility allocation. The norm system regulates the form of some, but not all, of these reports. Regulation applies to the underlying conceptual apparatus by which individual transactions are classified, the principles for valuation (e.g. the principles for valuing property) and the periods used for reporting (e.g. the financial year). The procedural system has the freedom to produce more reports than those demanded by the norm system. But their content is often based on the regulated structure, the regulated valuation principles and the regulated accounting periods. This means that internal reporting in an organization reflects external interests more than internal ones (Johnsen and Kaplan 1987).

The norm system only determines the use of the regulated reports to a very limited degree. Regulation is primarily orientated towards the handling of surpluses and deficits. The norm system therefore has very little control over how accounting is used. Regulation contributes mainly to ensuring actors' access to similar types of information, irrespective of the organization being examined. Unfortunately, there are only a few studies of how accounting is used in organizations. The few studies which have been carried out do show, however, that accounting fulfils more functions than are normally attributed to accounting as an institution. For example, accounting affects power, legitimacy, ideology and conflict in organizations (Mellemvik *et al.* 1988). Accounting is therefore a regulated system in the world of ideas and in simple models. Elsewhere, the relationships between accounting, decision-making and responsibility must be considered ambiguous (March 1987).

Municipalities are organizations where decision-making procedures have been based on accounting for a long period of time. They are built on the assumption that the elected politicians decide a budget which specifies the orientation, scope and financing of the operations to be implemented by the civil service. Accounting is presented as having the purpose of reflecting the actions that are carried out, and highlighting problematic situations by reporting discrepancies between the budget and the accounts. Moreover, accounting is meant to support the auditors when they make judgements about the discharge from responsibility of the politicians and civil servants with regard to the activities carried out during the year. In other words, the normative rhetoric on accounting has created procedures where accounting is perceived as an instrument for steering municipal operations. These procedures and their intended co-ordination reflect a basically mechanistic view of how accounting for actions implemented is related to decisions on future actions and their implementation.

The fact that organizations apply these procedures does not, however, ensure that the interrelationships work as described in the normative rhetoric. Normative accounting rhetoric is influential, which means that large amounts of money are invested to reform accounting systems. But reforming procedures and talking about how to use accounting are a far cry from the actual uses of accounting. Many of the reforms carried out are, therefore, relatively problem-free adaptations to the rhetoric rather than solutions to specific organizational problems.

REFORM AS LEARNING

In reform processes accounting is often presented as a goal orientated instrument built on a technology with clear cause-and-effect relationships. But in practice accounting is both formed and used in more ways, and more subtle ways, than the normative rhetoric claims. It is therefore difficult to understand accounting reforms as processes driven by local problems and rationality. It might be more useful to try to understand what environmental forces affect accounting norms. One approach is to see the process as a learning process.

According to Levitt and March (1988), organizational learning is routine based, history dependent and goal orientated, but the procedures formed by the learning process are a reflection of what is considered suitable and legitimate rather than a result of rational calculations and choices. Organizations learn in two ways: through their own experience and from the experience of others. Learning through an organization's own experience includes experimenting, as well as interpreting the results of these experiments. Learning from others' experience may take place in various ways, from compulsory to voluntary learning.

A norm system has a limited potential to learn about the norms it is reforming. It cannot experiment in the instrumental sense of the word, as it does not in fact behave according to the norms for which it is responsible. Thus a norm system has to learn from others' experience. Such experience may come from the regulated procedural system and from procedural systems in other contexts and countries.

In its pure form, a norm system can learn from a procedural system in at least two ways. First, the norm system forces the procedural system to implement given norms and interpret the experience of this implementation. This is quite a realistic picture of how the norm system learns, as the whole point of accounting norms is to regulate and, with the help of auditors, monitor how the accounting procedures are carried out by organizations in the procedural system. The second way for the norm system to learn is through organizations which are carrying out experiments of their own. These organizations may, in turn, have learned from their own experience or that of others. In either case, the norm system learns from organizations which break with existing norms.

But how does a system of norms learn to reform its norms? What triggers these learning processes, and when are they triggered? We will discuss these questions by using empirical data from two countries.

The empirical contexts

Norway and Sweden are often considered similar; when we inspect the ways in which their municipalities are organized, we mainly find similarities with regard to operations, organization and financing. Both countries passed legislation to regulate municipal organizations at an early stage. In Norway, such laws came into effect as early as 1837, while in Sweden the first Local Government Act was passed in 1883. Another important similarity is that the state influences municipal activities, both through norms, in the form of laws and regulations, and financing in the form of state grants. A third similarity is that the municipalities of both nations are organized into federations, intended to serve as their spokesmen in relation to the state and as their watchdogs in wage negotiations with the trade unions.

There are also some important differences. One is that the Swedish Local Government Act only covers the responsibility of the political organization, while in Norway legislation also stipulates that every municipality should have a representative to take on the administrative responsibility. This gives rise to another difference, which is that Norwegian municipalities, on the whole, are considerably smaller than their Swedish counterparts: Norway has nearly twice as many municipalities, although the population of Norway is only about half that of Sweden. Municipal taxation also differs: in Sweden there is no municipal tax ceiling, while in Norway there is a ceiling, and all the Norwegian municipalities have already hit it.

In both countries, the sections of the Local Government Act dealing with municipal accounting are extremely short and superficial. Instead of detailing legislation, the parliaments have authorized other organizations to regulate municipal accounting. In Norway, national ministries have always been responsible for norm-setting. These norms have the same effect as legislation, at they are generally compulsory. The first norms were issued in 1883, and since then have been reformed four times (in 1924, 1942, 1957 and 1971). In Sweden, the Swedish Association of Local Authorities (and its predecessors) have been responsible for these norms since the early twentieth century. However, the Swedish norms are merely recommendations, which gives the Swedish municipalities some freedom to formulate their own accounting procedures. The first norms were published in 1912, and since then there have been four reforms (in 1930, 1956, 1962 and 1987). With these differences between the norm systems in mind, we might expect Swedish municipalities to have more influence on the norms than their Norwegian counterparts. This makes it fruitful to discuss learning in the procedural system in order to understand the learning of the norm system. In doing so, we have chosen to disregard the norms which apply only to small municipalities in both countries.

Learning in the procedural systems

There has been, and still is, a great difference in the ways in which the norms regulate the municipal accounting procedures in the two countries. Since the early 1920s, municipalities in Norway have been more closely tied to the state than in Sweden. Norwegian municipalities have been seen as agents of the state, and have been forced to follow the norms very strictly. Consequently, a large number of auditors have been appointed to check that the norms really are being followed. In Norway, then, we can see that the norms affect the procedures to a very large extent. This observance of the norms primarily gives rise to accounting procedures that are carried out in accordance with the norms. A detailed examination of accounting practices does, however, indicate that there may be procedures which deviate from the norms. Mellemvik (1987), for example, reported that one municipality borrowed for planned investments but postponed the investments and used the borrowed funds to finance operating expenses.

In Sweden the norms are recommendations, and there are far fewer auditors than in Norway. In fact, it was not until after the publication of the 1956 norms in Sweden that a uniform accounting system was applied in most municipalities. One of the reasons for this harmonization was that the 1953 Local Government Act contained a section stating that municipalities were not allowed to decrease the sum of their 'wealth', as defined in the 1956 norms. This meant that Swedish municipalities were more or less forced to present their accounts in accordance with the norms in order not to violate the law. These norms therefore came to have a powerful effect on the procedures used for municipal accounting.

Although Norwegian municipalities follow the norms to a greater extent than Swedish municipalities and have their accounts approved by auditors, it is still extremely difficult in both countries to make comparisons, for example to compare expenditures for a certain type of activity, both between municipalities and within one municipality. Sometimes it is even difficult to compare data about the budgets with data about the accounting. Individual municipalities therefore change their accounting procedures themselves, not least because the norm system is so complex, and sometimes so ambiguous, that the different actors make their own interpretations of it. Furthermore, individual municipalities adapt the accounting system to suit their local interests.

The compulsory nature of the Norwegian norms and the size of Norwegian municipalities makes it difficult for Norwegian municipalities to experiment on a large scale. Swedish municipalities experiment more, and on a larger scale, than their Norwegian counterparts. All reforms of the Swedish norms, with the exception of the 1912 reform, have actually been based on experiments carried out in individual municipalities. The 1930 norms were largely based on accounting practices in the city of Malmö. The 1956 norms were based on an experiment in Stockholm, and the 1962 norms on one from Gothenburg. The 1987 norms were based on experience from a series of similar experiments in several municipalities. Accounting researchers were involved in all three experiments.

These experiments were not only part of a diffusion process within the municipal context. The experiment in Gothenburg which led to the 1962 norms was, in turn, based on norms developed by the Swedish Association of Mechanical Engineering Industries for its member organizations. The 1987 norms also have clear connections with industry, as they are almost exclusively based on terms taken from commercial accounting, including balance sheets, profit and loss accounts, and financial analyses. Experiments have also been carried out in which a municipality has been examined as if it were a corporate group, so that the municipal accounts also include the transactions of the companies owned by the municipality. On the basis of these experiments, the Swedish Association of Local Authorities, in consultation with some accounting researchers, drew up a new set of recommendations for municipal group accounting at the beginning of the 1990s.

Learning within the procedural systems in the two countries is different. The Norwegian municipalities basically have to learn from the system of norms and through carrying out small experiments. Swedish municipalities may follow the recommended norms if they wish, but some of them carry out experiments, even large ones, or learn from the experiments of other municipalities and other organizations. These experiments break with the prevailing norms, and therefore do not have their blessing. Yet some of these very experiments have served as models for subsequent reform processes.

Learning in the norm systems

When the first norms came into being in Norway in 1883, the state considered municipalities to be relatively independent organizations. The published accounting norms reflected this, for example by emphasizing that each municipality was free to formulate accounting reports that would be of use to local politicians. This concept of local independence has lived on into the present, but today it is in competition with a much stronger ideology that grew up in the early twentieth century. At that time, major municipal investments were made in electrical energy plants, financed by loans. However, in the depression following World War I, it became difficult for the municipalities to pay off these loans. The state then intervened and guaranteed the lenders that the loans would be repaid. This altered the relationship between the state and the municipalities. The municipalities were now seen as agents of the state, which should be controlled by the state. This view may have been reinforced by the fact that the Ministry of Justice was the body responsible for issuing the norms. The radical changes in the 1924 norms must be seen in the light of all this. These norms were considerably more extensive and complex than the previous ones, and they were formulated so as to be adapted to the state's need to control the municipalities. This ideological change gave rise to a clear hierarchy between state and municipality, and within this hierarchy there was a place for a system of norms to control municipal accounting. The legitimacy of the norms could be maintained by referring to the need for state control.

The next major norm reform came during World War II. The occupying German forces wanted more control of the municipalities, and they passed the most radical reform of municipal accounting in Norway. The previously established ideology, in which municipalities were seen as agents of the state, made the rapid, radical change possible.

Post-war independence brought a period of euphoria, and new discussions on municipal independence gained momentum. In the context of municipal accounting, this was reflected in discussions of the need for a new reform. A committee of three municipal officials was appointed. But, in addition, the municipal auditors' association forced through a seat for a representative of their own on the committee. This member's views on the existing norms and the need for reform diverged considerably from those of the municipal representatives. The municipal representatives considered there to be a clear need to adapt municipal accounting to local needs and wishes, while the auditors' representative found the prevailing norms excellent, and saw no need for change. When their report was submitted to various bodies for consideration, the responses indicated that the municipalities supported the proposal of the officials, and the auditors' organization supported its member's proposal. The Ministry of Finance and the Norwegian Central Bureau of Statistics responded that the 1942 norms had increased uniformity, and that they wished this high standard to be maintained in the future. As the committee failed to reach an agreement, time passed, and eventually a new committee was appointed, composed of entirely different actors. It included one representative from the ministry currently responsible for the norms, one from the Central Bureau of Statistics, and one municipal accountant. Not surprisingly, this group concluded that the current norms would do for the future as well. The 1957 norms were therefore basically a copy of the 1942 norms.

The next reform process came at a time when computers were coming into use. It was therefore partly concerned with adapting the 1957 norms to the conditions prescribed by computers. The committee responsible for this reform work consisted of six members, including three national civil servants, one municipal accountant and one municipal auditor. Once again there were discussions on adapting the norms to the demands of the municipalities, but once again the ideology which made municipalities agents of the state determined the results of the process. There were consequently no major changes in the norms.

The case of Sweden

The Swedish norms have developed in a completely different way. In the early part of the process, between 1883 and 1912, the only instruments were the Local Government Act, which stipulated that municipalities had to keep accounts, and the Swedish Central Board of Statistics, which requested certain types of data. However, the information they were able to collect was of such poor quality that it was meaningless to try to compile it for the various municipalities. The issue then became a political one, and in the early twentieth century, under duress, the newly established Swedish Town Federation began to develop accounting norms for towns and cities. It was feared that the state would regulate municipal accounting if the municipalities did not do it themselves. The ultimate aim was to create order in the municipalities, and facilitate comparisons of the expenditures and revenues of various cities. The Swedish Town Federation organized a group of municipal officials to carry this out and their work resulted in the 1912 norms. These norms did not however have much impact on accounting procedures in the cities.

Still, ambiguities of accounting posed a problem. It was altogether too easy for municipal treasurers to embezzle funds from the municipal treasuries without being discovered. Such criminality began to mount. Some municipalities even went so far as to demand guarantees from their treasury in the form of a cash deposit. Disorganized accounting and white-collar crime resulted in the Swedish parliament threatening to take over the formulation of norms. The reaction of the Swedish Town Federation was to contact the newly established Swedish Association of Municipal Treasurers, a highly exclusive debating society for city treasurers. The Association eagerly took on the job, debating both the principles and the technical aspects of the subject.

Public debate gave rise to an ideology implying that municipal accounting should not only be uniform but also satisfy the demand that the inhabitants of a given municipality would receive fair treatment. When it came to fair treatment, discussion centred around two main phenomena. First, no single generation was to be permitted to consume what an earlier generation had built up, and second, that the taxpayers should not subsidize activities mainly financed by tariffs, for example in the production of electricity. The funds of the municipality and the actual expenditures for the various activities had to be accounted for separately. Advanced accounting techniques, including depreciation on investments and distribution of interest income, were needed in order to carry out these ideas. These techniques were being discussed at the time in the business world and ideas from that context were transferred to the municipal sector.

There was general consensus within the Association of Municipal Treasurers as to all but the practical formulation of the norms. In fact, the two actors who had been most active in the discussion had also been active in promoting reform work in their own municipalities. One of them put forward a new accounting proposal in his municipality, and the other had actually implemented a change in Malmö, his home municipality. After a debate lasting several years, it was decided that the experience gained in Malmö should serve as the prototype for the 1930 norms. These norms were highly advanced, but also very ambiguous.

Although many cities tried to follow the norms in principle, their inherent ambiguity was so great that municipal accounting remained highly hetero-geneous until well into the 1950s. At that time, municipal operations had expanded greatly, and the Swedish parliament had adopted a decision to merge small municipalities into larger units. Over two decades, the number of munici-palities decreased by 90 per cent. The parliament still stayed out of the regulation of municipal accounting, but once again coerced the Town Federation into reforming the system of norms for municipal accounting for the new municipalities. The parliament, however, amended the Local Government Act, which affected municipal accounting. Municipalities were obliged to account for their wealth, which had been desired even when the 1930 norms were drawn up. A method was needed to achieve this, and the 1956 norms consisted mainly of this method. They were otherwise more a continuation of the 1930 norms than a true innovation. The 1956 norms were also based on experience from one municipality, the city of Stockholm, where an experiment had been carried out. The new norms had a sound theoretical basis, thanks to the efforts of an accounting researcher who had taken an interest in municipal accounting. With his assistance, the technology in the new norms was virtually perfected, and they were also presented extremely pedagogically. The new norms were implemented in most municipalities in Sweden, and were considered a great success.

The next reform produced the 1962 norms, which were mainly related to cost accounting within the framework provided by the 1956 norms. Once again a municipal experiment, this time in Gothenburg, served as the prototype. This experiment, led by a researcher in business administration, was based on cost accounting in the mechanical engineering industry. The 1962 norms were also a great success, not least because they made it possible to computerize day-to-day accounting. It is interesting in this context to observe that although Gothenburg was the prototype for the 1962 norms, the city of Gothenburg did not actually adapt its accounting to the new norms for cost accounting.

Thus municipal accounting in Sweden changed over the course of a decade from being heterogeneous to homogeneous, despite the fact that the Swedish Association of Local Authorities had no means of coercion available. What the Association did have was a strong desire to control municipal accounting. It had to use the means available. One was adapting the rhetoric of municipal accounting to current ideologies of equality and justice. Another was writing study materials and running courses. A third was serving as consultants to the municipalities. A fourth was to computerize accounting techniques and, through their ownership of a computing company, to offer to computerize the municipalities' accounting systems for them.

The more municipalities adopted the 1956 and 1962 norms, the more the norms were criticized. In the late 1970s and early 1980s, severe criticism was voiced. The common denominator of this criticism was an ideology of professional business practice. It was also often implied that the basis of the prevailing norms, i.e. control of the concept of wealth, was both overly complex and oversimplified. One reason was that inflation eroded the value of wealth when accounting was in purely nominal terms. Another was that the municipalities were incorporating most of their fee-charging operations into companies, in order to avoid control of their wealth.

Many different actors took part in this debate, including members of parliament, municipal officials, and researchers in business administration. Many municipalities also experimented with their financial reporting. These experiments often won the sympathy of the politicians as these gave more insight into municipal budgets. Once again the national politicians entered the arena, claiming that the Town Federation should reform municipal accounting. But in contrast with the past, they now referred to existing experiments and to corporate accounting.

The public debate also shifted. People began more and more to discuss the public sector in terms of whether or not it was 'business-like', and the ideology of professional business practice gained more and more supporters, even within the Social Democratic Party. As the current norms, like the previous ones, had been legitimatized through open, often ideological discussions, the new criticism also developed in this way. It was public and was often dispersed along with descriptions and justifications of the local experiments, in articles, books, and conference papers. Common elements in these experiments were a view of municipalities as corporations and the use of commercial models to describe them in the accounting system. These changes were not technically difficult to achieve, as the main components had already been developed and implemented in the norms of 1930 and 1956.

Experiments with new models and criticism of the current norms led to the Town Federation's dropping their defence of the current norms at a rather early stage in the discussion. Instead, they invested in co-operation with the experimenting municipalities, and with the accounting researchers who had participated in the experiments. The 1987 norms were the result of this co-operation. They correspond largely to the Bookkeeping Act which applies to Swedish industry. In addition, the process of developing municipal corporate accounting was initiated. In other words, municipal accounting in Sweden has followed in the footsteps of Swedish commercial accounting.

CLOSED OR OPEN LEARNING PROCESSES?

The learning processes described are quite different. The Norwegian accounting system has been shaped through a closed learning process, while the Swedish accounting system has been shaped through an open process.

The closed learning process

The Norwegian norm system has always been part of the state. However, it was not until the depression of the early 1920s that the state began to see municipalities as its agents, which was reflected in the 1924 norms. Since the norms were supported by legislation they were adopted by the munici-palities. The ideology of municipalities as agents of the state, along with compulsory norms and control by auditors, created a hierarchical account-ing system, the legitimacy of which was virtually unchallengeable. The only actor to succeed in changing these norms between 1924 and the present was the German occupation forces. During the 1920s, the municipal accounting system had been formulated as a hierarchical system in which the system of norms controlled the procedural system, and thus the Germans only had to take control of the system of norms in order to change the entire accounting system.

The resulting accounting system was a closed and hierarchical one in which there was no room for learning other than the municipalities' compulsory learning of the norms. As the norm system is distanced from the municipalities where the accounting is actually done, it is difficult for the norm system to learn anything from the experience of the municipalities. As the norms are compulsory, no individual municipality can experiment; and so the system of norms cannot learn anything in this way, either. The Norwegian municipal accounting system has turned into a closed system, which has difficulty in learning from within. Probably another strong actor in the surrounding world or a change in ideology would be required to achieve a change in its way of learning.

The open learning process

The Swedish accounting system has been involved in a different type of learning process. The Swedish system of norms, embodied in the Swedish Association of Local Authorities and its temporary allies, is separate from the state, and the state has only been able to force the norm system into action by threatening legislation. The system of norms has been relatively powerless, and has not been able to coerce individual municipalities into following its recommended norms by punishing deviant behaviour. Municipal accounting has been a matter of local interest, and individual municipalities have been able to experiment on large or small scales. Some of these experiments, especially those which have deviated most from the norms, have served as models for later reform processes. The largest experiments, such as the one in Gothenburg, were often parts of even larger processes of diffusion, in which some parts of the accounting systems used in industry have spread to individual municipalities and then on within the municipal context.

The choices available to the norm system for reacting to the experiments were either to defend the norms or to initiate a process of reform. The system could not react by taking disciplinary measures against the municipalities. Yet it also had to react to the threats of the state which were repeated at regular intervals.

The experiments of the municipalities and the threats of the state to legislate were, however, not the only phenomena contributing to normative changes. Societal ideologies have also played an important role, as they have endowed accounting with meaning and a basis for discussing both the existing accounting system and alternatives to it. Uniformity and justice were the dominant ideologies from the 1920s through to the 1970s. During the late 1970s discussions about control of activities in municipalities began, and a new ideology of uniformity and professional business practice began to take shape. It dominated public debate on municipal control throughout the 1980s.

The major changes in municipal accounting have taken place when there has been a conflict between norms and ideology. While the experiment in Malmö was the main innovation in the history of Swedish accounting and served as the basis for the 1930, 1956 and 1962 norms, the experiments which led to the 1987 norms were more directly based on corporate accounting. This latter reform led to rapid changes in the accounting systems of most municipalities; the norms were powerful since they were clearly formulated, based on practical experience and suited the dominant ideology. Thus, learning in the Swedish municipal accounting system was tied to ideologies in society, and took place in several steps. The learning process began through experiments in the individual municipalities. Experience from experimenting municipalities was then diffused both to other municipalities and to the norm system. When a certain experiment was considered exemplary by the norm system, and when it reflected current ideology, it became the model for a reform process and diffused back to the municipalities.

Hierarchy or ideology

The concept of hierarchy facilitates understanding of the Norwegian learning process. From the start, the system of norms was incorporated into the state, and therefore acquired the power of a national authority. When the municipalities were allotted the role of agents of the state, the function of accounting shifted from primarily satisfying the needs of the municipality to primarily satisfying the needs of the state to monitor the municipalities. With the support of its power, the norm system ensured that accounting was carried out in accordance with the norms. The effect was obvious. The municipalities essentially followed the norms, but this meant that no alternatives could develop within the framework of the system. Only one single actor, more powerful than the Norwegian state, actually managed to make the only change after 1924. When the closed system does learn, learning begins at the top of the hierarchy.

Ideology is the best concept to use to understand the Swedish learning process. The absence of a clear hierarchy between the state and the municipalities meant that accounting was not a natural link in their interplay. Instead, accounting was based on an ideology which stated that municipalities are to be relatively independent of the state. The state was therefore unwilling to be responsible for the norms. And the legitimacy of the norms did not come from state power but from the fact that the norms reflected societal ideologies. When municipalities perceived this link, they essentially followed the norms.

But when the municipalities perceived a conflict between norms and ideologies, more and more municipalities deviated from the norms by carrying out independent experiments or by following the example of some other municipality. This type of learning led to the development of considerable heterogeneity in municipal accounting systems on the one hand and a wide variation of alternatives to the prevailing norms on the other. In this situation the state threatened to intervene, and so stimulated reform. The norm system had good potential for reform. There was an ideology to use, there were various alternatives which had proven possible to implement, and the norm system could also involve one or more of the actors who had carried out the experiments. The norm system had direct access to practical experience. In the open learning process there is no clear hierarchy with the system of norms at its top. Instead, individual municipalities generate learning processes on their own initiative to which the norm system must then relate.

The two learning processes studied here differ from one another in various ways, but they also have one important similarity: the influence of the environment. The closed model is characterized by the norm system's inability to learn, except when someone takes command of it. In the open model, the accounting system is appraised on the basis of ideologies in the environment, and radical reforms come into being when these ideologies change. This means that irrespective of what model we discuss, the norms for accounting are strongly associated with the environment. In the closed model, this coupling takes place via the norm system and in the open model via the procedural system. The impact from the environment makes it difficult to assert that either individual organizations or the norm system selects the accounting system. Rather, they adapt norms or procedures to whatever suits an external ideology. Thus power over the accounting system is external to the system itself.

12 Reform and power

In the opening chapter of this book we described a number of assumptions on which the notion of administrative reform is based. The essential idea of reform is that, by making deliberate goal-directed choices between organizational forms, reformers can successively create new forms which improve operations and thus lead to better results. Implicit in this idea is a belief that individuals can wield considerable power over organizational forms as well as over behaviour and results. In previous chapters we have questioned this idea by challenging some of the assumptions on which the notion of reform is based. In this concluding chapter we look at the implications that our observations have for the issue of reform and power. We begin by examining the assumption of the reformers' power over organizational forms and operations, discussing the causes of reforms as well as their content and consequences. These last include possible effects on people's perceptions of organizations. In a second section we discuss the role of reforms in opinion-building, and we question the assumption that reforms are primarily a matter of organizational practice and change.

REFORMERS AS AGENTS

The idea of reform is an idea about the power wielded by individuals in positions of leadership – the idea that organizations change as a result of the activities of reformers. The reformers' conceptions and intentions are thought to control the form of the organization, and consequently its operations as well. If reform is assumed to be the only possible kind of change, the implication must be that organizations are static in the absence of reforms. At any rate changes not backed by reformers are not the same thing as reforms. All this suggests that different reformers are likely to produce different kinds of reform, that the identity of the reformer is important. If power is defined as the capacity of individuals to transform their intentions into practical action, then it seems that reformers must be powerful people.

If they are to be really powerful, reformers ought to be in a position to see that reforms do occur, to determine their content, and the reforms should be implemented and should produce the intended effects. But as we have seen in the previous chapters, the reformers' position does not tend to be that strong.

Reform initiative

Although reforms are often described as depending on the energy and drive of individual reformers, we found that in many organizations reforms are remarkably common and apparently easy to initiate. For instance we have described how Swedish state agencies and municipalities seem to expect new reforms all the time and to regard them as entirely legitimate.

In many large organizations reforms are routine. We could even say that they are an integral part of the institution known as the formal organization in its modern version. We have come to expect adaptation and change, particularly administrative change, in this setting. We have also come to expect the big changes to be directed and controlled by organizational leaders. Large organizations often include a 'development division', whose task is to consider, propose and implement reforms. There are also special organizations which sell reforms: management consultancy is a large and expanding field. There can be many powerful incentives to reform in the shape of problems, solutions or forgetfulness. Reforms do not necessarily lead to satisfaction and so may not pre-empt the need for reforms in the future. On the contrary, the implementation of a reform may provide a strong incentive for new reforms. Seldom does it generate a state of equilibrium.

The strong links between administrative forms in organizations and institutions in society at large attests to the relative openness of modern organizations. Organizations openly display their formal structures, processes and ideologies. An open organization is one whose administrative forms are available to the scrutiny of many people inside and outside its boundaries, people to whom these forms are of interest and whose positions make their opinions both legitimate and important to the organization. Outward openness means that the organization encounters external norms regarding acceptable organizational structures, processes and ideologies, and that it has sufficient incentive to adapt itself to these. And its very openness facilitates such adaptation: it is easy to see which forms are legitimate, and the openness of other organizations encourages imitation. When external norms change, or when an organization is obviously unable to match prevailing norms, then its capacity for adapting its organizational forms becomes crucial.

But the routine nature of reforms, together with their institutional ties, leave little leeway for reformers. Of course there must be people who drive reforms, if any such are to take place, but the fact that a reform actually happens may have little to do with these people. Either they appear to be interchangeable – if they had not pushed the reform, someone else would have done, or there are norms that compel them to push it – a management that always refuses to reform poses a serious threat to its own and its organization's standing.

Thus initiative on the part of reformers does not appear to be the main reason why reforms happen. The routine nature of reform and its institutionalization certainly makes action easy, but it limits the freedom of choice of the individual actors. Our concept of 'institutional environments' implies the dispersion of power, and this very dispersion gives rise to reforms. The fact that reforms happen is thus often an expression of the powerlessness rather than the power of organizations, managements and reformers.

Not much personal power is required to initiate reforms. To keep reform off the agenda, on the other hand, calls for a concentration of power. We have shown how radical reforms in Norwegian municipal accounting systems could be averted by associating the system with the state and its legislation. Only when new people acquired power over the state did any major reform occur. A comparison of accounting systems development in Swedish municipalities and in the SKF corporation reveals a similar difference between relative openness and reform on the one hand and a more closed system and an absence of reform on the other (Bergevärn 1989). Given a concentration of power, the powerful can of course still say yes to reforms whenever they want to. But the same factors that stimulate reforms render the reformers powerless.

Power over content

If reformers are to have power, they must enjoy independence in their intentions, i.e. they must themselves determine the content of the reforms they promote. In previous chapters we have indicated a number of factors which reduce the freedom of reformers to determine the content of reforms. What the reformers wish to accomplish is determined to a large extent by general institutionalized notions about the possible and desirable shape of organizations – notions widely held by those in such positions as allow them to be reformers.

Furthermore, irrespective of their own wishes, the reformers are generally forced to formulate the content of their reforms so as to make them acceptable to others, including the reformees. Although not necessarily describing how organizations actually work or are going to work, reforms are part of an organization's external image, of the organizational presentation. So reforms must be presentable: they must agree with what is considered good organization.

Ambiguity and complexity are both common characteristics of organizations, and often very useful ones too, encouraging survival and growth. But even a reformer who recognizes the value of these qualities would find it difficult to present a reform with just this thrust. Instead, if their reforms are to be accepted, reformers are usually obliged to argue in favour of rationality, clarity and simplicity. Moreover, it is difficult to drive reforms in any direction except towards more modern forms or increased rationality. It may also be difficult to go against whatever is in fashion at the time. Reforms are thus part of an inherent contradiction in the concept of modernity: this involves ideas about free choice, but as only certain organizational forms are considered 'modern', choice is actually being limited.

We have also indicated that reform solutions tend to come as part of a package: if you define the organization as part of a particular institution, you are also limiting yourself to choosing among certain possible organizational forms. If, for example, an organization is perceived as being, or as about to become, a company, then certain administrative forms are automatically given, because they are prescribed either by law or by current ideas on the nature of such organizations. It is more difficult to combine elements from many institutions in reforms than it is to combine them in organizational practice.

There are plenty of ready-made solutions to the problem of how to design organizations, which makes it difficult to choose new solutions of one's own. Ready-made standard solutions make it easy to initiate reforms, but difficult to control what they will contain.

As we found in the case of the public modernization programmes and the Active County Council reform, reformers – particularly if their power base is weak – may need to minimize their own influence over the content of a reform in order to make it acceptable and to see it implemented at all. The Active County Council reform was considered acceptable and successful by evaluators both inside and outside the organization, because the reform's promoters actively refrained from shaping its content. In other words reformers can affect the extent of a reform's success by relinquishing any power over its content. If the people at whom the reform is aimed are also allowed to participate in formulating its content, the chances of its implementation increase (Lien and Fremstad 1989), but this procedure does not give the reformers much power. The reform with the greatest chance of success is the one that involves some development which would have taken place anyway or which has even taken place already. The ambition to succeed can thus result in reforms which simply describe and interpret organizational change, rather than controlling it.

We have seen how the organization's institutional ties limit the power of reformers over the content of their reforms. But something which at least in principle could give the reformers a little more power would be the presence of several competing institutions. If an organization is regarded as a public agency, there are limits to the reforms that can be suggested for it, but if the reformers choose to look upon the organization as a business enterprise, they are free to make other and different proposals. Reformers do have power over the content of their reforms insofar as they are able to choose between institutional models. However, the risk then is that this power will be offset by a lack of power over the effects of the reform. That is the subject of the next section.

Power over effects

The purpose of administrative reform is to generate new administrative forms, which in turn will change the operations of the organization and thus its results as well. It may be comparatively easy to alter the form of an organization, provided that the new arrangements do not clash too sharply with its institutional identity, and that they match changes in general, institutional norms reasonably well. Such changes in organizational forms can even occur without any preceding reform. But a reform can also meet hard resistance if its content conflicts with the organization's institutional identity. For example, attempts to persuade courts of law to assume the values and processes of the business world, perhaps by giving priority to efficiency, would probably encounter as much resistance as attempts to get companies to imitate the structures, processes or ideologies of the law-court system. In our study of three-year budgeting we saw that it was easier to introduce new rationalistic techniques of control in public agencies with rationalistic traditions than in those imbued with other kinds of professional values.

Organizations can of course change their institutional affiliation almost completely, but there is every indication that this is normally a slow and intractable process which cannot be achieved by way of isolated reforms. In the case of the savings banks it took several decades. Even in an organization like Swedish Rail, which was originally a combination of state authority and business enterprise, attempts to redefine the organization in the direction of a single institutional affiliation met with considerable difficulty (Brunsson *et al.* 1989). It did not become possible to shift it slightly towards the business enterprise conception until the late 1980s, when the business institution was enjoying a boom in public opinion.

Many studies have reported a high level of conflict in connection with reforms (March and Olsen 1983). In the studies reported here, however, conflict has generally been noticeably weak or non-existent. This may be because the substance of the reforms had been adapted to what the reformers felt they would be able to implement. No single reform implied any sudden or radical change in the organizations' institutional setting, and they were all in line with popular ideas at the time.

There are many reasons why reformers should want to avoid conflict. If they lack sufficient power resources to promote their own ideas, conflict could lead to unpredictable results. Reformers may thus be tempted to adapt the content and ambitions of their reforms to what seems reasonably likely to be attainable, rather than taking a chance on bigger but less certain benefits.

But reformers who want to succeed often have to adapt more than the content of their reforms, they have to adapt the reform process itself. In the various Scandinavian programmes for modernizing the public sector we have seen how the reformers tended to act as guides rather than commanders. Powerful norms in organizations and their environments dictate not only what organizations should look like but also how changes should be made. And these norms often imply that change should be effected by way of reforms, that it should be controlled, made explicit and displayed to the world outside – all of which can expose or increase conflict and thus make change more difficult.

In the cases reported here it did prove possible to change some organizational forms, although it was sometimes a slow business. For example, organizational charts were redesigned, budget processes were altered and new goals and ideas proclaimed. But it turned out to be much more difficult to use the new administrative forms to influence anything except purely formal aspects of operations in the desired direction. And it can prove more difficult still to affect organizational results by introducing reforms; reforms often have effects other than those the reformers say they have in mind.

One problem in achieving intended effects has to do with how the contents of reforms are determined. We have indicated that the contents of reforms, both their problems and solutions, are often determined more by general norms, by trend-setting notions and popular opinion than by the practical situation of the organization to be reformed. Then we cannot expect that the intended effects will be easy to reach in this organization.

We have also argued that organizations are good at distinguishing between the formal and the informal, and at producing ritual and hypocrisy. These qualities protect the operations of the organization from many of the demands imposed from above and from the outside, and they protect operations from being affected by reforms. So they are qualities that fill reformers with despair. But they can also offer some consolation. The very fact that organizational operations are so difficult to change by reform means that organizations are also resistant to the mistakes of reformers. Administrative reforms are seldom the main cause of an organization's demise. Moreover, decoupling between organizational forms and operations can contribute to the failure of a reform, in the sense that it does not succeed in changing operations as intended – which makes it easier to start reforming all over again.

Reformers may not be very interested in the effects of their reforms on operations. This may be because their aims have changed in the course of the reform process, or because their aims are more short-sighted than they claim. In the case of SJ, for example, it was expected that effects would appear in the distant future, and there was very little interest in identifying the effects of earlier reforms and learning from them. The Active County Council case gives us an example of effects that were, so to speak, part of the reform. When the reformers described the reform, they talked not only about its aims and the new forms, but also about its effects. 'Effects' were things that occurred before and during the reform, and which could thus be used as internal and external propaganda for the reform; they were not things to be investigated after the reform had been implemented.

Similarly institutions not only embrace certain ideas about values, forms and behaviour: they also contain strong ideas about effects. For example, efficiency is sometimes regarded as an integral part of the institution known as the business enterprise, rather than a result that has to be demonstrated empirically. Efficiency is simply expected to materialize as soon as the organization has adopted the 'business enterprise' form. In these cases reformers have no need to treat behaviour and results differently from any other part of their reforms. To gain acceptance, reforms have to proclaim 'good' aims, forms, behaviour and effects; implementing such reforms holds out the promise of guaranteeing these virtues.

Actors or agents

To sum up, we have presented a picture of reformers here which is considerably less heroic than the one generally associated with the idea of reform. The reformers' opportunities for deciding to launch a reform are often severely limited, and so are their chances of determining its content. Moreover it is difficult to achieve the more profound effects which reformers generally claim as their goal. Reforms may constitute part of some more comprehensive change, but are not apt to steer it. Reformers appear as agents rather than actors, as agents of a development which would generally have taken place whether or not they had intervened. They seem to be easily interchangeable. Their position as reformers does not appear to give them anything like the power that the idea of reform would suggest. The main reason for this impotence is that organizations do not function as instruments, as prescribed by the individual-rational model on which the traditional idea of reform is based. The aim of many reforms is to improve organizations as instruments for their leaders. But reforms are difficult to realize simply because even in reform processes, this is not the way organizations work.

This does not stop many people from believing that reforms are important, nor does it always prevent fierce conflict about reforms and about who should be reformers. This may not depend entirely on the fact that the idea of the 'powerful reformer' is taken seriously: people may also consider reformers to be important because they are aware of effects other than those we have been discussing so far. They may be considering the effects of reforms on people's conceptions of reformers, of specific organizations or of organizations in general. These effects will be addressed in the next section.

REFORM AS OPINION-BUILDING

The concept of reform refers to a relation between thought and action, between ideas and practice: by planning and implementing administrative reforms the practices of an organization can be reshaped in a certain intended way. And the idea of reforming, and the ideas which comprise the substance of a reform, originate in an analysis of the problems and opportunities of the organization's practice. The thinkers – the reformers – are to affect the doers – the reformees.

We have argued that the immediate connection between reform and practice may be a weak one, and that reforms belong more to the world of ideas than to the world of practice; sometimes they can be best understood as ideas only. But demands and criteria in the world of ideas are different from those in the world of action. If the substance of a reform is to match criteria for 'good' ideas, it will for instance be characterized by rationality, clarity and simplicity. But this will make it more difficult to apply in practice: successful practice is often characterized by exactly the opposite qualities. This is one of the reasons why it is difficult to achieve the effects on behaviour and results that reformers like to talk about.

Reforming the environment

Instead of effects on practice, reforms may have effects in the world of ideas: they may affect people's image of the organization. We have seen in several of our cases that by reform people can acquire new ideas about the meaning and purpose of their organization and begin to feel that they understand its operations better. Reforms may also affect attention. Both inside and outside the organization they may direct attention towards the area being reformed and towards the particular problems, values and solutions raised by the reform. They can draw attention to some especially problematic or unsatisfactory aspects of the organization's practices. But reforms can also give hope of future improvements. Reforms can even create the impression that improvements have already been made, since they are prone to generate talk of change among both reformers and reformees.

When effects occur in the world of ideas rather than in the world of action it means that actual reforms are violating another common assumption of reform, namely that the reformees and their activities are the sole target of a reform. Reforms which remain in the world of ideas may instead have important effects on external parties. It is often easier to influence the way an organization is perceived by outsiders than to affect the views of its members, since outsiders generally have less first-hand experience of its operations. Those who have no direct contact with organizational operations are probably most easily convinced: it was presumably easier to persuade the ministry and the government of the excellence of the new SJ than to convince the general public or SJ's customers, who may not even have heard of the reform. Reforms may make a greater impact on the managements of other organizations, who recognize the language of reform, than on the public or the consumers. In other words it seems to be more difficult for élites to manipulate the masses by mediating images which do not reflect reality (Edelman 1971) than it is for them to convince one another of ideas in a highly abstract world where empirical aspects do not carry much weight.

It is possible in principle to imagine that the behaviour of organization members could be affected by the appearance of new organizational forms, even if people are not convinced of the rightness of a reform as such. New forms might induce new types of behaviour. At least this is the idea underlying the concept of the perfect bureaucracy. However, if a reform is meant to affect the opinions of external parties, then it is essential to its success that it be made acceptable to these parties. This is a further reason for adapting reform contents to general external norms rather than to the specific situation of the organization to be reformed. A reform designed in this way is well fitted for influencing outsiders, but it is less well adapted to internal implementation.

Change or stability

We also question the assumption that reform and change are closely related. On the contrary, reforms may contribute to stability. Reforms may prevent change in several ways. Reforms increase people's awareness that change may take place. If the changes are controversial and if the power of the reformers is not very strong, this may obstruct the process of change by activating resistance and providing the enemies of the reform with a forum in which they can oppose it. Many big changes in society take place without much prior discussion, and many of the most hotly debated areas are never subjected to any great change (Edelman 1971). It is easier to combine reform and change in uncontroversial areas, while in controversial areas the risk is great that attempts at reform will simply make for stability.

This stabilizing effect of reform can make reform popular with the opponents of specific changes. The opponents can activate other people's opposition to the change by trying to present it as a deliberate attempt at reform on the part of certain reformers. Another conceivable method of stopping a change could even be to present it as one's own idea for a reform. Furthermore, as we noted in Chapter 3, proposing a new reform can be a way of preventing the implementation of an earlier one. The counter-strategy for those who do want change is to try to achieve it without reform.

So reformers whose reforms are controversial may find that their re-forming ambitions actually counteract change. But this does not necessarily mean that the reformers will be hopelessly unpopular: their efforts at reform show that they are trying to change things, and this will probably be perceived as positive by those who want change. Moreover, the changes do not happen, which is comforting for those who do not want them. Failed reforms may thus provide a successful way of handling and responding to the contradictory demands to which reformers and organizations may be exposed. Reform becomes a kind of functional hypocrisy: reform talk can make stability in action more acceptable.

Perhaps the most important stabilizing effect of reforms is that they tend to reinforce prevailing ideas about organizational forms. Since reforms tend to be entrenched in generally accepted ideas, they may result in more people becoming – or pretending to become – convinced that these same ideas are good and also correct descriptions of a given organization. Reforms also help to reinforce the more general image of how organi-zations work (Sahlin-Andersson 1989a). Reforms confirm and reproduce images of organizations as systems that can be controlled from above, systems in which management or some other group of reformers possesses great personal power and can bring about and direct change, and in which administrative forms represent important instruments of change.

At the same time the result of reforms poses a potential threat to this picture of the organization as controllable and reformable from above. If it becomes clear that a reform has failed, the idea of powerful leadership might be called in question. But there are various ways of avoiding this threat, as we indicated in Chapters 5 and 6. For example, people may confess deviations from the norm but still avoid rejecting it as an ideal, or they can talk as if the reform has been implemented without changing their behaviour. We have also noted that organizations and reformers often avoid evaluations of the effects of a reform, for example by locating them far in the future. Another possibility is that the leaders who have failed resign, thus confirming the idea that management is very important. A third possibility is to formulate reforms in such a way that they cannot fail, perhaps by adapting their content to changes which would anyway have taken place, or to what appears attainable.

The Active County Council case provides a clear example of this last type of reform. Since attempts to control organizational operations were probably doomed to failure, the main thrust of the reform was that organization members should not comply with rules imposed centrally and, since changes in various directions could be expected, change in general was defined as part of the reform. But the reform definitely emanated from management, clearly emphasizing the importance of the managers. At the same time it helped to create a well-defined identity for a heterogeneous and change-prone organization, making the county council look like a single coherent and enduring organization, despite all the signs to the contrary.

The power of perceptions

If reforms affect the prevailing image of individual organizations and of organizations in general, then their implications for power are crucial. When reforms project an image of powerful reformers, and of change as something controlled by individuals, then they are putting responsibility – credit or blame – for the actions of organizations on the reformers. As reformers are either members of management or at any rate have its support, reforms also help to endow management with responsibility. Reforms may represent one way in which leaders can demonstrate their own importance to the organization's development, and thus also their own responsibility. Their aspirations to responsibility may persuade them to choose explicit reform as a way of affecting developments rather than trying to change things more discreetly, or they may decide to introduce reforms coinciding with changes already under way. The personal responsibility of those we call leaders is an essential aspect of institutions such as 'democracy' and 'organization'; it is also at the core of modern, secularized ideologies emphasizing the power and responsibility of human beings in general. The power and responsibility of leaders is a fundamental notion that constructs explanations of what we see going on around us, as well as apparently providing us with the instruments of change. It is also naturally reflected in the idea of organizations as instruments, and as open to reform.

Thus, by undertaking reforms leaders can reinforce their own responsibility, while also influencing other people's ideas about how the organization works. They can nurture an illusion of hierarchy and rationality which generates meaning and the power to act. But the unrealistic element in this illusion can lead to powerlessness in those who believe in it too strongly, regardless of whether they are leaders or led, or outsiders. Those who want to change or influence the activities of an organization may easily be misled about how to do it, believing change is best effected by replacing the management, altering the administrative forms, making reforms. If those who want change do not understand how to achieve it, this too promotes stability.

If it is true that reforms are opinion-builders while reformers are relatively powerless, the paradoxical result is that the image of formal organizations as instruments and of reformers as heroes, will be reinforced despite every indication that the picture is largely an inaccurate one. Reforms then simply obstruct any learning based on reality.

Reforms as a whole will then continue to attract sizeable resources into administration, into 'managing' organizations by adopting the 'right' forms – even though the aim of many individual reforms is said to be just the opposite. In many organizations huge administrative resources go into more or less continuous reform activities. Higher administrative costs benefit the administrators, but the benefit they bring to producers, consumers or financiers is more questionable.

To sum up, we have drawn a picture of reformers as people with considerably less power than the idea of reform implies. The limitations refer not only to what reformers can do, but even more to what they can say and perhaps even to what they can think. Administrative reform is determined to a large extent by culturally conditioned rules and institutional values; the reformer's prison walls are mental rather than physical. The most important of these rules and values is the very idea that it is possible to control and reform organizations. This idea is hard to abandon, not only for reformers but for all those who want to live in the world of formal organizations.

References

Abravanel, H. (1983) 'Mediatory myths in the service of organizational ideology', in L.R. Pondy, P.J. Frost, G. Morgan and T.C. Dandridge (eds) *Organizational Symbolism*, Greenwich, CT: JAI Press.

Akerlof, George A. (1976) 'The economics of caste and of the rat race and other woeful tales', *Quarterly Journal of Economics* 90: 599–617.

Anton, T.J. (1967) 'Roles and symbols in the determination of state expenditures', *Midwest Journal of Political Science* 11: 27–43.

Argyriades, D.C. (1965) 'Some aspects of civil service reorganization in Greece', *International Review of Administrative Sciences* 31: 297–307.

Aristotle (384–322 BC) (1985) *Nicomachean Ethics*, translated by Terence Irwin, Indianapolis, IN: Hackett.

Back, S. and Lane, J.E. (1988) *Den svenska statsbudgeten*, Lund: SNS.

Baier, V.E., March, J.P. and Sætren, H. (1986) 'Implementation and ambiguity', *Scandinavian Journal of Management Studies* 2 (3–4): 197–212.

Basu, K., Jones, E. and Schlicht, E. (1987) 'The growth and decay of custom: the role of the New Institutional Economics in economic history', *Explorations in Economic History* 24: 1–21.

Beeton, D. (1987) 'Measuring departmental performance', in A. Harrison and J. Gretton (eds) *Reshaping Central Government*, New Brunswick/London: Transaction Books, 77–89.

Bendor, J. (1977) 'Confusion between developmental and evolutionary theories', *Administration and Society* 8(4): 481–514.

Bentzon, K.H. (1988) *Fra vækst til omstilling – modernisering af den offentlige sektor*, Copenhagen: Nyt fra Samfundsviden skaberne.

Berger, P., Berger, B., and Kellner, H. (1973) *The Homeless Mind: Modernization and Consciousness*, New York: Random House.

Berger, P. and Luckmann, T. (1966) *The Social Construction of Reality: A Treatise in the Sociology of Knowledge*, New York: Doubleday.

Bergevärn, L.E. (1989) 'Processer och krafter kring företags och kommuners omformning av sin redovisning', Paper presented at Conference on Administrative Reforms, Grythyttan.

Bergevärn, L.E. and Olson, O. (1987) *Kommunal redovisning då och nu: Om längtan efter likformighet, rättvisa och affärsmässighet*, Lund: Doxa.

Bergevärn, L.E. and Olson, O. (1989a) 'Processer och krafter kring företags och kommuners omformning av sin redovisning', Paper presented at Conference on Administrative Reforms, Grythyttan.

Bergevärn, L.E. and Olson, O. (1989b) 'Reforms and myths: a history of municipal accounting in Sweden', *Accounting, Auditing and Accountability* 2(3): 22–39.

Bergevärn, L.E., Mellemvik, F. and Olson, O. (1989) *Learning in and around Municipal Accounting*, Bergen: Norges Handelshøyskole/Stencil.

Berman, M. (1983) *All That is Solid Melts into Air: The Experience of Modernity*, London: Verso Editions.

Brown, R.G. (1979) *Reorganizing the National Health Service: A Case Study in Administrative Change*, Oxford: Blackwell/Robertson.

Brown, R.H. (1977) *A Poetic for Sociology*, Cambridge: Cambridge University Press.

Brown, R.H. (1987) *Society as Text*, Chicago, IL: University of Chicago Press.

Brunsson, K. (1988) *'Hur stor blev tvåprocentaren?'* Erfarenheter från en besparingsteknik, Rapport till ESO (finansdepartementet), Ds 1988: 34.

Brunsson, N. (1982) 'The irrationality of action and action rationality: decisions, ideologies and organizational actions', *Journal of Management Studies* 19(1): 29–44.

Brunsson, N. (1985) *The Irrational Organization: Irrationality as a Basis for Organizational Action and Change*, Chichester: Wiley.

Brunsson, N. (ed.) (1986a) *Politik och ekonomi: En kritik av rationalitet som samhällsföreställning*, Lund: Doxa.

Brunsson, N. (1986b) 'Politik och handling', in N. Brunsson (ed.) *Politik och ekonomi*, Lund: Doxa, 19–44.

Brunsson, N. (1989) *The Organization of Hypocrisy: Talk, Decisions and Actions in Organizations*, Chichester: Wiley.

Brunsson, N., Forssell, A. and Winberg, H. (1989) *Reform som tradition*, Stockholm: EFI.

Brunsson, N. and Jönsson, S. (1979) *Beslut och handling: Om politikers inflytande över politiken*, Stockholm: Liber.

Brunsson, N. and Rombach, B. (1982) *Går det att spara? Kommunal budgetering under stagnation*, Karlshamn: Doxa.

Burns, T. and Stalker G. M. (1961) *The Management of Innovation*, London: Tavistock.

Cameron, K.S., Sutton, R.I. and Whetten, D.A. (eds) (1988) *Readings in Organizational Decline*, Cambridge, MA: Ballinger.

Campbell, C. and Peters, B.G. (eds) (1988) *Organizing Governance, Governing Organizations*, Pittsburgh, PA: University of Pittsburgh Press.

Carroll, L. (1907) *Alice's Adventures in Wonderland*, London: Macmillan.

Child, J. (1977) 'Organizational design and performance: contingency theory and beyond', in E.H. Burach and A.R. Negandhi, *Organization Design, Theoretical Perspectives and Empirical Findings*, Kent, OH: Kent State University Press.

Child, J. and Kieser, A. (1981) 'Development of organizations over time', in P.C. Nystrom and W.H. Starbuck (eds) *Handbook of Organizational Design* (vol. 1), Oxford: Oxford University Press, 28–64.

Christensen, T. (1985) 'Styrt endring og planlagte konsekvenser? – en studie av omorganiseringen av den sentrale helseforvaltningen i 1983', Tromsø: Institutt for samfunnsvitenskap.

Christensen, T. (1987) 'How to succeed in reorganizing: the case of the Norwegian Health Administration', *Scandinavian Political Studies* 10(1): 61–77.

Christensen, T. (1989) 'Forutsetninger og effekter: restruktureringen av den sentrale helseadministrasjonen i Norge', in M. Egeberg (ed.) *Institusjonspolitikk og forvaltningsutvikling: Bidrag til en anvendt statsvitenskap*, Oslo: Tano, 186–206.

Coase, R.H. (1937) 'The nature of firm', *Economica* 5: 386–405.

Coase, R.H. (1960) 'The problem of social cost', *Journal of Law and Economics* 3: 1–44.

Cohen, M., March, J.G. and Olsen, J.P. (1972) 'A garbage can model of rational choice', *Administrative Science Quarterly* 1: 1–25.

Colvin, P. (1985) *The Economic Ideal in British Government*, Manchester: Manchester University Press.

Crozier, M. (1964) *The Bureaucratic Phenomenon*, Chicago, IL: University of Chicago Press.

Crozier, M. (1988) *Comment réformer l'Etat?* Paris: La Documentation Française.

Cyert, R.M. and March, J.G. (1963) *A Behavioral Theory of the Firm*, Englewood Cliffs, NJ: Prentice-Hall.

Czarniawska, B. (1985) 'The ugly sister: on relationships between the private and the public sectors in Sweden', *Scandinavian Journal of Management Studies* 2(2): 83–103.

Czarniawska-Joerges, B. (1987) *Reformer och ideologier*, Lund: Doxa.

Czarniawska-Joerges, B. (1988a) *Att handla med ord: Om organisatoriskt prat, organisatorisk styrning och företagsledningskonsultering*, Stockholm: Carlsson Bokförlag.

Czarniawska-Joerges, B. (1988b) *Reformer och ideologier: Lokala nämnder på väg*, Lund: Doxa.

Czarniawska-Joerges, B. (1988c) *Ideological Control in Non-ideological Organizations*, New York: Praeger.

Czarniawska-Joerges, B. (1988d) 'Power as an experiential concept', *Scandinavian Journal of Management* 4(1–2): 31–44.

Czarniawska-Joerges, B. (1991) in P. Frost, L. Moore, M. Louis, C. Lundberg and J. Martin, (eds) *Reframing Organizational Culture*, Newbury Park, CA: Sage, 285–97.

Czarniawska-Joerges, B. and Jacobsson, B. (1989) 'Budget in a cold climate', Accounting Organizations and Society 14 (1,2): 23–39.

Dahl, R.A. and Lindblom, C.E. (1953) *Politics, Economics, and Welfare*, New York: Harper & Row.

Dente, B. and Kjellberg, F. (eds) (1988) *The Dynamics of Institutional Change*, London: Sage.

Dente, B. and Regonini, G. (1980) 'Urban policy and political legitimation: the case of Italian neighbourhood councils', *International Political Science Review* 2: 187–202.

DiMaggio, P. and Powell, W.W. (1983) 'The iron-cage revisited: institutional isomorphism and collective rationality in organizational fields', *American Sociological Review* 48: 147–60.

DiTomaso, N. (1985) 'The managed state: governmental reorganization in the first year of the Reagan Administration', in R.G. Braungart (ed.) *Research in Political Sociology*, Greenwich, CT: JAI Press, 33–72.

Dowling, J.B. and Pfeffer, J. (1975) 'Organizational legitimation', *Pacific Sociological Review* 18(1): 122–36.

Downs, G.W. and Larkey, P.D. (1986) *The Search for Government Efficiency: From Hubris to Helplessness*, Philadelphia, PA: Temple University Press.

Draft Bill (1986/87) 'Regeringens proposition: Ledning av den statliga förvaltningen' (1986/87: 99).

Dyson, K. (1980) *The State Tradition in Western Europe*, Oxford: Martin Robertson.

Eckhoff, T. and Jacobsen, K.D. (1960) *Rationality and Responsibility in Administrative and Judicial Decision-Making*, Copenhagen: Munksgaard.

Eckstein, H. (1982) 'The idea of political development: from dignity to efficiency', *World Politics* 34: 451–86.

Edelman, M. (1971) *Politics as Symbolic Action*, New York: Academic Press.

Egeberg, M. (1984) *Organisasjonsutforming i offentlig virksomhet*, Oslo: Aschehoug/Tanum, Nordli.

Egeberg, M. (1987) 'Designing public organizations', in J. Kooiman and K.A. Eliassen (eds) *Managing Public Organizations: Lessons from Contemporary European Experience*, London: Sage, 142–57.

Egeberg, M. (ed.) (1989a) *Institusjonspolitikk og forvaltningsutvikling: Bidrag til anvendt statsvitenskap*, Oslo: Tano.

Egeberg, M. (1989b) 'Effekter av organisasjonsendring i forvaltningen', in M. Egeberg (ed.) *Institusjonspolitikk og forvaltningsutvikling: Bidrag til en anvendt statsvitenskap*, Oslo: Tano, 75–93.

Etzioni, A. (1964) *Modern Organizations*, Englewood Cliffs, NJ: Prentice-Hall.

Etzioni, A. (1988) *The Moral Dimension*, New York: Free Press.

Fayol, H. (1916) 'Administration industrielle et générale: prévoyance, organisation, commandement, contrôle', *Bulletin de la Société de l'Industrie Minérale*, Paris: Dunod.

Feldman, M.S. and March, J.G. (1981) 'Information in organizations as signal and symbol', *Administrative Science Quarterly* 26: 171–86.

Forssell, A. (1989) 'How to become modern and business-like: an attempt to understand the modernization of Swedish savings banks', in *International Studies on Management & Organization* 19(3): 34–48.

Forssell, A. (1992) *Moderna tider i sparbanken*, Stockholm: Nerenius and Santérus Förlag.

Fry, G.K. (1988) 'The Thatcher Government: the Financial Management Initiative and the "New Civil Service"', *Public Administration* 66: 1–20.

Fürth, T. (1983) 'Från folkrörelseförvaltning till myndighets tillsyn – organisationssyn och teknikval i socialförsäkringens historia', in B. Abrahamsson and D. Ramström, *Vägen till Planrike*, Lund: Studentlitteratur.

Galbraith, J.R. (1973) *Designing Complex Organizations*, Reading, MA: Addison-Wesley.

Galbraith, J.R. (1977) *Organization Design*, Reading, MA: Addison-Wesley.

Glaser, B.G. and Strauss, A.L. (1974) *The Discovery of Grounded Theory*, Chicago, IL: Aldine.

Goldwin, R.A. (1986) 'Of men and angels: a search for morality in the Constitution', in R.H. Horwitz (ed.) *The Moral Foundations of the American Republic* (3rd edn), Charlottesville, VA: University Press of Virginia, 24–41.

Goodsell, C.T. (1985) *The Case for Bureaucracy*, Chatham, NJ: Chatham House.

Government Memorandum (1984) 'Regeringens skrivelse till riksdagen om den offentliga sektorns förnyelse' (1984/85: 202).

Gray, A. and Jenkins, W.I. (1985) *Administrative Politics in British Government*, London: Harvester.

Grønlie, T. (1989) *Statsdrift*, Oslo: Tano.

Hamilton, A., Jay, J. and Madison, J. (1787–8/1964 edn) *The Federalist Papers*, New York: Pocket Books.

Hanf, K. and Scharp, F. W. (eds) (1978) *Interorganizational Policy Making*, London: Sage.

Hannan, M.T. and Freeman, J. (1977) 'The population ecology of organizations', *American Journal of Sociology* 82: 929–64.

Hannan, M.T. and Freeman, J. (1984) 'Structural inertia and organizational change', *American Sociological Review* 49: 149–64.

Hansen, H. Foss (1989) 'Moderniseringens effektivitet', *Nordisk Administrativt Tidsskrift* 2: 189–212.

Harrison, A. and Gretton, J. (1987) *Reshaping Central Government*, New Brunswick/Oxford: Transaction Books.

Hastings, S. and Levie, H. (eds) (1983) *Privatization*, Nottingham: Spokesman.

Heckscher, G. (1952) *Svensk statsförvaltning i arbete*, Stockholm: SNS.

Högheim, S., Monsen, N., Olsen, R. and Olson, O. (1989a) *Action Research in Accounting*, Bergen: Norges Handelshøyskole Stencil.

Högheim, S., Monsen, N., Olsen, R. and Olson, O. (1989b) 'The two worlds of management control', *Financial Accountability and Management* 5: 163–78.

Hood, C. (1979) *The Machinery of Government Problem* (Studies in Public Policy No. 28), Glasgow: University of Glasgow.

Jacobsen, K.D. (1964) *Teknisk hjelp og politisk struktur*, Oslo: Universitetsforlaget.

Jacobsen, K.D. (1966) 'Public administration under pressure: the role of the expert in the modernization of traditional agriculture', *Scandinavian Political Studies* 1: 159–93.

Jacobsson, B. (1984) *Hur styrs förvaltningen? Myt och verklighet kring departementens styrning av ämbetsverken*, Lund: EFI Studentlitteratur.

Jansson, D. (1987) *Investeringskalkyler i empirisk investeringsforskning*, Stockholm: EFI Forskningsrapport.

Johnsen, T. and Kaplan, R. (1987) *Relevance Lost: The Rise and Fall of Management Accounting*, Boston: Harvard Business School Press.

Jönsson, S. A. (1988) 'Decentralization in local government: horizontal or vertical coordination?', in I. Lundahl (ed.) *Economic Change and the Local Planning Process*, Stockholm: Swedish Council for Building Research, 66–120.

Jönsson, S.A. (1989) 'Reformer underifrån – eller hur man övervinner organisatorisk glömska', Paper presented at Conference on Adminstrative Reforms, Grythyttan.

Jönsson, S.A. and Lundin, R.A. (1977) 'Myths and wishful thinking as management tools', in P.C. Nyström and W.H. Starbuck (eds) *Prescriptive Models of Organizations*, Amsterdam: North-Holland.

Kaufman, H. (1956) 'Emerging conflicts in the doctrine of American public administration', *American Political Science Review* 50: 1057–73.

Kaufman, H. (1976) *Are Government Organizations Immortal?* Washington, DC: Brookings.

Kaufman, H. (1977) 'Reflections on administrative reorganization', in J.A. Pechman (ed.) *Setting National Priorities: The 1978 Budget*, Washington, DC: Brookings.

Kay, D. A. and D.J. Thompson (1986) 'Privatisation: a policy in search of a rationale', *The Economic Journal* 90: 18–32.

Keeley, M. (1988) *A Social-Contract Theory of Organizations*, Notre Dame, IN: Notre Dame University Press.

Kelman, S. (1985) 'The Grace Commission: how much waste in government?' *The Public Interest* 78: 62–82.

Kimberley, J.R. and Miles, R.H. *et al.* (1980) *The Organizational Life Cycle*, San Francisco, CA: Jossey-Bass.

Knott, J.H. and Miller, G.J. (1987) *Reforming Bureaucracy*, Englewood Cliffs, NJ: Prentice Hall.

Kooiman, J. and Eliassen, K.A. (eds) (1987) *Managing Public Organizations: Lessons from Contemporary European Experience*, London: Sage.

Körberg, I. (1990) *Sparbankernas historia*, Stockholm: Läromedelsgruppen.

Krasner, S.D. (1988) 'Sovereignty: an institutional perspective', *Comparative Political Studies* 21: 66–94.

Landau, M. and Stout, R. (1979) 'To manage is not to control, or the folly of Type II errors', *Public Administration Review* 39: 148–56.

Lawrence, P. and Lorsch, J. (1967) *Organization and Environment*, Cambridge, MA: Harvard University Press.

Leazes, Jr., F.J. (1987) *Accountability and the Business State*, New York: Praeger.

LeGrand, J. and Robinson, R. (1984) *Privatization and the Welfare State*, London: Allen & Unwin.

Levitt, B. and March, J.G. (1988) 'Organizational Learning', *Annual Review of Sociology* 14: 319–40.

Lien, S. and Fremstad, J.K. (1989) 'Organisering av organisasjonsendring', in M. Egeberg (ed.) *Institusjonspolitikk og forvaltningsutvikling*, Oslo: Tano, 225–40.

Lindblom, C. (1959) 'The science of "muddling through"', *Public Administration Review* 19: 79–88.

Lindé, C. (1982) *Departement och verk: om synen på den centrala statsförvaltningen och dess uppdelning i en förändrad offentlig sektor*, Lund: Studentlitteratur.

Lundberg, E. (1957) *Produktivitet och räntabilitet*, Stockholm: SNS.

McClelland, D.C. (1907) 'The two faces of power', *Journal of International Affairs* 24(1): 141–54.

March, J.G. (1978) 'Bounded rationality, ambiguity, and the engineering of choice', *Bell Journal of Economics* 9: 587–608.

March, J.G. (1981a) 'Decisions in organizations and theories of choice', in A. Van de Ven and W. Joyce (eds) *Perspectives on Organizational Design and Performance*, New York: Wiley, 205–44.

March, J.G. (1981b) 'Footnotes to organizational change', *Administrative Science Quarterly* 26(4): 563–77.

March, J.G. (1987) 'Ambiguity and accounting: the elusive link between information and decision making', *Accounting, Organizations and Society* 12: 153–68.

March J.G. (1988) *Decisions in Organizations*, Oxford: Basil Blackwell.

March, J.G. (1989) 'Exploration and exploitation in organizational learning', Stanford CA: Stanford University, manuscript.

March, J.G. and Olsen, J.P. (1975) 'The uncertainty of the past: organizational learning under ambiguity', *European Journal of Political Research* 3: 147–71.

March, J.G. and Olsen, J.P. (1976) *Ambiguity and Choice in Organizations*, Bergen: Universitetsforlaget.

March, J.G. and Olsen, J.P. (1983) 'Organizing political life: what administrative reorganization tells us about government', *American Political Science Review* 77(2): 281–97.

March, J.G. and Olsen, J.P. (1984) 'The New Institutionalism: organizational factors in political life', *American Political Science Review* 78: 734–49.

March, J.G. and Olsen, J.P. (1989) *Rediscovering Institutions: The Organizational Basis of Politics*, New York: Free Press.

Marx, K. (1845/1976) 'Theses on Feuerbach', in K. Marx and F. Engels, *Collected Works* (vol. 5), London: Lawrence & Wishart, 3–5.

Mellbourn, A. (1986) *Bortom det starka samhället*, Stockholm: Carlsson Bokförlag.

Mellemvik, F. (1987) *Kommunenes lån – et regnskapsmessig problem?* Oslo: Universitetsforlaget.

Mellemvik, F., Monsen, N. and Olson, O. (1988) 'Functions of accounting – a discussion', *Scandinavian Journal of Management* 4(3/4): 101–20.

Metcalf, L. and Richards, S. (1987) *Improving Public Management*, London: Sage.

Meyer, J.W. and Rowan, B. (1977) 'Institutionalized organizations: formal structure as myth and ceremony', *American Journal of Sociology* 83: 340–63.

Meyer, J.W. and Scott, W.R. (1983) *Organizational Environments: Ritual and Rationality*, Beverley Hills, CA: Sage.

Mill, J.S. (1861/1962) *Considerations on Representative Government*, South Bend, IN: Gateway Editions.

Mintzberg, H. (1979) *The Structuring of Organizations*, Englewood Cliffs, NJ: Prentice Hall.

Moe, T. (1984) 'The new economics of organizations', *American Journal of Political Science* 28: 739–81.

Morrisey W. (1986) 'The moral foundations of the American Republic: an introduction', in R.H. Horwitz (ed.) *The Moral Foundations of the American Republic* (3rd edn), Charlottesville, VA: University Press of Virginia, 1–23.

Mosher, F.C. (1965) 'Some notes on reorganizations in public agencies', in R.E. Martin (ed.) *Public Administration and Democracy*, Syracuse, NY: Syracuse University Press, 129–50.

Nisbett, R. and Ross, L. (1980) *Human Inference*, Englewood Cliffs, NJ: Prentice Hall.

North, D.C. (1984) 'Transaction costs, institutions, and economic history', in E.G. Furubotn and R. Richter (eds) *Zeitschrift für die Gesamte Staatswissenschaft (Journal of Institutional and Theoretical Economics)* 140(1): 7–17.

Nystrom, P.C. and Starbuck, W.H. (1981) *Handbook of Organizational Design*, Oxford: Oxford University Press.

OECD (1987) *Administration as Service: The Public as Client*, Paris: OECD.

OECD (1989) *Survey of Public Management Developments 1988*, Paris: OECD.

Offe, C. (1987) 'The utopia of the zero-option modernity and modernization as normative political criteria', *Praxis International* 7: 1–24.

Olsen, J.P. (ed.) (1978) *Politisk organisering*, Bergen: Universitetsforlaget.

Olsen, J.P. (1979) 'De nordiske lands offentlige forvaltning i 1980– og 1990–årene: noen perspektiver', *Nordisk Administrativt Tidsskrift* 60(1): 257–73.

Olsen, J.P. (1986) 'Foran en ny offentlig revolusjon', *Nytt Norsk Tidsskrift* 3: 3–15.

Olsen, J.P. (1988a) 'The modernization of public administration in the Nordic countries: some research questions', *Hallinnon Tutkimus (Administrative Studies)*, Finland: 2–17.

Olsen, J.P. (1988b) 'Administrative reform and theories of organization', in C. Campbell and B.G. Peters (eds) *Organizing Governance, Governing Organizations*, Pittsburgh, PA: University of Pittsburgh Press, 233–54.

Olsen, J.P. (1988c) 'Reorganisering som politisk virkemiddel, og statsvitenskap som arkitektonisk våpen', in J.P. Olsen *Statsstyre og institusjonsutforming*, Oslo: Universitetsforlaget, 61–76.

Olsen, J.P. (1988d) *Statsstyre og institusjonsutforming*, Oslo: Universitetsforlaget.

Olsen, J.P. (1989) *Petroleum og politikk*, Oslo: Tano.

Olson, O. (1987) *Kommunal årsrapportering – Om utviklingen til nå og et alternativ*, Oslo: Bedriftsøtronomens Forlag.

Olsson, U. (1985) 'Vi behöver en ekonomi med mänskligt ansikte', in *Dagens Nyheter*, 12 May.

Peters, B.G. (1988a) *Comparing Public Bureaucracies: Problems of Theory and Method*, Tuscaloosa, AL: University of Alabama Press.

Peters, B.G. (1988b) 'Introduction', in C. Campbell and B.G. Peters (eds) *Organizing Governance: Governing Organizations*, Pittsburgh: University of Pittsburgh Press, 3–15.

Petersson, O. and Fredén, J. (1987) *Statens symboler*, Uppsala: Maktutredningen.

Pfeffer, J. (1978) *Organizational Design*, Arlington Heights, IL: AHM Publishing.

Pfeffer, J. and Salancik, G.R. (1978) *The External Control of Organizations: A Resource Dependence Perspective*, New York: Harper & Row.

Poggi, G. (1984) *The Development of the Modern State*, Stanford, CA: Stanford University Press.

Polanyi, K. (1968) *Primitive, Archaic and Modern Economics: Essays of Karl Polanyi* (edited by G. Dalton), NY: Doubleday.

Pressman, J. and Wildavsky, A. (1973) *Implementation*, Berkeley, CA: University of California Press.

Renck, O. (1971) *Investeringsbedömning i några svenska företag*, Stockholm: EFI.

Richardson, A.J. and Dowling, J.B. (1986) 'An integrative theory of organizational legitimation', *Scandinavian Journal of Management Studies* 3(2): 91–110.

Romanow, A. (1981) 'Case studies of organizational change: a review', Stanford, CA: Stanford University, manuscript.

Rombach, B. (1986) *Rationalisering eller prat*, Lund: Doxa.

Rombach, B. (1989a) *'Kvalitetsuppfattningar i svenska landsting – presentation av enkätresultaten'*, Paper presented at the 'Kvalitet i kommuner och landsting' conference in Göteborg, 1–2 February 1989.

Rombach, B. (1989b) *Mätning av servicekvalitet i offentlig sektor – en kritisk granskning av attitydundersökningar i sjukvården* (Research Paper 6398), Stockholm: EFI.

Roness, P.G. (1979) *Reorganisering av departementa: Eit politisk styringsmiddel?* Bergen: Universitetsforlaget.

Rothstein, B. (1986) *Den socialdemokratiska staten* (Arkiv avhandlingsserie 21), Lund: Studentlitteratur.

Røvik, K.A. (1987) 'Læringssystemer og læringsatferd i offentlig forvaltning: en studie av styringens kunnskapsgrunnlag', Tromsø: Institutt for samfunnsvitenskap, manuscript.

Sahlin-Andersson, K. (1989a) 'Reform: visionärens reningsbad', Paper presented at Conference on Administrative Reforms, Grythyttan.

Sahlin-Andersson, K. (1989b) *Oklarhetens strategi*, Lund: Studentlitteratur.

Sait, E. McChesney (1938) *Political Institutions: A Preface*, New York: Appleton-Century-Crofts.

Salamon, L.M. (1981) 'The goals of reorganization', *Administration and Society* 12(4): 471–500.

Savings Bank Act (1955) Stockholm: Svensk Författningssamling (SFS) No. 416.

Scharpf, F.W. (1977) 'Does organization matter? Task structure and interaction in the ministerial bureaucracy', in E.H. Burack and A.R. Negandhi (eds) *Organization Design: Theoretical Perspectives and Empirical Findings*, Kent, OH: Kent State University.

Schick, A. (1977) 'Zero-base budgeting and sunset: redundancy or symbioses', *The Bureaucrat* 6: 12–32.

Scott, W.R. (1983) 'Introduction', in J.W. Meyer and W.R. Scott *Organizational Environments*, Beverley Hills, CA: Sage.

Scott, W.R. (1987) 'The adolescence of institutional theory', *Administrative Science Quarterly* 32: 493–511.

Seidman, H. (1980) *Politics, Position and Power: The Dynamics of Federal Organization* (3rd edn), New York: Oxford University Press.

Selznick, P. (1957) *Leadership in Administration*, New York: Harper & Row.

SFS (1965) *1965:600 Allmänna Verksstadgan*.

Simon, H.A. (1955) 'Behavioral model of rational choice', *Quarterly Journal of Economics* 69: 99–118.

Simon, H.A. (1957) *Administrative Behavior: A Study of Decision-Making Processes in Administrative Organization*, New York: Macmillan.

Sjöblom, S. and Ståhlberg, K. (1987) 'Att utveckla förvaltningen: en beskrivning av förvaltningsreformskommittéer i Finland åren 1975–1987', *Hallinnon Tutkimus* 4: 263–72.

Sjöstrand, S.E. (1985) *Samhällsorganisation*, Lund: Doxa.

Smircich, L. and Morgan, G. (1982) 'Leadership: the management of meaning', *Journal of Applied Behavioural Science* 18(3): 257–73.

Smircich, L. and Stubbart, C. (1985) 'Strategic management in an enacted world', *Academy of Management Review* 10(4): 724–36.

Söderlind, D. and Petersson, O. (1986) *Svensk förvaltningspolitik*, Uppsala: Diskurs.

SOU (Statens Offentliga Utredningar, Reports of the Official Inquiry Commissions) (1983) *1983:39 Politisk styrning – administrativ självständighet*, Stockholm: Betänkande av Förvaltningskommittén.

SOU (1985) *1985:40 Regeringen, myndigheterna och myndigheternas ledning*, Stockholm: Huvudbetänkande från Verksledningskommitén.

Starbuck, W.H. (1982) 'Congealing oil: inventing ideologies to justify acting ideologies out', *Journal of Management Studies* 19(1): 91–102.

Starbuck, W.H. (1983) 'Organizations as action generators', *American Sociological Review* 48(1): 91–102.

Steinman, M. and Miewald, R. (1984) 'Administrative reform: introduction', in R. Miewald and M. Steinman (eds) *Problems in Administrative Reform*, Chicago, IL: Nelson-Hall, 1–9.

Stinchcombe, A.L. (1965) 'Social structure and organizations', in J.G. March (ed.) *Handbook of Organizations*, Chicago, IL: Rand McNally.

Tell, B. (1974) *Investeringskalkylering i praktiken*, Lund: Studentlitteratur.

Thomas, G.M., Meier, J.W., Ramirez, F.O. and Boli, J. (eds) (1987) *Institutional Structure: Constituting State, Society, and the Individual*, Beverley Hills, CA: Sage.

Tolbert, P.S. and Zucker, L.G. (1983) 'Institutional sources of change in the formal structure of organizations: the diffusion of civil service reform, 1880–1935', *Administrative Science Quarterly* 28: 22–39.

Wagner, P. and Wittrock, B. (1989) 'Social science and the building of the early welfare state: transformations of discourse and institutions interlinked', Uppsala: The Swedish Collegium for Advanced Study in the Social Sciences, manuscript.

Wass, D. (1985) 'The civil service at the crossroads', *Political Quarterly* 50(3): 227–41.

Weber, M. (1971) *Makt og byråkrati*, Oslo: Gyldendal.

Weber, M., Roth, G. and Wittich, C. (eds) (1924/1978) *Economy and Society*, translated by E. Fischoff *et al.*, Berkeley, CA: University of California Press.

Weick, K.E. (1979) *The Social Psychology of Organizing*, Reading: Addison-Wesley.

Weick, K.E. (1983) 'Organizational communication: toward a research agenda', in L. Putnam and M. Pacanowsky (eds) *Communication and Organization*, London: Sage.

Weizsäcker, C.C. von (1984) 'The influence of property rights on tastes', *Zeitschrift für die Gesamte Staatswissenschaft (Journal of Institutional and Theoretical Economics)* 140(1): 90–5.

Wildavsky, A. (1964) *The Politics of the Budgetary Process*, Boston: Little Brown.

Williamson, O. (1981) 'The modern corporation: origins, evolution, attribution', *Journal of Economic Literature* 19: 1537–68.

Williamson, O.E. (1975) *Markets and Hierarchies: Analysis and Antitrust Implications*, New York: Free Press.

Williamson, O.E. (1981) 'The economics of organization: the transaction cost approach', *American Journal of Sociology* 87: 549–77.

Williamson, O.E. (1985) *The Economic Institutions of Capitalism*, New York: Free Press.

Winther, S. (1987) 'Reorganisering og modernisering – en introduksjon', *Politika* 19(4): 374–84.

Wittrock, B. and Lindström, S. (1984) *De stora programmens tid: Forskning och energi*, Stockholm: Akademilitteratur.

Wolin, S. (1960) *Politics and Vision: Continuity and Innovation in Western Political Thought*, Boston: Little, Brown.

Woodward, J. (1965) *Industrial Organization: Theory and Practice*, Oxford: Oxford University Press.

Zucker, L.G. (ed.) (1988) *Institutional Patterns and Organizations: Culture and Environment*, Cambridge, MA: Ballinger.

Index

DATE DUE

MAY 0 5 1999			

Demco, Inc. 38-293